Sojourner to Stoner

The Journal

Gordon Schwerzmann

Copyright © 2023

All Rights Reserved

Dedication

For my late wife Astrid Schwerzmann, who left everything behind in the old world to come to the new world for me and to my son Nils, who left this new world to explore and discover exotic Asia and now lives and teaches in China

Acknowledgements

This book would have remained a jumble of incoherent notes without the encouragement and tough-love criticism of Fanny Lee. Thank-you for all of your hard work, patience and love.

Once again, I am deeply indebted to Arden Gallagher for her indefatigable help in getting this book ready for publication. Without her advice, help, understanding, and love this book would have remained a figment of my imagination.

Table of Contents

Map of Travels i
Preface ii
Introduction 1
Thailand 4
    Chapter One: Thailand Entry 5
    Chapter Two: To Pod or Not To Pod, That Is The Question? 8
    Chapter Three: The Soldier Becomes a Freak 12
    Chapter Four: Bangkok After Dark: Walk on the Wild Side 16
    Chapter Five: Two Tickets to Paradise 21
    Chapter Six: Ayutthaya 25
    Chapter Seven: At Play In the Sands of Time 29
Laos 32
    Chapter Eight: Berlin Bleibt Deutsch 33
    Chapter Nine: The Soldier's Tale 36
    Chapter Ten: Dr. Tom Dooley 39
    Chapter Eleven: Alles Ist Schone 42
    Chapter Twelve: Swiss Miss and the Golden Boy 45
    Chapter Thirteen: The Painter's Tale 48
    Chapter Fourteen: Vientiane-The Last Day "Gotterdammerung" 50
Thailand II 52
    Chapter Fifteen: Chiang Mai 53
    Chapter Sixteen: Christine 57
    Chapter Seventeen: Jim Thompson, the CIA, and the Deep Silk State 61
    Chapter Eighteen: Show And Tell 66
    Chapter Nineteen: The Thai Image of Buddha 69
    Chapter Twenty: Musings on a Long Hot Train Ride from Chang Mai to Bangkok .. 75
    Chapter Twenty-One: Christine II: Anatomy of a Relationship 78
Malaysia I 81
    Chapter Twenty-Two: A Double Date 82
    Chapter Twenty-Three: The Holy Grail 85
    Chapter Twenty-Four: Malacca 'The Old Town' 87
    Chapter Twenty-Five: Celebrating Life and Honoring Death 93
    Chapter Twenty-Six: Malay Christians (Kristangs) 98

- Chapter Twenty-Seven: Let The Good Times Roll 100
- Chapter Twenty-Eight: And Now For Something Really Different 103

Singapore 108
- Chapter Twenty-Nine: The Freak Takes a Dare 109
- Chapter Thirty: Stamford Raffles: The Founder of Singapore 113
- Chapter Thirty-One: Lee Kwan Yew 118
- Chapter Thirty-Two: The Grand Tradition: A Tale of Three Raj Hotels 124

Borneo 130
- Chapter Thirty-Three: A Personal Fiefdom 131
- Chapter Thirty-Four: Frank Buck the American Myth of the Self-Made Man 135
- Chapter Thirty-Five: Borneo: Into the Heart of Lightness 138
- Chapter Thirty-Six: Ice Princess to Primeval Eve 151

Indonesia 156
- Chapter Thirty-Seven: Indonesia Entry 157
- Chapter Thirty-Eight: Old Batavia 160
- Chapter Thirty-Nine: Jakarta Stadium 165
- Chapter Forty: Kretek 170
- Chapter Forty-One: Sukarno 173
- Chapter Forty-Two: Borobudur: The Big Rock Candy Mountain 178

Bali 183
- Chapter Forty-Three: Land Of Milk And Honey 184
- Chapter Forty-Four: Confessions Of A Mushroom-Eater 187
- Chapter Forty-Five: Balinese Art 192
- Chapter Forty-Six: Jan De Troop - Synthesis of Art Nouveau and Javanese Art 198
- Chapter Forty-Seven: A New Etymology of a Familiar Four-Letter Word 204
- Chapter Forty-Eight: The Balinese Religion 209
- Chapter Forty-Nine: The Balinese Ritual Of Death 213
- Chapter Fifty: The Incredible Lightness and Darkness of Being 217
- Chapter Fifty-One: The Garden of Earthly Delights 222
- Chapter Fifty-Two: And Now Meet the Real Bali 227
- Chapter Fifty-Three: Durian 234
- Chapter Fifty-Four: Loetz's Going Away Party 237
- Chapter Fifty-Five: Sandra 242
- Chapter Fifty-Six: Bali: Farewell to Paradise 247

Indonesia II 250

    Chapter Fifty-Seven: Duo in Solo 251
    Chapter Fifty-Eight: The Kris 257
    Chapter Fifty-Nine: Down and Out In Jakarta 260
Singapore II 268
    Chapter Sixty: Singapore Redux 269
    Chapter Sixty-One: Two Swiss and a VW Bus 271
    Chapter Sixty-Two: A Liberated Woman, Berliner "Luft" And Lady Jane 275
Malaysia II 281
    Chapter Sixty-Three: Outcasts of the Islands 282
    Chapter Sixty-Four: An Ocean Too Far 288
    Chapter Sixty-Five: "The Searchers" Meet "Waiting For Godot" 294
    Chapter Sixty-Six: The Freak Becomes a Landlord 304
    Chapter Sixty-Seven: On Traveling 309
    Chapter Sixty-Eight: Dinner and A Movie 313
    Chapter Sixty-Nine: Wang Yu 316
Thailand III 319
    Chapter Seventy: Taxi Dancing 320
    Chapter Seventy-One: Paradise Regained 325
    Chapter Seventy-Two: Koh Siracha: Sheep And A Tall Buddha 330
    Chapter Seventy-Three: The Continuing Adventures Of Flash Gordon 333
Bibliography 335
Illustration Credits 349
About The Author 378
About The Book 379

Map of Travels

"Soldier to Sojourner" are my impressions of Korea, Japan, Nationalist China, Hong Kong/Macau, Philippines, and Burma. "Sojourner to Stoner" continues the adventure photographing the people, places and lifestyles of Thailand, Laos, Malaysia, Singapore, Borneo, and Indonesia.

Preface

Before we embark on this grand adventure, it will be enlightening to discuss a topic near and dear to my heart and what the reader must look forward to: what is a travel book? Now a typical travel book is usually a straightforward narrative where the author goes from point A to point B, regaling you with his many adventures along the way. These stories are mostly true (poetic license for others) and along this journey you will get to know the author and, most of the time, this will determine whether you like the book or not.

(How you cannot like such a personable, knowledgeable and understanding author like myself is beyond belief, but let's continue).

There are two themes in travel books, one is the "quest" theme: here the main character, the author, fictional character, etc. is on a search, it could be for the Holy Grail (If someone actually found the Missing Cup, it would go to Christies the next day; you can get anything you want in New York City), it could be for a lost gold city deep in the Amazon (it may be discovered tomorrow with all the deforestation down there) or it could be to discover where fabled Xanadu is (for Oz you need a really powerful Twister {or a subway token to see the real Oz as Pete Hamill so lovingly wrote about New York}).

The second theme of travel books is "the long way home".

There is a third type of travel book, as an alternative to the literary book, and that is the photo book. If I had to pick just one book that defines what America is, it would be Robert Frank's photo book "The Americans" (1959). Like De Tocqueville in the 19th century, who praised the study, hardworking farmer as the embodiment of American democracy; Jacob Riis in the early 20th century with his biting exposure of the poor in the slums of New York and Robert Frank in the latter half of the 20th century, all these writers and photographers were outsiders or immigrants to America. They looked at America with fresh eyes, seeing the whole forest, while we Americans can only see a tree or two.

Robert Frank was an immigrant from Switzerland, who traveled the length and breadth of our land ("From the New York harbor to the Redwood Forest, this Land is your Land, This Land is my Land" {Woody Guthrie}) capturing the soul of America: the crash materialism, the venial corruption of politicians, the racial divide, and especially the loneliness of our society. Old people huddled forlornly on crowded benches in sunny Miami, the lost aimless boredom of a Las Vegas gambler, and the endless highway that has no beginning and no end: the open road as a nightmare.

Historically when we think about great travel books, two books come immediately to mind. The first is the greatest of all travel books and that is an epic poem called "The Odyssey".

"The Odyssey" has survived for millenniums because it portrays Odysseus as an ordinary person that must use his wits to defeat the obstacles the gods send him. He is subject to all the strengths and flaws of human beings: brawny, cunning, lustful, callous, bloodthirsty, and loving, every emotion and action is justified in his journey to get home and what adventures he has! Every school kid knows the story of the cyclops and every male adult wishes he was bewitched by a beautiful Circe. "The Odyssey" is the prime example of "the long road home" type of travel book and everyone, including yours truly, has used passages for comparison with their own travels. Here the conventional wisdom says that it is not the goal or final destination, but the traveling itself. Therefore, the book has remained an enduring, readable classic.

In more modern times, the greatest travel book would be Jack Kerouac's "On The Road", where the author sets off to find America and, of course, this is a novel. Jack Kerouac's "On The Road" is the Bible of all the young backpackers, either hitching or wandering throughout America or the world and detailing their adventures. This was the one book that more travelers carried in Asia than any other book (I, however, carried "Lady Chatterley's Lover" for those hot and lonely "dark night of the soul" nights). "On The Road" introduces us to a great larger-than-life seeker Neal Cassady, the last cowboy who traded his horse in for an automobile. Neal, like Falstaff outshines Henry the Fifth, eclipses the author Kerouac with his outrageous nonstop energy and drunken reveries. Here the real hero is the road. Neal, for all his energy and magnetism, really has no personality; he only becomes alive when he is behind the wheel; when he is driving furiously, speeding into oblivion on Robert Frank's endless highway, never stopping to find his goal: America. When he does stop, the narrative fails and flounders. Neal deserts his sick friend Kerouac in Mexico City, and all his sexual escapades are pit stops: change the tires, fill it up, screw and drop the girl; there is no love, understanding or meaning. Neal will always be the driver and that is his private hell.

There is a movie version of "On the Road", but this is a lifeless cinematic dud, failing to capture the energy and restlessness of the road. There is a much better movie, which is an update of Neal Cassady for the 21st century, that does succeed in capturing the aimlessness, emptiness and loneliness of the road. However, it is not on the road at all, but in the air. This is "Up in the Air" starring George Clooney. Here the hero is middleclass (a perfect stereotype of a corporate businessman), laidback, knowing everything and getting all the perks as he substitutes flying for driving with the same dissolute results. There is even a parody of Kerouac in the movie, where everywhere Clooney goes, he takes a photo of a place with a life-size cardboard cutout of his niece and soon to be married fiancé, placed in front of supposedly scenic views of all the major American cities. You have this vacantly smiling, clueless couple standing in front of an airplane terminal, ("Having the time of our lives") and we see the same loneliness here that we saw in Robert Frank's photobook. America has just become a series of airports, Holiday Inns, cheap cafeterias, and monotonous strip malls. The endless highway is now the air and when Clooney steps out of that, everything is the same, whether it's New York, Kansas or San Francisco. This is the real emptiness of the landscape and the soul that reinforces the loneliness and desperation of American society today.

In my travel book, both literary themes are fused. I too am a soldier making my long way home and, on the way, looking for epiphany or enlightenment, a quest to give my life meaning. I also followed the third way, that of the photobook, capturing in photos what would fall flat and lifeless in prose. Seeing Asia with fresh eyes, the outsider trying to capture a traditional way of life, a period in time that we in America have lost in our relentless pursuit of money and fame. My separate photo book, also called (with great imagination) "Sojourner to Stoner: The Photographs" covers the same territory as my written travelogue. This is not, however, a slavish illustration of my written text ("See Jane Run" in fulsome detail and then showing a photograph of a snot-nosed girl running in the street). Rather there are two ways of seeing and experiencing: one is striving for an intellectual or aesthetic approach to a subject and the other a visceral and spontaneous approach to the same subject. Now I will discuss further in (excruciating) detail what my travel book is really all about.

What I am doing using a 25-cent word, is to "deconstruct" the travelogue. Webster has three definitions of "deconstruct": the first, to take apart or examine the composition to reveal flaws or biases; second, to adapt separate elements in a composition in a radically new way; and third, to demolish. In my travel books I use deconstruction in all three definitions to bring the experience of travel vicariously to the reader. The employment of straightforward narrative, stream of consciousness, nightmare delusions, drug reveries, fictional voices, play dialogue, and poetry; this varied approach keeps the reader on his toes and enriches the narrative. For example, a play in my first book "Soldier to Sojourner" presents a moral point of view without preaching or exhibiting a "holier than thou" diatribe and what better vehicle for this than the medieval Everyman morality plays. There good and evil are clearly defined, and the path is straight forward: salvation or damnation. Similarly, poetry is used where, instead of a florid description of a place, a poem would distill my thoughts in capturing the mood and better convey this to the reader. Expanding the genre to include philosophical and artistic discussions, political and economic discussions, biographies, fiction, mixed media (movie reviews, songs, etc.) eroticism and humor (satire, slapstick and dry) are the tools in my travel kit.

My favorite exploration is discovering the art and culture of the country; people are defined by the art they create. The great works of art, be it painting, sculpture, dance or music, show how religion or philosophy is transposed to a canvas or a stone carving. In Nationalist China, the great works of Chinese painting of the 13th and 14th centuries A.D. were all visual depictions of a world deeply influenced by the Tao philosophy. Similarly in Bali, you will discover that all art is a struggle between good and evil. Every country has its 15 minutes of fame, where art reflects the confidence of the artist amidst his country's golden age. In Bali, all art is religious in nature whether it's temple building, gamelan music, dance-drama or sculpture and painting.

Asia's religions and philosophies were fascinating to me, and it is important to explain what they are and how they influence the people (including myself) of the particular countries. Arriving in Korea as a Christian, but finding so many new answers to life's questions, I began to doubt my faith and to see if there were alternative ways or beliefs that would give me satisfaction and true understanding of my life and my goals. Thus, the book is a "Pilgrims Progress" of a young man exploring religion, the afterlife and the moral codes and philosophies that guide the people of Asia and adopting what works for me.

As far as the politics and the economic system that people live under ("This is a song of great political and social significance", as Janis quipped before belting out, "Oh Lord, Won't You Buy Me A Mercedes Benz") I have tried to be fair, not believing that our Western capitalist way of life is the panacea for Asia's problems and to be understanding, although at times it was exceedingly difficult to reconcile the present cruelty and oppression with the eventual goals that were set up to help these downtrodden masses. I do not use hindsight in my observations but look at the stark reality as it existed at that time. For example, democracy is not working in India: there is too much poverty, too many people and too little resources to lift the poorer classes out of extreme poverty. The traditional way of life was under assault by western consumer culture, by communism and by capitalism. There were a few success stories in Asia, but there were also glaring examples of abject failures. For every Yew in Singapore, there were the Marcos in the Philippines and the military junta in Burma. In Sukarno there was a man that tried to steer Indonesia toward a middle path, not kowtowing to capitalism or communism and that failed miserably as you will read in my chapter on Sukarno. I am a modern-day Hans Castorp (in my case traveling through dictatorships, guided democracies, tribal and religious societies, observing what works for the people that live in these places) naively going to the sanitarium in "The Magic Mountain" for a cure, but subject to all of the conflicting philosophies of communism, capitalism, nihilism, and religion.

The fictional first-person dialogue adds immediacy and poignancy to an otherwise "dry facts" account. For example, the narrative could have read, "the bar was chuck full of soldiers on R&R from Vietnam; they were really letting go and they deserved it." Instead, I chose to follow one fictional soldier and gave him feelings, thoughts, and actions that I would have had myself in his boots because I too am a soldier and live in his world.

Songs are referenced because songwriters are our modern update of the Romantic poets like Byron and Wadsworth. Our song writers create lyrics that elucidate joy, sorrow, jealousy, love and espouse political and social issues in a succinct, thought-provoking style with deep emotional fervor and heartfelt anguish and they must relate their message set to a catchy tune and keep it under four minutes to capture their fickle audience. Bob Dylan, Bruce Springsteen, Johnny Cash, Janis Joplin, Aretha Franklin, and The Beach Boys, just to name a few, wrote the anthems of our generation. So, quoting a song is just as valid as quoting a Keats or Shelley poem. It is ironic that we have come full circle: the original poem "The Odyssey" has only survived because it was sung, with lyre accompaniment, for hundreds of years before it was written down. Now our generation sings the songs, of which the best will be handed down, revised, adapted and cherished by future generations as immemorable cultural icons of a time long gone.

Movies are indispensable because they have a pulse on what is happening in our society and succinctly convey in two hours what authors take years to construct. We are a visual generation and if I had the artistic skills, this would be a comic book version of this travelogue, where the artist's vision and the photographer's vision meld into one meaningful experience.

The comparisons with contemporary American cities particularly my hometown, New York City, and artists and public figures from the 1970s are used to make sense of my understanding of Asia by juxtaposing American attitudes and responses and my personal history to emphasize and exemplify a point, not as a personal memoir, but as a way to see how we are all related as human beings.

In my first book I referenced Italo Calvino's extraordinary novel "Invisible Cities". Here Marco Polo is tasked by Chinese emperor Kublai Khan to survey his kingdom and report back to him on what he finds. Marco sets off and he observes the whole of Kublai's Kingdom and describes each city in such glowing terms that they become more real than the actual cities of the realm. After Marco finishes his imaginary descriptions, Kublai tells him: "however there was one city you did not describe and that is your home city Venice." Marco just smiles and answers "all the cities described in such vibrant colors are all aspects of my hometown of Venice." Similarly, New York City is a microcosm of all the Asian cities: the poverty, crime, over crowdedness, injustice and the aliveness of spirit. In my first book James Joyce's Dublin in "Ulysses" is an excellent example of an imaginary city. However, a better example would be a Western outsider looking at a strange and exotic oriental city, finding meaning in the mystery of the different layers of history that interplay and transform the present reality to create a fantastical imaginary city. This book is Lawrence Durrell's "Alexandria Quartet". Here Alexandria is the main character, the all-pervading presence in all four of these novels. This city is given a life of its own by an aesthetic sensibility that forever imprints on our minds a magical realism vision more real, exotic and mysterious than the actual flesh and blood Islamic metropolis will ever be. This "magical realism" approach of my travelogue is really my way of showing enthusiasm and awe at the wonders before me.

Meanwhile back to deconstructing the travelogue: two points are extremely important and make or break a book in my eyes. The first is total honesty with the reader and this honesty extends to my depicting eroticism in my book. I have been accused ("J'Accuse!" by Emile Zola) of practicing a double standard when it comes to my moral views on sexual behavior, being more severe in my application of morals to women than to men.

First, my description of sexual acts is a natural part of my humanity. I'm not ashamed of my body and as a writer there is nothing wrong or immoral about giving the reader graphic details of my relationships. To me, it is more honest to fully describe the sexual act rather than" and after he made love, he left the bedroom with a satisfying smile". That is more disingenuous and dishonest;

you really have no idea what the author actually feels in this "discreet" description of his lovemaking.

That I exhibit a "double standard" is blatantly wrong. Webster defines "double standard" as "a set of principles that applies differently and usually more rigorously to one group of people or circumstances than to another." I never felt myself morally superior to the prostitutes or the freaks and tourists that freely gave themselves to me in sexual relations. I was single and my relations with prostitutes was a business arrangement between two consenting adults. As far as including this eroticism in a travel book, there is no conflict of interest either. In fact, it adds another dimension to understanding the personality of the writer. If you cannot trust the writer because of his frankness in dealing with sex, why would you trust his other judgments about people, places, and ideals?

We beat this horse to death, and in closing, borrow the slogan of a failed nudist candidate for President of the United States: "What do I have to hide?"

In writing a really good travel book you must, above all else, be humorous. If, as when Eric Anderson sang" You've long been on the open road, you've been sleeping in the rain" ("Thirsty Boots"), you know the hardships, frustrations and boredom of getting to different places in your journey, so lighten up and learn to laugh at yourself, at others and at difficult situations to keep your sanity.

Now that we've talked about what a travel book should be, let's talk about what a travel book shouldn't be and that is a tour guide. Tour guides are great, carrying one with me as my faithful companion for two years, but you are not buying this book to find the cheapest hotel or best restaurant in some exotic locale or even the most architecturally significant shrine. You are buying this book because you identify with the author and vicariously put yourself in his shoes. His struggles are your struggles, but that doesn't mean you have to be dragged in the mud on a constant basis. Too many travel writers spend half of the narrative going into minute detail on their mode (or lack thereof) of transportation or their shitty accommodations. The energy and awe of travel is lost in these books because the writer must stand on the road waiting a ride for endless pages (and makes you stand {"are we there yet?} with him) or he can't get a shower, or he can't find dope after more tedious pages of "Waiting for the Man".

NO WHINING! What the reader wants is the thrill of discovering a ruined city, the gracious hospitality of locals towards yourself and an aesthetic appreciation of your desired destination.

Another trap many travel writers fall into is how cheap everything is, selling you on the wholesale version of travel (Such a deal! Only 25 cents a night for a room) as opposed to the retail version of the standard tourists' experiences. I drop these books immediately because they are boring! boring! boring!

Certain travel writers fall into writing prolix pontific prose, waxing poetic on a sunset or a beach. Sure, it's beautiful, but get over it, don't drool on for pages and pages extolling its wonders. The sunset and beach on Coney Island are also beautiful (and for many, only a subway token away) and you don't have to go to faraway places to appreciate nature's bounty. Traveling is about learning a new religion, philosophy, or way of life totally alien to you and to your normal existence. You are Virgil guiding all these naive Dantes from one circle to another, weaving a memorable experience of the places you are in and exploring.

A travel writer should also not sell you something: whether it's his conversion to Buddhism (If it works for me, it will work for you. Just sit with your legs crossed and repeat the word Omm! over and over for four hours each day, this time with feeling!), endless forays to get the best drug high or even the writer's moral superiority as an enlightened westerner as opposed to the backward traditional way of life. For example, a westerner only sees the evils of the caste system in India, yet it has given stability to that society for thousands of years.

Lastly there is the nostalgia rap: This was a golden time, and it can never be repeated: too bad suckers, you missed it, but I will make you envious of my adventures from that magical fairytale place. That's not what traveling is about; traveling is not about whether you went 50 years ago or today. You still go with the same enthusiasm for discovering the unknown and learning about yourself. If my book teaches you anything, it tells you to get off your ass and "Just Do It" (preferably in your Michael Jordan Nikes). It doesn't matter if you can't get the cheap hotels, the 50-cent fish dinner, or there's too many tourists in line ahead of you to see the Taj Mahal. Experience all this for yourself. There is a great line in the movie "Good Will Hunting" where Robin Williams is talking about Michelangelo and the Sistine Chapel and tells Matt Damon "sure you've read all the books, you know all about how it was painted, you can convince people that you know the beauty of the Sistine Chapel through detailed close up color images and can spout with grand authoritarianism on the symbolism of the painting, but you can't feel the absolute wonder of standing under that immensely high ceiling, looking up, not even making out the details, smelling the earthy, musty odor of the Chapel, just being there, that's the kick that travel is all about".

Now that I've given you a movie trailer of my personality, if you find me too opinionated, too critical of others or just plain nasty, stop here, save yourself the money and don't buy the book. However, you will be missing out on something ("Oh Baby, you ain't seen nothing yet! Here's something you never will forget!" {Three Dog Night}) and entreat you to continue reading. However, here is the test: if you agree with what I'm raving on about (You're a Better Man than I, Gunga Din") tell me or if you think " Who is this misanthrope anyway, is he completely out of his mind?", my email is gordonroyschwerzmann@gmail.com or better yet, buy the book and write a review of my book (books, in a solicited plug of my photography book) : whether you write a good or terrible review, it's all publicity to me. There are no bad reviewers, only disgruntled people entitled to voice their "wrong" opinions.

As Arlo Guthrie crooned, "I've been singing this song about "Alice's Restaurant" for 25 minutes and I could go on for another 25, I'm not proud." And I haven't even mentioned Dana Wynter once, but I'll stop for now, so you can dig into the grand adventure.

"Now brought to you live from a subterranean storage closet beneath Broadway in the heart of New York City (I Heart NY as my baseball cap logo shows) recorded in front of a live studio audience: Here's Gordon!"

Introduction

The picaresque and strangely fascinating adventures of Flash Gordon continues. This, of course, is Volume Two of the author's grand tour. And for those who have managed to finish Volume One "Soldier to Sojourner", the author now bestows his highest accolade to those intrepid readers: "atta-a-boy! and atta-a-girl!" For those they have not read "Soldier to Sojourner", that is a shame because you will be reported to the IRS for not listing the life changing experiences that the book so glowingly describes and there will be a penalty. However, if you do not itemize and use the standard form you will be safe, only duller.

The action now switches to Southeast Asia which is in a veritable Garden of Eden (or maybe a postcard from a beach paradise: "Having fun! Wish you were here!"). The Pilgrim's Progress is not a trial of fire and doubt, but a trial (and trail, "We're off to find the wizard, the wonderful wizard" or as they say in New York City," Waitin' on the Man") of dope. We follow the hero through other trials such as contracting hepatitis, bouts of diarrhea and dehydration and learning through trial and error, the proper user techniques of Asian toilets. Flash also has ecstatic mystical visions comparable to Hildegard of Bingen, Saint John of the Cross and Timothy Leary. The author immerses himself in Buddhism, Islam, Christianity, and nature beliefs, not to check the boxes, but to gleam from each faith something that will help him give meaning to his life.

Flash Gordon has rediscovered lost civilizations buried in the jungles, lived with former headhunters, enjoyed paradisaical beaches and fought off hordes of flies in stifling shoebox rooms. He has seen grinding poverty in overcrowded, fetid city slums and seemingly bucolic lush countryside. Our hero also hobnobbed with the wealthy in smokey dark cafes and glittering discotheques.

Like Volume One, the most important part of this book are the people that I met (notice the switch to the first person, more personable, down-to-earth narrative). I spoke with and listened to, drank with, and sometimes smoked dope with students, monks, businessmen, sailors, gangsters, artists, transvestites, farmers, former headhunters, bar girls and everyday ordinary people. Our conversations were about their religion, political ideology, and personal hopes and dreams. I traveled with stoned out freaks, tourists on a shoestring budget, bespectacled academics, ex-GIs and Peace Corps volunteers. Many of these were passionate seekers looking for answers in religion, philosophy, and lifestyles that they encountered on the road. Many expressed to me there must be more to life than a wife, job, and 2.5 kids (How do you have a .5 kid anyway?) in a house in the suburbs. The local people that I encountered in each country were open, friendly, and inquisitive; many wanted the things that we take for granted or are questioning: the all-pervasive religion of consumerism.

I have experimented with every type of drug and even reexamined my sexual identity. I have experienced calming beatitude and squalid ugliness. Through all this my outlook on life has changed, but I hope it has not clouded my judgment. If it has, "I blame it on society, I grew up poor, society made me a criminal"...wait, isn't that a line from a bad movie?

Throughout the book I tried to keep an optimistic outlook, to accept people as they are. Again, as in Volume One, I have found comparisons with the way the local people solve their problems, and the way Americans do (or don't, thank-you again Congress) and try to postulate possible solutions for these problems.

So, let's get on with the "living better through chemistry" adventure (in three-part- harmony and a cloud of smoke). "Who is that masked man?"

Grant Wood "American Gothic" 1930

"Well, Pa, what do you make of this guy?"

"I'll tell you, Ma; I'd get him working on the farm and have him clean out the pig barn: shit in and shit out."

Thailand

Thai temple in Bangkok 1972 (author's photo)

Chapter One: Thailand Entry

"I Whistle a Happy Tune": Anna sings in the Broadway musical "The King and I"

Bangkok's Canals 1900

After the crash of commercialism in Hong Kong, I was looking forward to the laid-back atmosphere of tropical languor that I had read about in Thailand. My imaginings of Bangkok as a tropical paradise with smiling women, long boats laden with fruit plying the wide canals, exotic temples, and colorful bazaars quickly dissipated in the smog-filled, traffic-congested ride from the airport to the city. I asked the cab driver for a hotel where hippies stay, and, of course, after he told me about this great hotel, he rattled off in quick succession: "You want ganja (marijuana)? You want good clean girl?"

When I nodded no, he seemed perplexed, but then he brightened, turning to me in a conspiratorial tone, whispering, "So you want young cherry boy?"

He dropped me at a small two-story wooden hotel with a large verandah overlooking a garbage strewn, fetid smelling canal. The verandah was something straight out of a Somerset Maugham novel: a wide high ceilinged white painted room complete with slow moving ceiling fans, potted palms, tables over-laden with bowls of exotic fruit and comfortably frayed wicker chairs. But instead of staid, genteel old Englishmen in rumpled white linen suits, nursing their gin and tonics, there were young American and French junkies staring emptily in space, nodding off their highs. The serpent had corrupted this paradise: the idealistic youth of my generation searching for life's meaning found their nirvana at the end of a needle.

I left this house of the living dead and visited the wats (temples). At one of the most beautiful wats, the Emerald Buddha Wat, which is all golden on the outside, while inside darkness was banished by hundreds of candles, leading up to the iridescent, grandiloquent Seated jade Buddha. I was befriended by a young Buddhist novice, who offered to show me around, ostensibly to practice his English. The Buddhist initiate and I sat in the shade of a large pipal tree (the tree Buddha sat under when he achieved nirvana), talking and laughing at the other foreigners—the Thais laugh at foreigners in a friendly way as a means to break the ice and be able to communicate with them. The initiate spoke of his experiences in the monastery and his doubts about becoming a real monk for life. He came from a very poor family, and as a dutiful son, he must take care of his parents when they get old, and that would be hard if he became a monk. He was fascinated with American culture: the music, movies, the big cars, but he was proud to be a Thai. Thailand was one of the few countries in Asia that had never been conquered by the west, and the people were not intimidated by foreigners. It was this fierce spirit of independence, coupled with their positive attitude toward life, which made the Thais a joy to speak and be with.

The ever-present heat enervated you so much that you had to visit the wats and pagodas in the mornings when there was a brief respite from the stiflingly humid, sweat-soaked, gasoline fume haze of the afternoon inferno. The gold roofs of the wats reflected dreamily in the brackish canals, dissipated noiselessly by the long-prowed skiffs of the fruit and vegetable sellers. The Floating Market is an insane jumble of hundreds of low skiffs selling everything imaginable. I rented a boat with an operator, and we plied the waterways, buying fiery prawns from one boat, beer from another, and delicious hairy red rambutans for desert from another skiff. By 11 AM, it was mostly finished. The housewives had bought their fresh produce, and the farmer vendors returned to their fields to harvest the next day's market.

A Canal in Bangkok 1972 (author's photograph)

Chapter Two: To Pod or Not To Pod, That Is The Question?

"Look, you fools, you're in danger! They're after all of us! Our wives, our children, everyone! **THEY'RE HERE ALREADY! YOU'RE NEXT!**"

Kevin McCarty screaming at the cars on the California freeway at the end of the 1956 "Invasion of the Body Snatchers"

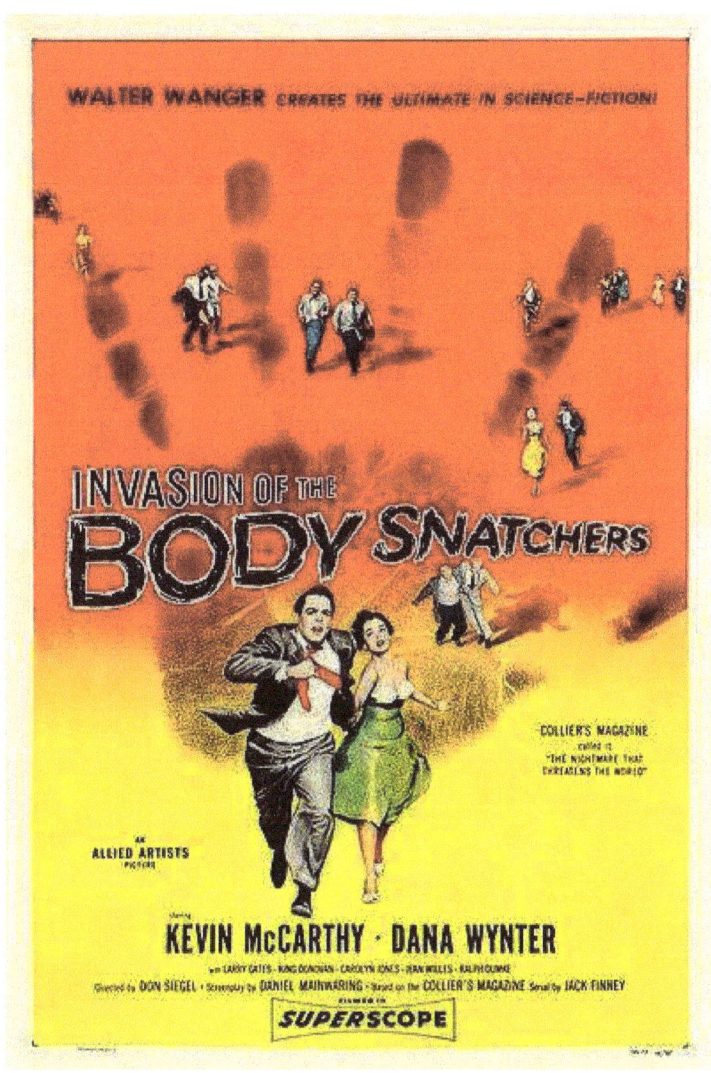

The original "Invasion of the Body Snatchers" Movie Poster 1956

"The Invasion of the Body Snatchers" is, in my not-so-humble opinion, the greatest science fiction movie(s) ever made ("The Attack of the Killer Tomatoes" is, however, a messy second). There are no evil slimy-green aliens, no germ warfare "Aliens", and thank God, Tokyo has not been destroyed again for the tenth time. Here the evil is more insidious: harmless floating spores from outer space that can replicate and replace any living life form. The spores grow in this cocoon pod that takes over your body when you sleep, and you are replaced by an emotionless, humorless, robotic automon (for some unknown reason, the pods do not affect Germans). You become a part of a collective mind community, where you all think alike and work together to destroy humanity (at first, I thought the pod people were a parody of our Congress, but since they can never agree on anything and they do absolutely nothing, it is not an apt analogy).

There were four "Invasion" movies made: 1956, 1978, 1993, and 2007. Why are these movies important, and what is their significance? The central core issue of all these movies is the individual pitted against a conformist society. This new society gives us universal peace (What will Miss America contestants aspire to now?), an end of hunger, and total acceptance of all races and creeds. In short, the pod people are offering us Utopia, a goal that mankind has always strived for but never achieved. All we have to do is give up our emotions, feelings of passion, hate, envy, and jealousy (on second thought, they may have something there).

The 1956 movie takes place in small-town America at the height of the "Cold War". The menace is a foreign "communist" takeover that will remake our society into a "socialist" (read soulless) prison, where the rights of the individual are crushed. That's a great interpretation if you are on the "right" side of politics. Now, if you are on the "left" side of politics, the pod people are demagogic McCarthyites that want to mesmerize you into their hysterical anti-communist fear-mongering agenda and brand any individual opposition as un-American (evil) communists. So, with this movie, you can have your cake and eat it too.

We now jump 22 years to 1978 San Francisco, the second "Invasion" movie. Here you have pod conformist American society attempting to destroy individual groups: hippies, gays, anti-war activists, radical blacks, Native American and eastern religious communities, and anyone at odds with our American homogenized shared values (one size fits everyone). Here the pod people have an animal instinct to preserve their way of life, a piercing scream that brings the mob to destroy this counterculture and keep our complacent "American Way" intact.

Donald Sutherland screaming and pointing at a non-POD individual: "Invasion of the Body Snatchers" 1978

The third 1993 "Invasion" is set in an army base. This is the time of the Gulf War, and the pod takeover of our military is a microcosm of our jingoistic war fever society. If you oppose this war, just like the opposition to the Vietnam war twenty-five years before, you will be crushed. The "girl power" heroine survives the clutches of the pod people, but a dying pod person gives her an ominous warning. As she escapes by helicopter from a pod-controlled army installation, he shouts at her, "Where you gonna go, where you gonna run, where you gonna hide? Nowhere! Cause there's no one like you left."

The fourth "Invasion" offers an interesting premise: the outer space spores can now "rewrite" your DNA via an alien virus that makes you a pod person. Presto, you have a new, improved human being. This was the time when cloning was being done (we all remember the cloned Korean sheep, bah!). Cloning promised a stronger, longer living, more intelligent human being: Nietzsche's "Ubermensch" meets "Better Living Through Biology". However, our "Rugged Individual" heroes don't want this new and improved mindless species and develop a cure to stop the pods (This is kind a like when Coca-Cola abandoned its original formula to become the "new, improved taste" Coca-Cola. However, we, as true red-blooded Americans, rejected this pod Cola- we want the old familiar take-the-paint-off-your-car-hood Coke, and we brought it back!).

Each generation finds new issues, metaphors, and political meanings in these movies. I am looking forward to a new "remake "of the "Invasion" franchise, where another "burning issue" will be idealized, satirized, or parodied.

I am not usually a conspiracy doomsayer (please don't listen to my ex-girlfriends), but I do believe that the 1978 "Invasion" movie really happened. Somehow after the original alien pods took over, they were replaced by counter-culture pod people (I think the original aliens had one too many marijuana tokes. Yah know this is San Francisco, with the flowers in your hair!), and these new, improved pod "heads" took over San Francisco. Before you dismiss me as crazy (what's that guy smoking?), just read any newspaper story or watch any TV report coming out of San Francisco. I'm sure you'll come around to my belief that these pod people are out to crush any individual or group that does not agree with their party pod line. Ironically, this is where the "Free Speech" movement began in Berkeley in the early 1960s. However, being humorless pods, they would not understand the subtle satire of the joke: "Everyone is entitled to their wrong opinion".

Chapter Three: The Soldier Becomes a Freak

"Mama Told Me Not To Come": Three Dog Night

The hilarious song about the reactions of a non-marijuana smoker at a pot party

Movie Poster from 1936 film "Reefer Madness"

Before I arrived in Bangkok, the countries that I had visited had no freaks, or as in Hong Kong, they were in the definite minority of travelers.

Everywhere I went, I stayed in "Traveler's Hotels". What I loved about these hotels were the interesting people: people on a spiritual quest, people learning about martial arts and herbal medicine, and scholars exploring cultural, economic, and political issues for their careers. I had little connection with a regular tourist, who came to the country for two weeks, took their photographs, ate at fancy restaurants, and stayed at luxury hotels without any or minimal interaction with the local people.

Here in Bangkok, the scene was altogether different. In Traveler's Hotels, everyone was a freak, and they were all stoned to some degree. What was most disturbing was the lack of meaningful conversation. Drugs were the only topic; how to get them, what was the best hash or grass, and how mellow your trip was. I felt like Kevin McCarthy in the 1956 movie "Invasion of the Body Snatchers". Someone had put pods by each traveler, and these grew into perfect replicas that had been turned *en masse* into stoner freaks (no passion or emotion, unless you count the heroin drool). I was outside and saw all of this, but there was nothing I could do. I could have started screaming like Kevin McCarthy, "They're coming for you; they're already here!" but the only response I would get would be, "Bad trip, huh? You should try this Buddha grass; it will mellow you out right away." I knew that the pods would eventually change me just like they did with McCarthy's girlfriend (Ah, Dana Wynter was a delectable "pea" in her pod).

I reminisced back about my college days. I had come from a home where no alcohol was kept; we had no beer or wine for dinner, and I was never drunk until I got to college. There I joined a fraternity that alternated with other fraternities so that every week we had a raunchy keg beer dance party. Drinking beer was how you met girls and enjoyed bull sessions with your frat brothers, and it became an integral part of college life. It made the insipid banter with vacuous coeds and the deafening party bands bearable and, after a while, fun. Drinking in the army was *de rigeur*: we all got together at the officers' club, and it was a comradery experience and a test of character: see who could get the most drunk and be at your job in a freshly starched uniform at 8 am, performing your duties efficiently and normally, whether you were hungover and had to excuse yourself every fifteen minutes to retch your guts out.

For the first couple of months traveling, beer and saki were the fuel to maintain lengthy discussions on myriad topics from philosophical systems (Taoism) to politics (communism in China) to understanding people (what makes the Japanese people tick?) Now I had a decision to make. Do I go with the flow or keep myself apart? At first, I just abstained. I saw the Bangkok

Floating Market, the principal Buddhists Wats, and museums, straight and by myself. At night I'd drink some beer and write in my journal. This soon got boring, and I thought I might test the waters with only my toes. I bought a small portion of hash from a fellow freak and got some rolling paper. I retreated to my room and rolled my first joint. I'm a cigarette smoker, but my secret is that I don't inhale tobacco. I smoke it like a pipe or cigar, swishing it in my mouth and then exhaling it. Smoking hash demanded a deep inhale and holding it in as a swimmer holds his breath underwater.

The following may sound like a kindergarten presentation: "See Jane Smoke Pot for the First Time" ("Kids, Do Not Attempt To Actually Smoke Marijuana, The Smoking is being performed by Trained Professionals in a Controlled Environment for Educational Purposes Only") but in this big country there must be at least one naive farmer in Iowa who reads this book (that's a stretch!) and would benefit from my in-depth IKEA by-the-numbers instruction on how to get high.

My first joint was hilarious. I took a deep hit and coughed madly while trying to hold it deep in my lungs. I didn't get high; I said to myself, "This isn't for me." But that night, I rolled a second joint, learning how to keep the smoke in without coughing too much. I got a mild sense of calmness and felt I didn't want to move; however, I did get up from my chair and check under the bed to see if there was a pod growing into my replicant, but there wasn't any there. The next day I had my third joint, and then the euphoria hit. I was still in control of my mind and my motor skills, but I had this beautiful sense of peacefulness and accepted everything around me with equanimity. Everything was the same; only it was now more agreeable: the heat, the cold showers, the inane conversations, and even the stall food tasted better.

Now I was ready for the Varsity Squad. I wanted to be a team player, and we were at the big game; I was going to do this for the Gipper. I rolled a large joint and shared it with a few freaks in our lounge area. We all got high; I was now one of them; "We have met the enemy, and we are theirs." My transformation into a Pod Replicant Stoner was complete ("Somehow, Toto, I don't believe we're in Kansas anymore").

When this state of high became the norm, I found that I could function very well on this supra-reality level. In fact, I felt it wasn't a good day unless, as the Rolling Stones song goes, I ran daily to the cupboard for "Mother's Little Helper". Even though being transformed into a Pod person with no emotion or passion, somehow, I still kept thinking to myself, "Where is Dana Wynter when I really need her?"

Dana Wynter in 1962

Chapter Four: Bangkok After Dark: Walk on the Wild Side

"One Night in Bangkok": Murray Head

Bangkok Nightlife (photo by Norbert Braun 2022, UNSPLASH)

Bangkok comes alive at night. I left the hotel with Marc, a drug zombie but also a former chef in France, who showed me the best places for Thai food. The fiery-hot chili-infected concoction of green, red, and black sauced food that is their national cuisine. We tasted "scorch your tongue" prawns in green chili sauce, "run to the toilet" chicken in red chili sauce and "give me another beer quickly" pork with black bean chili sauce.

My father had trained as a French saucier in Switzerland, so I was used to the different tastes of European haute cuisine, but Thai food blew me away (both in a discovery and bowel movement sense). This wasn't the half-rotten, garlicky cabbage, buried for a year in earthen jars in your backyard, kimchi that stunk up every bus in Korea. Thai food burned a hole all the way from your mouth to your rectum. A fiery bullet that I imagine is the trial version of passing kidney stones; however, with mounds of sticky rice and Singha Thai beer, the food was quite enjoyable, even though I had to carry a full roll of toilet paper with me everywhere I went.

Marc, when he wasn't totally stoned, was a great guide, and I learned to balance the milder coconut-based sauces with the "enfant-terribla" green chili sauce. Marc was thoroughly French and had a colorful way of describing in detail the different sauces (imaginative fulsome variations of merd!) The local fruits also helped: golden melt-in-your-mouth pineapples, fleshy lychees, and prickly succulent rambutans: all left a sweet relief in your mouth.

After a hot, sweat-inducing meal, we went to a hot, sweat-filled gym arena. Here we watched a singularly Thai sport: kickboxing, which is similar to American boxing, only on speed. Instead of the slowly grinding, clutch-induced exhaustion of American boxers as immortalized by George Bellow's New York City prizefighter paintings, here we have a stylized ballet of swirling arms and legs. The audience really gets into the fighters: yelling bets, screaming at favorites and shouting at the referee. The arena is a mini-Inferno of glaring and harsh electric lights, enveloped in the smokey haze of cigarettes and the tightly packed body sweat odor of the betters. For a few of the best fighters, there is a chance to make extra money as a stand-in extra in Thai kickboxing films. They would be one of the ten bad guys that, all at once, fight the skilled photogenic star of a Thai thriller.

Thai Kick Boxing (author's photo)

We escaped from this sauna into the relative cool of the night to head for the bars. Bangkok's sex scene is a huge chunk of the local economy, fueled mainly by American servicemen on R & R (Rest & Relaxation) from Vietnam. GI's get one week away from their mud-soaked hell to a paradise of American-style hamburgers, cheap booze, and an endless supply of beautiful "ladies of the night". This Thai version of legendary Storyville in New Orleans fulfills every man's desire: country and western clubs with honky-tonk music, complete with cowboy booted, Stetson-wearing cowgirl courtesans to Soul Clubs with funky bands wearing out Sly and the Family Stone and Marvin Gay. The music is usually without the "r's". Thai bands have trouble with the letter "r", so Thai bands when they sing: "Ready to Rock", it becomes "Letty to Lock". There are also mainstream Rock & Roll, Psychedelic, and Heavy Metal Rock Clubs that entice the white GIs and foreign sex tourists.

The girls are lined up on a stage, and for the right price, you can pick out bachelorette #10 with the flick of your finger. Thai women are gorgeous, without the hardness you often see in the Korean courtesans. The prices for an evening of paradise are too high for me, but the voyeuristic window-shopping here beats the jaded, over-made-up hookers in the cubby window holes of Amsterdam.

Bangkok is like the hole in a bathtub: everything goes down the drain, and that was the freak's fate. This was the end of the line for many freaks, as cruel as the senseless heroin overdose of a young black in a cold Harlem apartment or the intoxicated raving of a young Indian in a mobile home on the reservation. You could see them nodding off near the main Wats, staring motionless at a dish of fried rice, or just disappearing into their hotel rooms and not coming out for days.

Heroin was dirt cheap, brought down from the Golden Triangle (Laos, Thailand, and Vietnam) by slick Chinese businessmen to keep the prostitutes strung out and docile and to feed the addictions of young Western tourists.

As a bon-a-fide freak, I gave my fellow freaks a pecking order. The French were the worst. Most came from crowded, shithole cities like Marseilles or Calais, always strung out and keeping with their own countrymen. They were always out of money and constantly stealing from the other freaks. The French chicks used their sexy French-accented English and Chanel perfume to score rich Chinese businessmen (Oh, mon Cheri!) to pay for their extended Thai vacation. The French felt superior to the other freaks, with their dime store existentialist spouting or their idealization of the simple Thai life, as opposed to the corrupt bourgeoise society they left behind. Merd!

The British reflected their class society: there were the rich, upper class, hippie types, dressed in flowing white robes, dabbling with heroin and Buddhism. They stayed for a few months to soak up the sun, practice yoga, and get laid. An exception to the guys, Brit university gals were usually serious, articulate, and drug-free. The working-class Brits were different. They were down-to-earth and usually kept their highs to hashish. Many came from the post-industrial north. They had no future in Britain and were headed for Australia and a new life.

The Germans were divided into two stereotypes: the smug, obnoxiously superior-to-everyone type that has endeared them to all of Europe and the "romantic" type, as exemplified in "Meister Wilhelm" by Goethe: the wandering Siegfried and Brunhilda, here to learn about the people, religion, and customs of the Thai people. They were serious and intellectual, open to new ideas, and usually the best conversationalists, great companions for long bus and train rides.

The Aussies were the easiest to travel with. The guy freaks were either total stoners or beer party drunks. The sheilas (chicks) were either on a mission from God: they were on a pilgrimage to the U.K. for a job or to unite with the far away "motherland" or California party girls with a funny accent.

The Canadians with their red maple leaf patch sewed on their backpacks and the New Zealanders with their green Kiwi logo emblems usually spent the first hour when you met them justifying and emphasizing why they weren't American or Aussie. After they got that off their chests, they were fun, sharp, and usually in control of their drug and drink addictions (the Maple Leafs were just good ole guys and gals in flannel). The Kiwis had the most musical, lilting English accent that I ever heard (Riiightt maaaate, in three-part harmony).

The Americans ran the gamut from drooling heroin addicts, sex tourists, serious Buddhist disciples, mal-adjusted expatriates, California flower child hippies, Valley airheads here for fun in the sun, ex-GIs that would not or could not go home, and itinerant freaks. That's me, the wandering freak: I'm just the all-American kid from New York City.

Chapter Five: Two Tickets to Paradise

So, take off your thirsty boots
And stay for a while
Your feet are hot and weary
From a dusty mile
And maybe I can make you laugh

"Thirsty Boots" Eric Andersen

This classic folk song is about the hardships of the Freedom Riders down South in the 1960s, but it could just as easily be a depiction of the fear and suffering of the common 11 Bravo grunt in the jungles of Vietnam.

American soldiers in Vietnam

We got off of the plane, a bumpy Air Force cargo plane fitted with makeshift seats, direct from Da Nang. After six months in the boonies with insufferable heat, mosquitos, and Charlie shooting at us, Tom and I finally got our R&R. Most of our platoon took it in Australia, wanting round-eyed girls and cold beer, but I had heard so much about Bangkok that I had to see it for myself.

Tom was my best bro: we had been through ambushes, where we lost a quarter of our platoon, miserable monsoon-soaked days when nothing would dry, and endless nights hunched over sandbags waiting for Charlie (Viet Cong) to attack. Tom didn't give a shit where he went, as long as it was out of the jungle.

The USO got us set up with a clean hotel downtown. The sights and sounds blew my mind. I wasn't a farm boy rube: I'd been to Topeka and Frisco before we shipped out, but this was another world!

Tom and I had three things on our minds: eat a huge steak, get drunk, and get laid. We didn't care about which came first; we just had to do all three.

The streets were jammed with people selling everything under the sun. I bought a pair of Ray Bans; now I was incognito. Tom bought a cheap Japanese camera and proceeded to shoot everything in sight.

Tom was from Worchester, Massachusetts, a dirty mill town where upward mobility meant moving from a grocery clerk to the night shift at the local John Deere plant. He probably would have stayed there for life, marrying a factory girl or waitress and raising a bunch of kids, but the draft fixed that.

Me, I was from a small farming community in Kansas; my dad worked at Sears, and my mom took care of my two younger sisters and me. I had a girlfriend back home, Beth, but she was a born-again Christian, so we never had sex; she wanted to wait until we got married. Well, I didn't, and not knowing what I wanted to do with my life, Hell, I enlisted! "Kill a Commie for Christ" or some other asinine justification for wanting to get away from home. Having no job training or skills, I was classified 11 Bravo (infantry foot soldier), and boy did I step into it. If I was going to die in some god-forsaken jungle, at least I would have spent a week in paradise first.

We met some Navy slugs; boy, do they have a cushy job, just sitting in their ships, firing at Charlie from a safe distance, then going ashore in some exotic port, buying souvenirs and getting laid. Anyhow, they told us where to go for the best girlie bars and where to find those steaks. We had our steaks with good Thai beer and tequila shots. Then we went out to a girlie dance club. That first night out was fun, as much of it as I can remember. We were buying these cute Thai girls drinks and dancing to good ole rock and roll. The next thing I knew, Tom was leaning over me and saying something, trying to pick me up from the dance floor. I remember muttering something like; I knew it wasn't good for me to eat the worm at the bottom of the bottle. After heaving up my steak and the rest of my guts in the alley, Tom somehow got me home, and I slept until the next night, waking with a splitting headache, but the party must go on. After a cold shower and two Bloody Marys, I remembered the third thing on my list and was determined to find the girl of my dreams.

We landed at the Golden Rainbow Club, where the girls were all sitting at tables with numbers, waiting for a date. They were all gorgeous; this was the candy store of my dreams, and I had the quarter to pick anyone I wanted. After talking with a few girls and buying endless rounds of watered-down champaign, I settled on a beautiful, sweet, long black-haired girl. She was probably only 20 years old, with white chalk skin and soft pink lipstick-coated lips. She spoke a little English, definitely enough to tell me $20 a night for her company. Tom had found another long-haired beauty with fiery eyes; this one speaking broken English in short, clipped phrases. Tom and I went to their rooms in a nearby apartment and agreed to get together in the morning for breakfast.

My girl called herself Gloria, an English name to make it easy to remember her, but her real name was Su Lee, and I called her that. Her room was clean and compact: a large double-sized bed with a small lamp on a nightstand, a makeup table with a mirror, and a small wardrobe. It was the walls that were interesting; they were plastered with Western fashion models, displaying the latest European fashions and hairstyles. Best of all, she had a small balcony that overlooked a back alley, complete with potted plants, a table, and chairs. The bathroom was in the hall, and it smelled like cooked cabbage.

She quickly ran to the bathroom, and I was left gawking at the fashion models and smoking Camels on the balcony, watching old Chinese women cooking, washing clothes, and playing mahjong, a Chinese game that looked like a combination of checkers and dominos.

She came back in a kimono robe and brought me over to the bed, where she started kissing me and undressing me at the same time. She hung my clothes over a chair and then tucked me under the sheets, deftly turning off the bedside lamp, removing her robe, and seamlessly sliding into the bed beside me. Her long hair flowed over her breasts, small but large enough for my hands to encompass and my mouth to kiss her rigid nipples. She kissed my nipples and then worked her way down to my penis, first licking the tip with her tongue before moving her lips over the head. Her tongue lapped the tip while her mouth rocked rhythmically up and down. I was going crazy; it's all over now, baby blue, I'm goin' come. Suddenly she stopped and pulled me over her, helping me bring my penis into her bare shaved vagina. We moved together, her lips, arms, and legs now entangling mine. Her back arched to bring me completely in her. I came with a thrust that seemed like I was splitting her apart. She moaned quietly and continued to grind her hips, absorbing all of my pent-up juice and locking my penis until it was finally spent. I rolled over, drained, still reeling from our lovemaking. She kissed me again and then lay in my arms quietly. The darkness enveloped us while the sounds of mahjong tiles clacking echoed from below.

Chapter Six: Ayutthaya

Ruins of Ayutthaya (author's photo)

"It seems, in fact, that the more advanced a society is, the greater will be its interest in ruined things, for it will see in them a redemptively sobering reminder of the fragility of its own achievements. Ruins pose a direct challenge to our concern with power and rank, bustle, and fame. They puncture the inflated folly of our exhaustive and frenetic pursuit of wealth."
— **Alain de Botton,** <u>The Pleasures and Sorrows of Work</u>

My trusty, well-worn "Golden Guide to Asia" raved about a vast ruined city that was only about thirty-five miles from Bangkok. This was Ayutthaya, a former Thai capital city.

So, one bright morning I armed myself with my camera, a bag of rambutans, two large Singha beers, and a pack of Golden City Thai cigarettes, and I was off to discover Ayutthaya.

I felt like the American archaeologist Hiram Bingham, the discoverer of Machu Picchu in Peru. Instead of hacking through dense jungle and swatting malarial mosquitos, I boarded an overcrowded country bus, suffering crying babies, aisles clogged with bags of rice, and endless loud chattering from the farmers, to travel one and a half hours to my destination. When I arrived, I felt the joy of discovering a "lost" city (National Geographic, eat your heart out!). I found a bicycle rental shop and would see my first ruined Asian city in style, see Siam (Thailand) on your sleek Schwinn (bicycle).

Ayutthaya was founded by an adventurer of common origins named U Thong. The city was built on a peninsula, surrounded by three rivers and a later canal that made it into an island city. In its heyday in the fifteenth century A. D., it was one of the richest and most magnificent cities in Asia. There were hundreds of wats, temples, palaces, and canals, now mostly in a totally ruined state. The European merchants who visited this city called it the Venice of the East. It controlled a vast empire that spanned central Thailand, Laos, Cambodia, and down into the Malay peninsula. It was a busy commercial river port, trading with all of Southeast Asia and with major cities of medieval Europe.

Unfortunately, it attracted the envy of the Burmese kingdom and was thoroughly destroyed in 1767. Bangkok then became the new capital, and Ayutthaya was abandoned and forgotten.

I spent all day bicycling to different wats, ruined temples, broken colonnades, and palaces in various states of desolation. There was an imposing chedi (bell-shaped tower), which was about two hundred feet high, with trees growing out near the top. There was a prong (central tower) at Wat Ratchaburana, which still had its golden gilt Buddha standing tall in an arched niche. Near Wat Chai Yai Mongkon was a large reclining Buddha cast in bronze, with its eyes wide open, as if staring in disbelief at the destruction surrounding it.

I shot two rolls of black and white photographs of the destroyed monuments because B & W gives a more powerful contrast and lets your eye focus on the fine details.

I was thoroughly exhausted, and my legs were sore (not to mention my butt) from peddling for six hours. By sundown, I had gone through my beer, rambutans, and half a pack of cigarettes. I boarded the last bus back to Bangkok. As the bus bumped along dusty roads, I reflected upon all of the destroyed cities in history: Genghis Khan, sacking city after city and massacring the inhabitants, like the Silk Road oasis cities of Samarkand and Bukhara, and the temples of Pagan that I described in my first book, in his blood-thirsty conquests. Allied bombers thoroughly destroyed medieval Nuremberg and Baroque Dresden. And the horrific destruction of Hiroshima and Nagasaki that brought Japan to surrender in WW II.

Destruction of Dresden in WW II (Photo by Richard Peter)

When I see this iconic photo, I can't help but remember the haunting lines from Percy Bysshe Shelly's famously ironic poem: 'My name is Ozymandias, King of Kings: Look on my works, ye Mighty, and despair!'

We in America are lucky that we never had a modern-era major war that ravaged our own country. But I reflected on war's horrors in Ray Bradbury's "The Martian Chronicles", where Los Angeles is obliterated by atom bombs. One house alone has music and an automated wake-up system that keeps playing every day. The house occupants were so pulverized by the blast that they left only black silhouettes on the outside wall, yet the taped band played on, a dissonant note in the complete silence of destruction.

Chapter Seven: At Play In the Sands of Time

Thai kids playing soccer on a beach (author's photo)

I convinced Marc, my French Freak friend, that we needed a little R & R from our 9-5 drug habit (To be honest, I had to bribe Marc to come, promising to share my Buddha grass, which I'd scored the night before.). A short two hours away by bus was Bang Saen Beach, a Middle-Class escape for Thai families from the heat and smog of Bangkok. We rented a small bungalow near the beach, complete with two rope beds, an outdoor outhouse, and a working ceiling fan.

I wanted to lose my pasty-white "Night of the Living Dead" complexion with some sun and surf. Marc, however, decided to stay stoned on my Buddha grass and to perform an in-depth analysis of the ceiling fan (At least it appeared that way, since he stared fixedly at it for hours, immobile and silent from his bed). As I left for the beach, I gave Marc my customary "Say Goodnight Gracie", getting no response as usual.

The beach was beautiful and unspoiled. There was no glitzy boardwalk, just a few stands selling drinks and snacks. The beach had fine yellow sand, clear waters, and no undertow from the surf.

I set up my towel and was immediately surrounded by dozens of Thai children, all yelling, "Falang! (Foreigner) Where are you from? What is your name?" After a while, they got used to me and ignored me. After a few days, I became a part of their group, kicking the soccer ball, building sand pagodas, and splashing them in the shallow waters.

Playing with these Thai children brought back memories of when I was their age (7 or 8 years old) and our monthly summer outings to Coney Island. My mother would take me on two trains and a subway ride to get to Bay Ridge, Brooklyn. Bay Ridge was largely Norwegian in the 1950s, and we mounted a Viking expedition of mothers, fathers, aunts, uncles, and dozens of blonde tow-head kids to Coney Island (Instead of a dragon head longboat, we all piled on the local RR subway train). The beach was jam-packed, but we conquered a small section of the beach without shedding a single drop of blood. I spent the entire day in the water, eating Nathan's hot dogs with French fries sprinkled with vinegar and losing at SkeeBall. At the end of the day, I was sunburnt and vividly embarrassed. All of the kids changed out of their bathing suits. My mother and aunt held a white beach towel around me and told me to take off my wet, sandy bathing suit and get dressed in my normal clothes. There I was, naked to the world, with people streaming all around me and only partially hidden by the towel. If I wasn't red from the sun, I surely was from my bare body being brazenly exposed to the eyes of the world!

We stayed at my aunt's apartment, where I met her son. He was older, a teenager, about seventeen, and apparently always got into trouble. My aunt, however, was pretty clever; she used to bribe him to stay home and not hang out with his juvenile delinquent friends by buying him a pack of Lucky Strikes and a comic book. Now I was beginning to understand why the Vikings couldn't keep control of America after first stumbling on to it.

While at Bang Saen Beach, I had great Chinese stall food and spent my nights reading and talking to my pet rock since Marc was still intently studying the ceiling fan.

Meanwhile, back at the beach, I thought of all of those innocent Thai children – how long before "Along Comes Jones, tall, lanky Jones". How long before our "superior" western culture (sex, drugs, and rock & roll) corrupts them with the promise of a better life? This will not be accomplished with the gun and horse that the Spanish wielded to conquer the Aztecs and Incas, but with the irresistible lure of indoor plumbing, electricity turned on by a switch, and a shiny automobile in their driveway. Change is inevitable, but can it be accomplished in a truly Thai fashion? Buddhism shaped the Thai character - will that be lost on the altar of Capitalism? Will the seedy nightlife of Bangkok sex clubs engulf this pristine beach?

I and my fellow freaks are mere glowworms in this Garden of Eden, visible but not a threat to the Thai lifestyle. The real vipers are the CIA agents, building up the Thai Army and bribing government officials to resist communism. Then there is the Japanese businessman selling his Honda motorcycles with exorbitant credit terms. Lastly, there are the Chinese and Thai entrepreneurs, getting the prostitutes, drugs, and clubs to make Thailand an international sex tourist destination.

We left Bang Saen after two weeks. I had a Hollywood tan, gained five pounds, and had remained drug-free for that period. Marc is, well, Marc: the drug addict only used the beach as a change of scenery. I gave him the window seat on the bus back to Bangkok; he seemed content because now he had a moving picture to stare blankly at.

A typical Thai Beach

Laos

Monument for Fallen Heroes-Vientiane (author's photo)

Chapter Eight: Berlin Bleibt Deutsch

(Berlin Remains German)

Gene Pitney: Town Without Pity

A Russian tank rolls triumphantly down a Berlin Street, passing a wall inscribed with "Berlin bleibt Deutsch" (Berlin remains German) April 1945

I had just gotten back from two weeks at the beach and felt relaxed and ready for a new adventure. At the hotel, someone mentioned they had a great time in Laos. The only thing I knew about Laos was that that was where Dr. Tom Dooley had set up a clinic there in the 1950s. He treated the Hill Tribes people, actively converting them to Christianity, exemplifying the life of Christ by his example of selfless love and helping and treating them at no cost. Visiting Laos sounded like a good idea, and I determined to clean up my act and take my show on the road. The next night I left the Bangkok train station for the overnight train to Vientiane. I love train rides, especially at night, because it makes me think of Germany and the Berlin Troop Train, where we passed by old East German towns and empty highways and finally arrived at dawn at the Hauptbahnhof (central train station) in West Berlin. The Berlin Troop Train was an American train, patrolled by American Military Police but operated by the German Railroad, which carried American military and government officials from Frankfurt to Berlin nonstop. This train was not subject to East German customs and regulations but could not stop anywhere in East Germany outside of West Berlin.

I arrived in Vientiane in the early morning. The train station was very crowded. People had all their belongings with them and seemed to be leaving Vientiane in a hurried manner, like rats deserting a sinking ship. There was a siege mentality here; people were very anxious to get out. It reminded me of the stories that old Germans had told me about April 1945, when they knew the Russians were coming. They may have scrawled on the walls: "Berlin bleibt Deutsch" (Berlin remains German), but they all knew the "Gotterdammerung" was coming.

French Indochina Travel Poster 1931

I flagged down a pedicycle and asked him to take me to a cheap hotel. The hotel was an old French Colonial Government building that had been converted into a hotel, with peeling ochre stucco walls and rusted wrought iron balconies in a vaguely Art Deco style. This was in the heart of the old part of Vientiane. Like the rest of Vientiane, there was an air of decay and shabbiness in this hotel. However, my room was luxuriously furnished with a big brass bed, my own toilet, and the proverbial ceiling fan. Another great thing about the hotel was that it had a beautifully walled-in patio with tables and tropical palms. There was a large broken fountain, which was filled with brackish water and discarded cigarette butts. Here we congregated in the late afternoon, drinking bitter French espresso and eating croissants. We exchanged stories, got info on traveling, and paired up for dinner and Vientiane nightlife. Speaking of nightlife, there was even an American-style discotheque, which alternated playing American pop music and French chansons.

Currently, Laos is a dangerous place for foreigners. The kingdom was a former French colony that was equally divided between the communists (Pathet Lao), who controlled the southern half of the country, and the other half was run by the drug lords in the north. Added to this, the CIA also had a share of the pie, running clandestine air operations, arming Hmong tribesmen to fight the Pathet Lao, and bribing officials to maintain a policy favorable to US interests. In the middle was the King, with his small army, trying to hold it all together. The only thing that made sense of all this was a routine by that famous duo: "Well, this is a fine mess you've gotten us into," said Ollie to Stan. You could not leave Vientiane; here, you were relatively safe. The countryside was extremely dangerous. There was a Danish backpacker that was killed near the Mekong River by the Pathet Lao because he was blond, and they thought he was an American.

The hotel had a cast of characters that begged for a modern-day Somerset Maughan to chronicle their expatriate lives. I can only portray a fleeting glimpse, a snapshot of a moment frozen in time, like when you see an angelic vision of a hauntingly beautiful Puerto Rican girl entering as you are leaving the subway car on the uptown IRT Local. Her longing expression: the eyes that spoke of sadness and loss and how you would give everything just to take her in your arms and say, "It's alright, I'm here to save you and myself", and then the subway door closes, and she is gone forever.

On the first floor, Room 3, there was an ex-army captain, Terry, whose story follows.

Chapter Nine: The Soldier's Tale

Country Joe and the Fish: "I Feel Like I'm Fixing to Die Rag"

This "gallows' humor" song mocks all aspects of the Vietnam war: the war profiteering, the right-wing government paranoia, and the heartbreaking consequences of this senseless war.

Two Women, French Indochina 1895

It is no wonder that French and later American soldiers fell in love with these lovely women.

"Vietnam was a hell hole. You went on endless patrols through mud, got bitten by mosquitos, and sweated through the insufferable tropical heat. All that, and you couldn't trust anyone. You enter a village, and you only find old men, women, and children. The young men were all in the Viet Cong, hiding in the jungle. Many of the houses were booby-trapped, and the villagers saw us as the enemy. Everyone in the platoon was either hysterically tense or numbed by drugs. When you were on patrol, Viet Cong snipers killed your friends; others died in a flurry of grenades in close explosive bursts, and then Charlie melted away back into the jungle. You were walking, side by side, with your best buddy, and suddenly, he fell down dead with a bullet in his head. Why him and not me? The Viet Cong is a vengeful God manipulating fate: there is no good or bad, right or wrong, just a coin toss to decide life or death. You lead these scared young kids; you're supposed to have the answers, but you don't. The orders come down to secure this sector of the jungle, and shit flows downhill. You lose three GIs taking this shithole village. The minute you leave, the Viet Cong come back, coerce the villagers, rob them of their meager food, booby trap their homes and force the young men into their ranks. Then you come back to Saigon, and it's honky-tonk America. A bar on every corner, endless booze and drugs, and beautifully delicate women. Gorgeous women that you didn't stand a chance to date back home; now yours for the night for a ten-dollar bill. We turned Vietnam into a Sodom and Gomorrah that reflected the bankruptcy of our own "superior" American society.

Somehow, I managed to survive, living one day at a time, hardening myself and striving to protect my men. I didn't give a shit over meaningless ideologies of communists versus free men and how righteous our fight was. It's all just bullshit. When it came time to go back to the States, I stayed on because there was no one waiting at home for me. My parents wouldn't understand. My friends, who were in the Service, were gone, and there was no special girl waiting for me. I was angry. I knew I wouldn't fit in; I might even kill someone if I went back home. Then they told me I couldn't stay in Saigon, so I took a flight to Vientiane and got here to this cheap hotel and started drinking.

I went out one night to a small bar, where I met An Li. She was a "cherry" girl, fresh from the southern provinces, which she left to escape the Pathet Lao. Like many young girls coming here found out, there were no jobs, and she became a hostess in this bar. I wasn't the first to have her, but I caught her while there was still innocence left in her eyes and demeanor. She wasn't a hardened zombie like most of these hostesses; she still had hopes that she could leave this "life", start a dress-making shop or work in a hair salon to escape. Then fate threw us together. Was it love? I didn't know. All I knew was that I wanted to protect her and maybe make some sense out of all this shit. Getting her away from the madame was expensive and ugly. Dealing with her goons, fighting them in the fetid alley behind the bar, endless payments to the madame with no resolution in sight. Finally, we agreed on a price, I paid it, and she was truly free. We lived together in a dream, absorbed only in ourselves and hidden away from the sordid reality that surrounded us.

We married in Laos, but then the bureaucratic nightmare began, trying to get her a visa for the States. There were endless forms to fill out, meetings with corrupt officials, payments to this magistrate or another, lost paperwork, and more payments. We are still waiting, and it's been going on for six months now. God knows if we're ever going to get the right paperwork to the right corrupt official for the right baksheesh money. "I just know that I love her and won't leave here without her."

Chapter Ten: Dr. Tom Dooley

1 Be still, my soul: the Lord is on thy side.
Bear patiently the cross of grief or pain.
Leave to thy God to order and provide,
who through all changes faithful will remain.
Be still, my soul: thy best, thy heavenly Friend
through thorny ways leads to a joyful end.

2 Be still, my soul: thy God doth undertake
to guide the future surely as the past.
Thy hope, thy confidence let nothing shake;
all now mysterious shall be bright at last.
Be still, my soul: the waves and winds still know
his voice who ruled them while he dwelt below.

3 Be still, my soul: the hour is hastening on
when we shall be forever with the Lord;
when disappointment, grief, and fear are gone,
sorrow forgot, love's purest joys restored.
Be still, my soul: when change and tears are past
all safe and blessed, we shall meet at last.

BE STILL, MY SOUL"

German spiritual hymn by Katharina Amalia von Schlegel (1697-1768)

English translation by Jane Borthwick 1855

As I mentioned before, the only image that comes to mind when thinking of Laos is Dr. Tom Dooley. When I was a young teen, our minister at Montgomery Presbyterian Church in my hometown had preached about him, calling him a selfless human being that was sacrificing his life for the welfare of the Laotian people, both as a doctor and as a Christian spreading the love of Christ.

Today his legacy is somewhat diminished because of his lies about communist torture and his cooperation with the CIA. However, if you look at the man in total, you see his devotion and love for the people of Laos outweigh these less significant detractions. Did he have flaws: yes, but he rose above them, working tirelessly, "Do this for the poorest, and you do it for Me," as Christ said. Here is Tom Dooley's story.

Dr. Tom Dooley was a Roman Catholic doctor in the US Navy in Vietnam, working with refugees. He inflated his role in this humanitarian work, saying, "To be a humanitarian, you've got to run it like a business. You gotta have Madison Ave., T. V., and radio." His "self-aggrandizement" helped him to get more funding and political backing to help more people. Before, he had personally treated about a hundred patients a day; with this self-advertisement, he received funding to build a network of clinics that treated over five hundred people a day.

In 1958 he left the Navy and decided to go to Laos because he was, in his words, the only "bon-a-fide" doctor in a country of three million people. He founded an international medical cooperation organization, MEDICO. MEDICO built three hospitals and treated up to a thousand patients a day. Dr. Dooley worked in the hills near the Chinese border because there were sick people there. Furthermore, the tribespeople there were indoctrinated by anti-Western propaganda from Red China, and he felt they needed a loving Christian message. He was recruited by the CIA to share the information received from the refugees. He fabricated atrocities by the Viet Minh. Why did he do this? I believe he felt empathy for the refugees, and the more grotesque the suffering, the more financial support he would get to treat more people. He worked tirelessly, going from 180 to 120 pounds, continually working, even though he was sick with intestinal worms and malaria.

He wrote two bestselling books about his experience in Laos: "Edge of Tomorrow" and "The Night They Burned the Mountain." Again, he helped the CIA by telling them about military movements in the hills. His daily work consisted of traveling from village to village, treating illnesses, spreading his Christian faith, and helping Laotians with sanitation and medication advice. He died of cancer in 1961 at the age of 34.

Dr. Dooley's legacy is one of exemplary duty and love for the Hill People of Laos. He saw himself as an American patriot, and for everything he did for the CIA, he never took any money. He said, "I did this because it gave me more freedom to do my work and a little less harassment."

When President Kennedy founded the Peace Corps, he cited Dr. Dooley as a glowing example of what the Peace Corps could aspire to and the success that could be achieved.

Dr. Tom Dooley in Loas

Chapter Eleven: Alles Ist Schone

("EVERYTHING IS BEAUTIFUL")

"What a Wonderful World": Louis Armstrong

The Vientiane Outdoor Market (author's photo)

I was alone, walking around and trying to capture the mood and rhythm of the old city. The old crumbling, peeling yellow painted French Colonial Government Buildings, the soot-covered white wat temples, and the colorful two-story stucco houses in saturated blues and pastel yellows and pinks. There is a main tree-lined avenue, culminating in the French-built Monuments des Muerte. At the other end of the boulevard is the bustling market. This market is huge and sells everything from food to drugs to black-market electronics. As I was walking through the market, I was approached by this incredible laughing German who came up to me and said, "Isn't this wonderful?" "Isn't this beautiful?" Hans was in his mid-thirties, potbellied with his blonde-brown hair in a ponytail. He was dressed in a flowery shirt and Chinese fisherman pants, but what stood out was his animated, outgoing manner. You could not help but feel at ease with this vivacious "teddy bear". He invited me to his house, which was the bottom floor of a brightly painted blue bungalow, to meet his Lao wife and assorted relatives. The music was blaring from the kitchen, and in his bedroom, the walls were filled with photos of naked women. He offered me a hashish smoke, and we sat down in his crowded kitchen, filled with relatives and chattering children, and talked about Vientiane. He told me that there was quite a large expatriate colony here, with many Germans, Dutch, and a few Americans. He had come from Germany, looking for easy women and cheap dope. He first landed in Bangkok but found the sex and drug scene too overwhelming for him and moved on to Laos. He had been a handyman and carpenter back in Germany, and what little money he made was with his hands, fashioning furniture for the restaurants, billboard signs, and odd jobs to eke out a marginal existence. He had met this lovely Lao woman and married her. This was also the story of many of the other expatriates, who had gone native like himself, married Lao women, and lived hand-to-mouth without any direct source of income. He had no life back in Germany, and here the dope was cheap, and the authorities left him alone. For better or worse, this was his life now, and he really loved his wife and the no-hassle lifestyle.

Hans told me of a restaurant where I could get the best French food in Vientiane and a little about the political situation. It seemed that the Communists had taken the upper hand, and there were daily rumors that Vientiane would be captured. I asked him what he would do, and he just shook his head and said, "Life is beautiful; who knows?" Clearly stoned, I thanked him and headed back to my hotel. As I entered the hotel, I met Ally, the Swiss woman who lived in 3C. This is her story.

French Indochinese Tourist Poster 1931

Chapter Twelve: Swiss Miss and the Golden Boy

"The Needle and the Damage Done": Neil Young

Jeff was a typical all-American Boy, blond, blue-eyed, tall, good-looking, and sharp-witted. We met in an Amsterdam youth hostel. He was taking a break from his PhD program in History, and I was spending the summer traveling around Europe before I would take up a boring apprenticeship in a pharmaceutical company in Zurich.

He wasn't into drugs then, just an occasional hashish smoke, which was legal in the drug cafes in Amsterdam. He was always trying new things: eating a "rijsttafel" meal, the Indonesian smorgasbord of spices, sauces, meats, and vegetables, or sampling Guyana stews, all the while chatting up Indonesian and Guyana expatriate immigrants from the former Dutch colonies. He passionately studied the masterpieces of the Rijks Museum and the anthropological artifacts of the Troppen Museum. We hit it off and started living together, exploring ourselves as well as discovering the strange new world around us. The catalyst that changed him was a bag of psilocybin mushrooms that "opened his mind" and revolutionized his goals. School meant nothing; he was determined to find God in the form of Buddhism. I fell head-over-heals for him. We quickly got married in a civil service, and for our honeymoon, we bought two tickets to Paradise: the cross-country bus, filled with hippies from England that went from London (through Amsterdam) to India. The bus was a veritable candy store of drugs. Everything from speed to hashish to LSD and what you couldn't find on the bus, you could find in the countries you passed through: heroin in Turkey and hashish in Iran, Afghanistan and Pakistan. The trip became a hazy high that blurred the monotonous desert landscapes we drove through. We both thought we could control this habit, having each other for support. We had a higher goal: to find God in the Lotus Land of Southeast Asia. After a short stay in Bombay, where India's poverty freaked us out, we took a plane to Bangkok. We took lessons in Buddhism with monks and lived in a wat. We were heavily into meditation and discovering ourselves; these few months were the happiest time we ever had. During this magical time, we stopped the heavier drugs. Opium and heroin were omnipresent in Bangkok, but we had each other and were studying the precepts of the "rightful path" of Buddhism. But then Jeff saw opium as the means to Enlightenment, and he became heavily addicted. My practical Swiss upbringing kept me off the hard stuff, just an occasional hashish buzz. Besides, I couldn't get too high: I was his support pillar. I realized that opium wasn't the doorway to nirvana but a destructive dead end. We had to make a clean break: leave our so-called junky friends and the endless merry-go-round of shooting up in the morning and the stupefying nodding-off in the afternoon. We took a train to Vientiane to dry out, but Jeff found more heroin in the market, and it got out of control. We were going to go dancing with you tonight, but he was so desperate for drugs that I had to lock him in our room. "I don't know what to do: he doesn't eat, we don't make love anymore, and he is wasting away."

She was sobbing, I tried to console her, and we went to a nearby chai café, where she could continue to lay bare her feelings. I told her that I'd accompany her back to her room and try to talk some sense into Jeff.

We arrived back at the hotel and found the door broken open, and Jeff was nowhere in sight. He had taken what money he could find, undoubtedly, to get his hands on opium or heroin to feed his desperate habit.

Ally broke down, crying uncontrollably. I told her I'd find him and bring him back. I left her and headed for the market; that's where I had scored my hashish. It was dark now, and the market was empty, but there were small cafes still open. The first two were empty of foreigners, but the third one had a forlorn familiar face: Jeff was glazing off in space, lost in his private heroin heaven.

"Jeff, what are you doing? Ally is worried sick about you. Come on, let's go back to the hotel."

"Hey man, I got some great stuff; you want a snort with me?"

"Jeff, I'm goin' take you back to Ally."

"No way, Gordo, I stole her money and am ashamed to face her; besides, she locked me in, and I busted up the place to get out."

"It'll be okay; she'll forgive you. You can't stay here; they're closing soon, and where are you gonna go?" I got him up and shouldered him because he was wobbling on his feet. We staggered out, and I half carried him through the silent streets; he was limp and easy to control.

I finally got him back to his room; Ally had stopped crying, her eyes puffed, but when she saw him, she ran up to him and grabbed him, kissing him. Jeff was crying now, repeatedly droning, "I'm sorry, baby."

"Everything will be alright; here, lie down." He was soon quiet, lost in his reverie. "Goodnight, Ally; if I can do anything for you, don't hesitate." She thanked me and shut the door; she had her own demons to deal with now and knew I could not help her with these.

Chapter Thirteen: The Painter's Tale

I went out to see a few temples, but here too, there was an air of decay and abandonment. There were very few monks, and it seemed that everyone was leaving due to the foreboding that Vientiane would be attacked. I walked around the Old City and tried to follow the advice of that potaholic German Hans. The French were exploitive colonists that used their colonies for their own gain and did not share the wealth with the natives, nor did they educate them, but they did leave their cuisine, and there were a handful of small cafes that served real French food. Then the miracle happened. I had been for seven months without a piece of bread, and here was a French-style bakery that made real French baguettes. I found the restaurant that Hans had raved about, and the food was delicious. I indulged myself every night. Once steak (from water buffalo) and pomme frites, other times escargots in garlic-butter sauce and topped off with real demitasse French coffee. When not eating, I spent my time in the dusty outdoor coffee cafes, drinking endless cups of espresso and watching life go by, as if I were in a Parisienne cafe. When I returned to the hotel, I saw Ian, our resident painter, and this is his story.

A Painter's Tale

"It's impossible to go home once you see Paris…Texas." a film by Werner Herzog

"I was raised in Glasgow, a gritty soot-covered city in Scotland. I went to the Art Institute, a dark-stained colossus that was designed by a famous architect, Rennie MacIntosh, who thankfully gave up his profession to move to the south of France, painting luminescent landscapes and flowers.

I showed promise in my painting and participated in a few "group" shows that gave me rave reviews. However, I found everything here grey and depressing: the weather, the drab concrete box buildings streaked with rust, the listless, strung-out heroin addicts, and the deadening malaise of yet another economic depression. I had broken up with my girlfriend Tanya, another artist, who I accused of being a sellout, working as a graphic designer at a good salary, advertising for beer and sportscar companies.

With nothing going for me here, I thought I might become the new Gauguin. Tahiti was out, too far away and expensive. So, I looked around and talked to several people, who told me that

Bangkok was the goal: cheap living, lots of drugs, and loose women. Oh, and by the way, it might reinvigorate my artistic vision.

I was totally seduced by Thailand: the steamy climate, harsh bright sunlight, and endless fields of green and colorful flowering markets. My art was infused with this lushness. They say that the Eskimos have over thirty words to describe snow: fresh soft snow, old blue glacial snow, translucent ocean snow, and so forth. I felt the same way about the variety of greens: the dusty blue-green ferns lining the murky canals, new shoots of ivory green rice, and the emerald green of tropical jungles. I never felt so creative; my canvases radiated day glow colors: landscapes so real, they popped out of the canvases. I even sold some of these paintings to foreigners and had a gorgeous sunlit studio.

Then everything went to shit; I started hanging out at the bars, meeting a lot of expats, cheap whores, and even cheaper drugs. I painted less and less, caring more for football scores back home, getting high, and getting laid. This went on for days, weeks, and months, losing track of all time until I woke up one morning and saw myself in the cracked mirror of my wretched hotel room. I had very little money and no ambition and felt terribly lost. I knew I had to clean up my act, and so I followed a decisive impulse and came to Vientiane. I've been clean now for two months, still craving company, but I'm eating now and started painting elementary stuff: flowers and trees. The vision is not here yet, but my magical sense and feeling for color is taking hold of me again, and that's the path I'm going to follow. Here, let me show you my latest work."

Chapter Fourteen: Vientiane-The Last Day "Gotterdammerung"

The destruction of Berlin in May 1945

The city was tense and teetering on panic; there had been fighting nearby, and you could see the smoke of artillery fire in the distance. Everything was uncertain; would the city fall, and if so, how would I get out?

The day before I left Vientiane, I went to my favorite nightclub. Here the booze and the women were as plentiful as when I first arrived. There was a celebration in progress, and everyone was drunk and singing. The bar girls were doing a lively business; the dance floor was packed with sweating, gyrating couples. However, I was the only foreigner, and the f*in de siècle* atmosphere of the nightclub reminded me of the German Army staff watching a performance of Wagner's "Gotterdammerung" in March 1945, oblivious to the irony of the Russians fast approaching the Brandenburg Gate for their own Russian version of the fall of the Nazi "gods".

Hashish prices were a bargain at the market, but I was subject to Thai Customs, so I passed on that deal. Ally and Jeff had already left, hoping a change of scenery would save their relationship; the ex-Army Captain Terry and his Lao wife were still in bureaucratic purgatory and couldn't leave. Ian lived in his own private world, painting incessantly with his newfound creativity. I imagined my expatriate German friend Hans still thought, "Everything is beautiful."

I took one last trip to the French bakery and, with a baguette in hand, headed for the train station. The station was like the Berlin Zoo after a Russian aerial bombing: animal cages were blown open, and protective fences were destroyed. There were monkeys and giraffes running wild, and the roar of preying lions could be heard echoing through the empty streets. People were running everywhere, frantically purchasing tickets, collecting baggage, and rounding-up family members to board the train in time. I was lucky to book a second-class ticket, but there was standing room only in the train car. Panicked Laotians tried to take all of their worldly possessions with them, and you had to stand motionless, sandwiched between over-stuffed suitcases and crying children.

As the train pulled out of the station, we could hear the artillery shelling in the distance. I didn't know where the fighting was coming from, but I hoped it wasn't in the direction our train was going. If the Pathet Lao stopped the train, I was sure to be pulled off as a foreigner and, when they saw my passport, killed because I am an American. I remembered reading with horror about the partition of India upon independence. There were trains filled with Hindu men, women, and children fleeing Pakistan for India. When the trains arrived in India, every man, woman, and child had been slaughtered. However, we were fortunate: the further we traveled from Vientiane, the less we heard of the din of combat and the more we heard of the incessant crying of children on the train.

Crossing the Mekong River, the boundary between Laos and Thailand, I saw a bunch of Thai youths zestfully playing soccer on the sandy banks of the low-tide river. Maybe there was hope - people could go on with their normal lives as usual, and the impending carnage next door would pass them by, like the goat blood-splattered doors of the Jews in Egypt that kept their firstborn sons safe from the vengeful Angel of Death.

Thailand II

Thai Spirit House (author's photograph)

Chapter Fifteen: Chiang Mai

"I Left My Heart In San Francisco": Tony Bennett

This is the way I felt about Chiang Mai.

Thai Dancers 1900

Talk to any Thai, and they will tell you that Chiang Mai is the most beautiful city in Thailand; it is also reputed to have the most beautiful women in Thailand. Enterprising Chinese and Thai bar owners go to North Thailand, around Chiang Mai, to get girls for the Bangkok sex clubs. They "buy" daughters from poor rice-farming families, promising factory or domestic help jobs to the naïve teenage girls. They then bring them back to Bangkok for a life of prostitution.

I got back from Laos and, without skipping a beat, was back to being stoned 24/7. After about two weeks of this steady regimen, I determined to break from this heavy drug scene (all dope and no travel makes Gordon a dull boy) and tried to find a companion to accompany me to the fabled Chiang Mai in the north of Thailand. The response was less than enthusiastic, "Hey man, why should I leave this junk paradise?"

"Yeah, that sounds groovy, but I can't go now. I gotta see a man; maybe next week." So, I went to the nearby cafe to find new prospects, looking for fellow Freaks that I had traveled with. It was a hot, humid afternoon, and there weren't many people around in the café. I guessed everyone was getting high in their rooms, and vampire-like wouldn't venture out until the nighttime. I saw one freak that I had smoked with and started my spiel, but to no avail. Then I heard a voice behind me, saying, "I'll go. I planned to visit Chiang Mai soon." I turned around, "It's a girl, my Lord, in a Flatbed Ford, slowing down to take a look at me" (Eagles: "Take It Easy") Mira, Mira Senorita." She was medium height, a brown-haired girl in a sarong with a white peasant blouse. She was cute in a fresh sense: deep blue eyes with rosy cheeks and a perky, pouty mouth. She said her name was Christine, and she was from Vancouver, B.C. I introduced myself and said, "I thought all Canadians wore flannel and lived with moose in the forest."

"Well, my flannel is at the dry cleaner, and I couldn't get my pet moose, Clyde, past Customs. But I do have my maple leaf sewn on my backpack, so I won't be mistaken for one of those loud-mouthed, obnoxious Americans."

"Well, that fried my Canadian Bacon Ass." We both laughed and started talking, planning our great expedition. Christine had been in Bangkok about a week, having come up from Malaysia. She was lively and self-assured, but it was those two blue loadstones that bewitched me: "My, My," said the spider to the fly, "Jump right ahead, and you're dead!"

The trip would take about thirteen hours on the train, and we decided to treat ourselves royally by booking second class instead of the totally overcrowded third class. We bought Chinese stall food, fruit and since she avoided stoners (Moi?), I bought extra beer. The journey was hot and stifling, but we talked about what we wanted to see in Chiang Mai. We arrived late at night and got a pedicab to a traveler's hotel. We booked separate rooms and met some fellow Freaks, who told us what to see and do here.

We met for breakfast, and since we were staying outside of the old city, we rented bicycles for a day-long tour.

Chiang Mai's old city is surrounded by earthen walls in various states of decay and is partially encircled by a shallow moat. There are four old fourteenth-century gateways; each had a special purpose. One gateway had a large plaza just beyond the gate, where festivals were held; another gate, where the dead were taken out, and yet another was the entrance to the old king's garden.

East Gate of the Old City of Chiang Mai

The largest temple, Wat Chedi Luang, has a huge bronze Buddha surrounded by his disciples; the temple stands next to a huge pipal tree, the tree that Buddha sat under for forty-nine days to achieve nirvana. There is a Wat monastery complex, Wat Phra Sing, which has a venerable Buddha statue, famous for its supposed healing benefits.

What makes Chiang Mai so interesting is that it's a real city: young Thai school kids, in their white tops and blue pants and skirts, going and coming out of school, orange-clad monks chanting sutras on the streets, and ordinary Thais going about their daily lives. This isn't a fossil city like Williamsburg, but an alive city, where religion was a daily part of life like medieval Nuremberg.

I told Christine that this was the same type of ambiance I felt when I visited San Francisco in 1967; instead of Wats and Buddhist images, you had rainbow-painted Victorians and stately nineteenth-century churches. Here you have silk and lacquer shops; there, you have used clothing, record, and head shops. People were friendly in both places, and you could turn the corner here and find a Buddhist temple festival, while in Frisco, you could turn a corner and chance upon a street festival with live music and handmade handicrafts.

We had been pedaling around for the whole day, and I told her, "Only mad dogs and Englishmen" stay out in the hot tropic sun, and I was going back for a cold shower and a Singha beer. She, too, was tired, and we pedaled back to the hotel, agreeing to meet for dinner later.

Chapter Sixteen: Christine

"Waiting For A Girl Like You": Foreigner

This has to be one of the greatest "Waiting for Godot" true love songs ever written.

Proserpine: Dante Gabriel Rossetti 1874

We were both exhausted, saddle-sore, and probably dehydrated when we got back to our hotel. I took a shower, drank about a gallon of water, and met her for dinner at a local Thai restaurant. We didn't get to know much about each other on our way here due to the over crowdedness and the loud chattering of our fellow passengers in our train compartment. We were now refreshed and relaxed (I had not smoked hash since Bangkok and was feeling haze-free alert). I asked her why she was traveling and what her goals were on this journey. "I graduated from university and had a good job working for the government. I had a steady boyfriend but felt confined like I was missing something in my life, so I got a flight to Singapore and traveled around Thailand, Malaysia, and Singapore. I met a lot of travelers, but most were stone heads, only interested in drugs, which is not my thing."

"Did you study anything about Buddhism?"

"Yes, I even took a weeklong seminar at a Buddhist ashram school, and I had practiced yogi back in Vancouver."

"And how are you progressing with this teaching?"

"The meditation really relaxes your mind, making you open, but it's very difficult to desist from material pleasures; life is so full of endless possibilities that to see it all as an illusion doesn't really work for me."

"And did you find out what "that thing" you thought was missing from your life?"

"No, and it frightens me that I may never find it. In high school, I used to think it was the local sports jock; in university, I thought it was a meaningful career; however, at work, I got no satisfaction, and my boyfriend just wanted to get married and have kids."

"So, traveling has not given you "inner peace?"

"On the contrary, traveling frees you from responsibility: you do what you want, stay in paradise as long as you want. You're free, isn't that what life is all about, you say to yourself, and are serenely content. But somewhere in the back of your mind, you see this as maya, an illusion that will disappear once you're back to the daily grind."

"But don't you think that all these experiences and people you met, these random dots of life, will help you connect them into a meaningful picture that allows you to have the same freedom working 9-5 as you would traveling around Chang Mai – freedom is in your mind to control.

Buddhism and Christianity preach that you must use this freedom to do good whether it's helping people or working toward a specific goal for you and no one else."

"But isn't that selfish – to "cultivate your own garden" as Voltaire wrote?"

"Not if you see this "garden" as a microcosm of the universe. Nature is alive and is flowing all around us. We must find a way to experience this flow or consciousness. We must tune our senses to the right frequency to see the natural order of life- the consciousness that makes us feel how we fit into this flow or way as the Taoists say."

"And are you part of this flow?"

"Sometimes I feel that all living things have God in them, in a pantheistic sense, and I am part of this wonderful experience, but then reality kicks in. For example, the Taoists believe that nature should be unfettered. A river should run its course, yet a dam, which would help poor farmers irrigate dry land and produce more crops or provide electricity for a lightless village, interrupts this natural flow, and the Taoists would not build it. I see the poverty and lack of basic necessities, things we take for granted-and I say, you're dammed (no pun intended) right, I'd be an eager beaver (pun intended) to build that dam." She laughed, and we continued our dinner, talking over our day's adventures.

I walked her to her room and was about to say good night when she asked if I wanted to come in for a while. I followed her in and shut the door; we looked intently at each other, and I grabbed her and kissed her. I pushed her back, kissing and touching her. I unbuttoned her blouse, kissing her and loosening my belt. She undid her skirt and pulled her panties down, and I dropped my pants down to my knees. I spun her around and spread her legs apart, kicked off my trousers, her hands on the table as I rushed to find her vagina. I found it and thrust in, holding her body as we started moving at a frantic pace. I must have come in less than two minutes but kept moving in her until I felt her body quiver. I pulled out and turned her around, kissing her until we were both out of breath. We fell onto the bed and held each silently until we fell asleep.

In the morning, we continued our bicycle odyssey, visiting lacquer and silk shops, stopping for endless cups of chai to keep from overheating.

Christine and I pedaled by a Buddhist shrine, where they were staging a dance drama. Thai dancing is beautiful to watch because of the elaborate costumes and intricate headdresses. We asked a Thai who spoke English, and he said the dance was dramatizing an old folk story. Watching the dancers, you see elaborate arms, hands, and finger positions that delineate characters, situations, and plot development. In the West, ballet primarily emphasizes the feet, while here, the eye movement and stylized upper body positioning were the elements by which the audience judged the dancer's skills. When this dance is performed at the royal court, the plots are all from the Hindu epic, the "Ramayana". Here the dancer shows humor, honor, bravery, and fear by stylized body movements, not by facial expressions. I told Christine that this was a great learning lesson, which I could borrow to spice up my Motown dance routine ("I'm just a dancing fool", as Frank Zappa sang and strutted his stuff).

Chapter Seventeen: Jim Thompson, the CIA, and the Deep Silk State

Eurythmics: "Sweat Dreams"

Here was a self-made American who made his dreams a reality

Jim Thompson in Bangkok 1965

While I was accompanying Christine on her shopping foray, "Here, hold this, please; which silk scarf looks better on me? The shimmering orange one or this deep purple one that glistens jewel-like in the sunlight?" I looked at all these silks in the store; I thought of the American that Time magazine praised as "the man who almost single-handedly saved Thailand's silk industry". This man was Jim Thompson.

Jim Thompson was a great example of a self-made American man. He was a spy, working in Southeast Asia during and after World War II with the Office of Strategic Services (OSS), a precursor of the CIA. He was a failed businessman, losing money on an investment hotel in Bangkok and was near-broke.

Then he saw an opportunity to invest in a silk company. Thailand used to be a major silk producer, but the war and the Japanese occupation all but destroyed that production. He pioneered the idea that the company should create a dynamic new style of silk: vibrant jewel-tone patterns and bold color combinations in dresses, sweaters, and scarves. To make this project a success, he would need to make a "quality" product. Instead of the huge factories that were producing hundreds of yards of silk bolts daily (which was happening in my home state of New Jersey, in the water-turbine-run silk factories of Paterson), he would give thousands of poor Thais a chance to make a good living. His company was founded as a cottage industry: the silk was produced in Thai homes using handlooms. This gave Thompson the opportunity to keep quality-control high and enabled the mostly Thai women and mothers, the principal weavers, a chance to be well-paid breadwinners and still maintain a stable family life.

"Silk Loom Jim Thompson House photo D Ramey Logan.jpg from Wikimedia Commons by D Ramey Logan CC-BY-SA 3.0"

The company struggled for the first few years, and then a fortuitous event occurred. Margaret Landon wrote a best-selling book: "Anna and the King of Siam" (Thailand). This story was about a young English tutor and her unfulfilled love for the king of Siam.

Irene Sharif was a New York costume designer who, with a theatrical agent Fanny Holtzman, convinced Rogers and Hammerstein to create a Broadway play based on the book. Miss Sharif traveled to Thailand and was awed by the beautiful silk fabric that Thompson was making. She ordered the entire show's costumes using Thompson's creative silks.

The play ran for three years on Broadway and revolutionized the fashion world. Now everyone in America wanted similar silk dresses and even used this vibrant-colored silk for curtains, tablecloths, and upholstery fabrics in interior home decorations. This ensured Thompson's success; his silk now set the standard for quality all over the world.

Now that Thompson was rich, he decided to build his dream mansion. At Princeton, Thompson trained as an architect, and he had a vision of what his "dream house" should be. He traveled all over Thailand and bought six old Thai teak wood houses of different sizes and designs, had them dismantled, floated the pieces down the river, and then re-assembled them on a peaceful canal near his weavers. The largest of these houses was a one-hundred-year-old weaver's shop with old, polished floors and ironwood columns, which now became his main living room. He connected the six houses, raised the combined structure on a platform, and created an interior staircase, as opposed to the outside staircases, which were typical of Thai houses.

He filled the house with priceless antiques: carved teak doors, Buddhist statues, and paintings gathered from buying trips in Thailand, Laos, and Cambodia. The house is an airy, high-ceiling, teak-paneled home with low sofas decorated with his bright silk fabric. It is open to the breezes and the luxuriant tropical scenery and overlooks a verdant still-water canal. The Thompson house is now a museum that can be visited when in Bangkok.

"Main House of Jim Thompson photo D Ramey Logan.jpg from Wikimedia Commons by D Ramey Logan, CC-BY-SA 3.0"

However, the story ends tragically; Thompson was murdered by Malay Communists in 1967 while on vacation there, and his body was never found. However, his legacy was that of a self-made American who realized his vision both economically and artistically. He provided a good livelihood for thousands of poor weavers and restored a traditional Thai handicraft to worldwide prominence.

"Yes, Christine, I think the purple one suits you; it brings out the color in your cheeks."

"Yes, I think so too; I'll take it, now for the bargaining…"

Chapter Eighteen: Show And Tell

(A MEDITATION ON INNOCENCE LOST)

While Christine and I were exploring the old city of Chiang Mai, we went to the tourist office and found they were offering trips to a hill tribe village north of Chiang Mai. I had never seen any of the hill people, but I had read about them in Tom Dooley's book "The Night They Burned The Mountain". See Chapter Ten describing Dr. Dooley and the Hmong people of northern Laos.

Christine had to get some last-minute gifts and begged off. So, I, as Flash Gordon, discoverer of strange new worlds, proceeded alone. I got on a minibus in the early morning and departed for the hill tribe village. As I was riding through the countryside, I reflected on a school trip that I had when I was about eight years old. We went with our entire grammar school class to Strawbridge Village Museum in western Massachusetts. Here we saw how Americans lived 100 years ago. The village has a working farm, blacksmith shop, general store, and weaving center, all run by people in period costumes, who showed us by doing it, how people lived, worked and had fun in the old days. I was especially fascinated by the blacksmith shop and how they made the various nails, farming tools, and horseshoes. Growing up, we did not have a car in the family, so I did not get a chance to visit a zoo or a petting farm, or even a circus. So, as a young kid watching all of this was like seeing "Aliens from Planet 9". I never knew how they made butter, nor did I ever witness how cloth is weaved. The chance to see animals up close was very exciting, but the most fascinating thing I saw was cows being milked. As a kid growing up in the suburbs, I had no idea how milk was made; I only opened the carton and poured a glass. It was so strange to see the farmer pulling on the cow's udders and out spurted white milk ("Teacher, can you show me where the chocolate milk cows are?").

The bus to the hill tribe had nine people: a German couple with a small child, a middle-aged English couple, two Australian backpackers, a Thai tour guide, and me. After an hour and a half, we finally arrived at the village. There were thatched cottages where the people lived and a large open area where the people worked and congregated. All of the inhabitants were dressed in their native costumes, including the children. I thought of my mother's people, the Norwegians, and how each valley in the separate fjords had their own distinctive dress. These colorful costumes, however, were only worn for traditional weddings and important celebrations like First Communion. The guide took us around to show us what the villagers did: we saw women weaving, men in the rice fields, sowing the new crop, and women preparing meals and tending to the pigs and chickens in pens near the houses.

The guide explained that the men of the village spent some of their time farming and other times hunting in the jungle or fishing in the streams near the village. The villagers generally ignored us, which must have been very hard since everyone was gawking and snapping photos at everything they did. It was like we were at the Bronx Zoo, gazing at exotic animals. I thought to myself, "Damn, I didn't wear my colorful Hawaiian shirt and shorts, but I did have the camera hanging around my neck".

I tried to imagine how the village was before it became the poster child for Thai tourism. Were the villagers happier enriching themselves off of the tourists, or did they regret losing the traditional self-sustaining lifestyle of their ancestors? The weaving that the women produced was for sale, and they made money this way, rather than just weaving the clothes that they wore as in the other hill tribes. Once you travel further North in Thailand, you enter the "Golden Triangle", where the hill people raise opium as a cash crop. This opium is bought by enterprising Chinese businessmen for the sex trade (to keep the bar girls docile and dependent on their pimps) and to feed the addiction of western tourists. Raising opium gave the hill people much more money than just rice farming, which this village subsisted on. The Hmong tribespeople in northern Laos were given arms and money by the CIA to fight the communist Pathet Lao. It seemed that everywhere in the hill tribe country, the people were losing their paradise to western commercialism and ideologies.

While I was at the Bang Saen beach, I was deeply impressed by a book I read that described a similar situation: Peter Matthiessen's "At Play in the Fields of the Lord". This is a Paradise Lost tale of missionaries and mercenaries out to convert or save a native Amazonian Indian culture that had never seen a white man before. The missionaries want to convert the souls of the Indians to save them from eternal damnation. The mercenary originally wanted to wipe out the tribe, on the directions of his "Grande" rancher, who wanted their lands for cattle grazing. But he has a change of heart when he experiences their peaceful and bucolic lifestyle. Now he wants to save these people by arming them and having them fight back against the ranchers that are encroaching on their land. The missionaries failed to convert them, with some going insane, and the mercenary hero must corrupt their unique culture to rescue the tribe by giving them guns to fight the ranchers. However noble their intentions were, the end result is an Innocence Lost: a traditional way of life that the tribe can never go back to again.

I looked at the children and wondered what they were thinking about, facing a daily onslaught of camera snapping "Falang": They are like miniature adults, dressed like their parents and assuming the parents' responsibilities for taking care of younger siblings and helping their mother with her chores. Would they be satisfied remaining in the village when they see what the outside world offers them? Would the girls fall prey to unscrupulous men and become part of the Bangkok sex scene? And would the men fall into a life of crime in the cities since they had no marketable skills for a job? For now, they are just smiling, inquisitive, shy children, and this is how I tried to capture them in my photographs.

Thai Hill tribe Children (author's photograph)

Chapter Nineteen: The Thai Image of Buddha

Traveling all over Thailand, you see hundreds of images of Buddha in various positions, sitting, walking, standing, and reclining. What is amazing is the different faces of the Buddha. In America, when you go to certain black churches, you see Christ depicted as a black man. In South America, Christ and Mary are portrayed with a distinct mestizo (Indian and Spanish racial hybrid) face. When the Nestorian Christians and the Jesuits tried to convert the Chinese court to Christianity, Christ was presented as a Confucian scholar to show the continuity of ancient Chinese philosophy with the newer Christian morality.

Nestorian Christian image of Christ as a great Confucian scholar (9th century)

And let us not forget the typical American Protestant Christ portrayed in books and stained glass with a porcelain white face, light blond-brown hair, and blue eyes: a handsome Hollywood movie star. My favorite Christ, however, is the "Blinking Christ" sold in the souvenir shops near

Times Square; be advised that this is not some magical miracle; you must supply your own batteries to have your "strobe light" Christ.

However, in Thailand, the face of the Buddha adopted the cultural imagery of the various conquerors and trading partners. For example, near the Cambodian border in Western Thailand, you see the influence of Khmer sculpture (Thirteenth Century A. D.), the thick lips, and the enigmatic smile of the Buddha, as seen in Angkor Wat in present-day Cambodia.

Sandstone Khmer Bodhisattva 10th century A.D. Here you can see the enigmatic smile of Khmer and Thai Buddhas of that period.

The southern Thai kingdoms had extensive trading with Buddhist and Hindu kingdoms in Java in Indonesia. Here you see a face strongly influenced by Javanese facial characteristics. As trading partners, the stronger culture of the Javanese is reflected in the Buddha's likeness to Javanese sculpture, as seen in Borobudur in central Java.

Southern Thai Bronze torso showing Java (Indonesian) influence 9th century AD due to trade ties between the two Buddhist kingdoms in Sukhothai and Java

The Green Emerald Buddha in the Lan Na style Bangkok

Source	Own work
Author	กสิณธร ราชโอรส

The Lan Na Thai Buddha has a round face with lowered eyes, a sharp nose, and a small fleshy mouth. The Buddha bump is a lotus bud surrounded by large, coiled hair. This Buddha's face reveals Burmese influence because of the many Burmese invasions. The most famous representation of this style is the green emerald Buddha shown above, which was carved out of semi-precious stone and bedecked with jewels.

The U Thong style of Central Thailand spanned the centuries 1300-1500 and had three distinct styles as follows: Thong "A" style had just a bump, no flame, and separate straight eyebrows above the eyes. The face was round, and there was a line band below the hairline. Thong "B" style was an oval face, stylized flame bump, and banded eyes. Thong "C" style had a huge flame bump and huge eyebrows that met above the nose.

The first Thai national style was called the Sukhothai (Fourteenth Century A.D.). Here we see a style that is free from Cambodian as well as Burmese and Indonesian influences: an oval face with high eyebrows and a parrot-shaped nose. The bump is a flame finial, and the figure has curled, slightly smiling lips. This reflected the ascendancy of various powerful Thai kingdoms that created a distinctly ethnic Thai characteristic to Buddhist sculpture.

Sukhothai Walking Buddha 15th century

My favorite Buddha image is the fifteenth-century Sukhothai Walking Buddha. The pear-shaped face has a parrot-beak nose with a slender flame finial. There is a refined sense of movement: the stylized large, broad shoulders and long thin serpentine hands give the statue an overly feminine appearance, especially with the androgynous lower body and form-fitting garment that leaves the right shoulder bare. The right leg is slung, tango-style backward, giving the whole statue kinetic energy, as if it would walk off its pedestal at any moment!

From the eighteenth century onwards, the Buddha had a more uniform look: a flat pancake-shaped face with tall, tapering headdresses and fancy ornamental jewelry, especially on the winged earlobes. The late 18th century and the 19th century were times of peace in Thailand, and there was no new conqueror to impose their cultural image of the Buddha. So, this facial type remained the typical Thai Buddha face that you can buy in the souvenir shops of Bangkok today.

Chapter Twenty: Musings on a Long Hot Train Ride from Chang Mai to Bangkok

Countin' the cars on the New Jersey turnpike

They've all come to look for America

"America" Paul Simon

At first, it seems ironic that we would look to New York City, the most un-American city in the country, to find America. However, it is in New York that we see the new face of America that will shape the ultimate destiny of our country.

Photo by Pedro Gaberiel Miziara (UNSPLASH)

When I first started out from Korea, I wanted to discover the real Asia and, in the process, the real me.

I served my country and did what I was told. I was expected to go back to a normal life of job, family, and kids. And why shouldn't I follow this path? The American way of life, with all our material goods: big houses, expensive cars, state of the art-stereos and TV, and a secure job, was the envy of the entire world. Everyone I met on my travels wanted a slice of the American pie. So, what made me so dissatisfied with this way of life? Here in Buddhist Thailand, I found yet another way. Buddhism teaches that life is an illusion (maya): desires, joy, and fears must be overcome so that the individual soul can lose its identity and merge with the Universal Soul/Consciousness. Taoism has taught me to understand the natural order and flow of nature, which is all prevailing. Spinoza believed that God is in everything. Christianity preached that knowing God will make you free, and this freedom will show your love for your fellow man.

All these religious and philosophical ideas percolated in my mind. Everyone wants a simpler way of life, and we travel to see how we can find it.

Dope relaxes your mind, making it receptive to new ideas, but it offers a false reality. The dope becomes an end, instead of the means, for further discoveries.

All of these grand ideals butted up to the earthy reality of poverty, misery, corruption, and lack of basic necessities, like clean water, electricity, and sanitation.

Lenin and Mao transformed their societies, making them gods of the common man. The welfare of the people vs. the individual: in Russia and China, the people triumphed (however imperfectly realized).

Capitalism, communism, religion, and a traditional way of life are all fighting for the Soul of Asia. That's what makes traveling so important for me: I can observe and absorb this transformation firsthand.

How will this affect me? Will I find a new religion to give myself to, or will it be in the arms of the girl I'm traveling with? Or will I be the constant outsider: sampling the Epicurean delights and making sage and (hopefully) witty observations, a modern-day Montaigne in a self-made ivory tower. The people I admire most are the passionate loners that give themselves totally, the seekers that are never satisfied. Perhaps it is the journey to discovery, not the actual achievement of the goal. I only feel truly alive when I can throw myself, heart and soul, into an idea, task, or person.

Is this self-disillusionment, youthful idealism, or a moral cop-out (as Groucho Marx ironically said, "I wouldn't join any club that would have me.")? My favorite American novel is "Moby Dick" – Ahab is the consummate loner. He is obsessed with the White Whale, and what is this whale? Is it a symbol for all the evil in the world, or is nature incarnate that we all die trying to master? As a soldier, I saw firsthand the folly of imposing our value system on other people. As a traveler, I feel like a sponge, constantly absorbing new ideas, experiences, and people. Hopefully, I can wring out the ephemeral and save what is really meaningful.

Chapter Twenty-One: Christine II: Anatomy of a Relationship

"Goodbye My Almost Lover": A Fine Frenzy

"The Roseleaf" by Dante Gabriel Rosetti 1875

When we got back to Bangkok, Christine informed me that she would fly out in three days, going back to her normal life in Vancouver. We had only been together for about two weeks, but I really enjoyed her company. Here was a person that didn't mind getting sweaty and filthy to see something beautiful and, at the end of the day, would be alive and bubbly, eager to talk about it. She was serious and down-to-earth and just the person I needed to get me off dope (and fantasies of Dana Wynter). Who needs dope when you can discover the world together and have a loving relationship? Yet there was so much more that we needed to learn about each other, but now she was going, and we would never find out.

I wanted her to stay and put on the full-court press. I was the vacuum cleaner salesman that came to the house, spilled the dirt on the floor, and then proceeded to show how great the vacuum that I was selling was in picking up the mess. I told her, "Christine, you haven't really found what you want in life. Stay, and we can discover it together."

"That's all well and good, but I don't have any money. I'm running out, and besides, I have obligations at home."

"Well, how about this? Why don't you work for six months and then meet me in India; we could discover a true spiritual experience there. We would go to Benares, where the Hindus say if you die there, you escape the endless circle of reincarnation and go directly to the godhead, and then there's Kathmandu, with its lamas and Buddhist teachings: there is a whole world out there to discover! Come with me, and we'll find it together."

She shook her head and said, "That would be great, but I just can't do it now." I didn't make the sale, going down in flames.

I tried to understand her: after all, we had only known each other for a short time. Yet I saw we were two different people: she needed a framework to make her life meaningful, whether that framework was a job, family, or marriage: she didn't know exactly what she wanted, but she knew that she needed that stability.

I didn't feel that way. I saw myself as completely open to any experience, and I was willing to take the plunge wherever it went. But I understood her because I was like her in a way. My parents had struggled to get me a college degree, and I didn't want to disappoint them by living the life of a vagabond in Asia.

I briefly fantasized about how our life together would be. I would follow her to Vancouver ("And I didn't even have Hockey Skates", as Kathleen Edwards crooned) and get a 9 to 5 job. We will have an apartment in a funky neighborhood filled with Asian antiquities, and we will discover ourselves just like we discovered Chiang Mai together. Could our relationship have survived the petty domestic squabbles and the need to pay bills to maintain a lifestyle that we were both accustomed to? Is that what I really wanted? I didn't really know if I was ready for that conventional type of life; at least not now. There is still too much to learn and wanted to share that discovery with someone special.

Our last day was bittersweet, and as I accompanied her to the airport, I told her, "If you change your mind, you can write me and send the letter to the American consulate in Calcutta; that's where I pick up my mail. I could meet you anywhere in India." However, we both knew that this was a final farewell, and maybe it was better just to have the memories intact of a love that might have been.

After Christine left, the Bangkok drug scene lost any appeal (if it ever had any appeal), and I left Dodge for Penang, Malaysia. The long bus trip gave me time to reflect on my time with Christine, and for the first time since I left Korea, I felt lonely traveling alone.

Malaysia I

Street scene in Malacca (author's photo)

Chapter Twenty-Two: A Double Date

"Crazy Over You": Heart

The title of the song says it all

Evelyn de Morgan, Queen Eleanor & Fair Rosamund, 1880-1919, oil on canvas, 29 x 25.5cm. London, De Morgan Centre.

I arrived in Georgetown (the old colonial heart of Penang) and was immediately enchanted with this jewel of preserved time. I found a Traveler's hotel, met some freaks, and started exploring.

Dan (an Australian freak) and I met these two English tourists here on holiday from the UK. June was tall and willowy, with long straight blond hair and a cute face. What distinguished her was a mischievous pixie smile, which gave the impression that she was up to no good. Darcy was short, with close-cropped brown hair, an abrupt manner, and might have been pretty if she wasn't perpetually frowning. At first, I thought Darcy was a bull dyke and June her sex slave. Dan was always heavily stoned, so he didn't see them as strange. We had dinner together, and I was very wrong: they were both fun to be with and definitely not lesbian lovers. I suggested we all go to the beach in the morning.

I awoke and decided that I would not start the day stoned since they didn't do dope; however, this did not deter Dan. Dan was an Aussie that left home to find cheap dope, and he was in Paradise here. He was always carrying his chillum, lighting up 6 or 7 times a day: for the rest of the day, he sat staring out at the horizon. I seem to attract the "Night of the Living Dead" zombies, first Marc and now Dan; it's either my winning personality, or maybe I bore them to death: dope is their only escape.

We picked up the girls at their hotel and started walking around Georgetown. It is a beautiful old British colonial town with quaint squares, bubbly fountains, and dozens of small cafes and restaurants tucked in under overhang arches to keep diners from getting wet. The government buildings, grand hotels, and shopping arcades are all two- or three-story buildings, whitewashed, exuding an air of dignity and stability.

Then the comedy of manners started (we could have filmed this for a BBC comedy sitcom). There were all these outdoor food stalls selling Chinese, Malay, and Indian specialties, and the girls stopped at each one and chowed down. At first, I thought they had tapeworms, but then I remembered they were English, and everyone knows that English cuisine (if you can call it that) sucks, and this was the first time that they had really tasty food. And in the back alley, Dan was having his own breakfast of champions, a fully stuffed chillum.

We finally got to the beach, and I spread a beach towel for us. Five minutes later, June was up, playing social butterfly with a bunch of drunk Aussie volleyballers. Darcy wore a two-piece swimsuit, which really showed what a terrific figure she had. It was hot, and I suggested we cool off in the gentle, clear waters. We left Dan, who had assumed his Sphinx position, and didn't notice us leaving. The water was coolly refreshing. We were out about 50 feet, a little over shoulder level. We were facing each other, making small talk, when Darcy impulsively kissed me. It took me by surprise, but I recovered quickly, taking her face in my hands, French-kissing her. She started to massage my trunks, and I pulled them down to my feet; she slipped out of her bottom piece and held it in her hand. I was hard by then and turned her around, searching for her sweet spot. After some fumbling (wrong hole, GI!), I eased myself in. She leaned forward, and our heads and bodies started moving in unison. The cool water kept me erect, and her body undulated rhythmically with my thrusts. I came and pulled it out, turning her around, kissing, and holding her. We finally dressed ourselves in the water; my trunk was full of sand.

Dan was still there, guarding against some imaginary foe ("and we will fight them on the beaches") and barely acknowledged us. I imagined if he saw us, we would have seemed like two dashboard bobbleheads swaying in the breeze. June was now playing volleyball, oblivious to us.

I saw Darcy that night, and we had the chance to use a bed for the first time, and our lovemaking was even more satisfying. Both girls were off for Bangkok in the morning. I felt like a GI on a two-day pass with his girlfriend; the sweet memories will sustain me when I hit the trenches of the road again.

Chapter Twenty-Three: The Holy Grail

For the spiritual Holy Grail, I would recommend "Le Morte d' Arthur" by Thomas Mallory. However, if you want the popular, under two hours "Cliff Notes" version, watch "Indiana Jones and the Last Crusade". For the Grail as the ultimate high, any Cheech & Chong movie will do.

For the last three months, I have been continuously stoned, not the nodding off, drooling in your chai addiction, but my normal life was a "high life". I call this "The Grail" (blasphemously after the Holy Grail, which was supposed to have caught the droplets of Christ's blood while He was being crucified. The Grail was lost shortly afterward, but anyone who finds it and drinks from this chalice will be given immortality (i.e., the perfect high, in my definition).

"King Pelles' Daughter bearing the Holy Grail": Frederick Sandys 1861

King Pelles' daughter: "I thought you loved me, but it's only the dope that you want."

Author: "Not true, I do love you."

King Pelles' daughter: "Well if that's so, then choose it's either me or the dope."

The Author says to himself: "God I'm gonna miss that girl", grabs the chalice, pushes the girl aside and exits stage left.

The search for the Grail (the perfect high) consumes you. You are the pilgrim. You are always alert for the perfect high on this quest. You sit for hours on a beach absorbing everything: the hot sun, the sand in your trunks, the undulating, ever-changing surf, and the laughter of children around you. But you are not part of this scene; you are somehow standing above, looking down at yourself. You may want to speak, but the "you" down there does not. He is content to be a silent sponge, savoring the numbing hash high. When you finally rouse yourself, you're back on the search, asking yourself nervously, "Do I still have any hash left? Where can I get some more?" "Is it the magical Grail that has been obsessing you?" You find yourself examining each new purchase as if it were a fine wine: nice colorization, smooth smoking with a hint of spice aroma, and a pleasant aftertaste. You become nostalgic, "This is good, but when I was in _____, the hash was exquisite, with a rich bouquet, very little tannin, and a nuanced effervescent mellowness. Like a good wine, you take a small toke to wet the palette. Then when you think you have found the perfect high, you say, "Now I can really move on, get things accomplished, but is this really the Grail?" Like the surfer film, "The Endless Summer", there will always be a better wave on some exotic beach. The search becomes the reality, not your previous life or goals. You are waiting in your mind for a metaphorical "Magic bus" that will take you from London to India to the phantasmagorical paradise where the Grail awaits you.

You may think to yourself, "What a waste of a mind". However, the skills learned in appraising the qualities and grades of the hash will give me the expertise for profitable employment when I return home. I will write menus for fancy "haute cuisine" New York City restaurants. "Lightly braised Cornish breast in a glazed crackle crusting of Dijon mustard and English raw honey, suffused with a hint of fresh rosemary. Complemented with German white asparagus tips in a creamed ragout of roasted shallots and Neapolitan provolone. The chef recommends a dry Italian sauterne to set off the spice aromas."

Chapter Twenty-Four: Malacca 'The Old Town'

Sultan's palace 15th century A.D. (a reconstruction, now a museum)

Malacca is a gem, fought over by the Malays, Portuguese, Dutch, English, and Japanese. Malacca was originally a small fishing village until a Malay chief called Parameswara developed the city and made it a trading hub with all of Southeast Asia. In the 15th century A.D. he became the first Sultan of Malacca and sought Chinese protection against the more powerful kingdoms of Burma and Vietnam. He personally met Zeng He, the Chinese eunuch admiral, and became a vassal state of China (Zeng He is discussed in more detail in chapter Sixty-Four, "An Ocean Too Far").

The Chinese solidified their position by sending a princess, the daughter of the Ming emperor, to marry a Sultan of Malacca in 1460. Malacca prospered on the spice trade, and the Sultans became fabulously wealthy, making the city an international trading hub in spices, ivory, and Chinese silks. Unfortunately, this attracted the Portuguese from their trading base in Goa, India. The Portuguese conquered the city with a fleet of eighteen warships under Alfonso de Albuquerque in 1511. They fortified the port with huge stone walls (see below), but they failed to make this an international hub because they disrupted the internal trade in Southeast Asia, sending the valuable commodities exclusively to Europe. They also failed to control the Malay pirates, who attacked the commercial vessels which had previously been under the protection of Malay and Chinese warships. However, for over a hundred years, the Portuguese controlled the spice trade and sent back this precious cargo to Europe, thus putting Venice, which depended on the more expensive overland Asia route for their spices, out of business. The Jesuit missionary, Francis Xavier, spent time here, preparing for his proselytizing mission in Japan. The Portuguese had a trading center in Nagasaki, Japan, where they exchanged spices, Chinese silks, and ivory for Japanese silver.

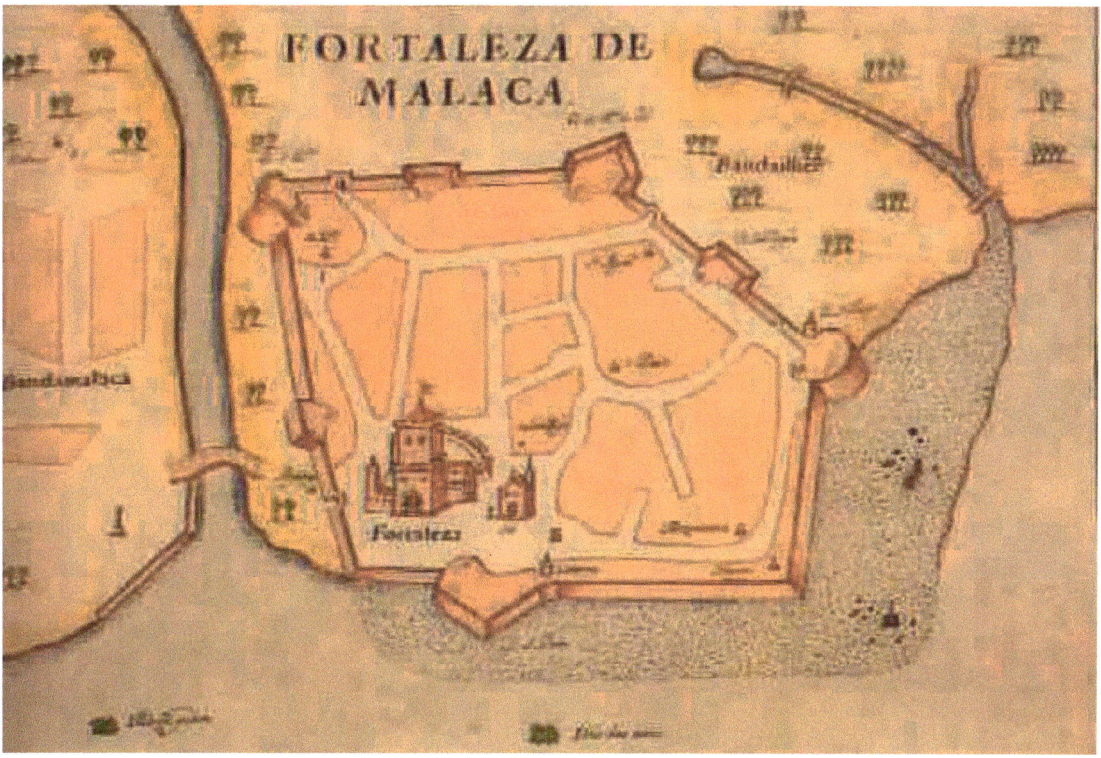

The Portuguese Fort 1630

The next conqueror was the Dutch, who were eager to expand trade opportunities from their base in Batavia in the Dutch East Indies. In 1641 they defeated a Portuguese fleet sent from Goa with the help of the Malay Sultan of Johor. The Dutch built up the city, further fortifying the fort and building the Stadthuys as their center of administration, which has now become the architectural symbol of Malacca. Again, the Dutch, like the Portuguese before them, did not make it an international trading hub because they had developed Batavia in Java as their premier port. However, they did control the spice and silk trade from the mainland of Southeast Asia.

Dutch East India Company vessels in Malacca harbor in 1775

In 1824 Malacca was transferred to Great Britain in exchange for a city in Sumatra. This was the heyday of Malacca. The British had vast rubber plantations and tin mines, and these goods shipped out of Malacca port, making the local merchants and port operators rich, enabling them to build their "mansions on the hill", which I discuss later in this chapter. The last conqueror was Japan from 1942-1945. After their World War Two defeat, the British took over again, and Malaysia finally gained independence in 1963.

These countries were just the external conquerors; the Chinese laborers were the American-style success story internally. The first Chinese came to Malaya in great numbers in the 19th century, brought by the British to work the rubber plantations and the bustling port. This was just like in America, where the first Chinese worked out west, building the transcontinental railroad. They saved their money in America and Malaya, becoming shopkeepers, laundry owners, and small-time financiers for their own countrymen. The next generation became local bankers, port operators, merchants, and factory owners. They bought over their wives and families and built their "mansions on a hill". They settled on Huerlin Street, their "Gold Coast". The next generation embellished these stately buildings. The port and exports were booming, but a change was in the wind. The British built up Singapore, and by 1900 it surpassed Malacca as the international shipping hub of Southeast Asia. Just like in Salem, Malacca's harbor couldn't handle the large cargo ships; in Salem, it was the decline of the whaling industry and the silting of the river that drove the merchants to a better harbor in Boston. In Malacca, the merchants couldn't compete with Singapore's easily accessible deep-sea harbor, newer docks, and cheap labor.

However, the present generation has lost their business acumen, more interested in keeping up appearances and devoting their lives to art and pleasure. As I walked around this faded glory district, I was approached by the owner of one of these dilapidated mansions. He was a middle-aged Chinese homosexual who did not work and spent his days seeking pleasurable company. He invited me in for a chai. I accepted and followed him in, past intricately carved Chinese doors through a dark narrow hallway that opened into a spacious two-story open-air courtyard, complete with a private Chinese altar shrine, surrounded by potted palms and a centralized marble fountain with a stone dolphin spouting water. We proceeded to a marble-floored alcove, to a shiny elm wood table with Chinese armchairs. On the walls were faded photographs of past ancestors and portraits of stone-faced Chinese families.

Interior of a mansion on Huerlin Street Malacca (author's photo)

We sat down, and he introduced himself as Hwe Li, and he lived here with various old aunts and uncles. One old "aunt" brought us chai and some sweet biscuits. He told me of his family: his grandfather had built this imposing mansion, and he started a thriving export/import business. His father took over the business, but most of his customers took their rubber and tea to Singapore. The business had seriously declined by the time he took over from his father. There is still a small storefront shop, but now the business only does a little local trade. He was a painter and brought out a canvas for me to see; it was a nicely done realistic harbor scene of Malacca's port. He asked me if I was interested in purchasing the painting, and I told him I was traveling and could not carry anything like that, but I sincerely complimented him on his work. He then asked me to dinner, but I lied, saying I was meeting a girl for dinner. I wasn't interested in a homosexual tryst and excused myself and left.

As I walked back to my hotel, I was reminded of Thomas Mann's "Buddenbrooks". This book details the rise and fall of a 19th-century merchant family in Bremen, Germany. The first generation built up a successful business empire. The second generation tried to sustain the business but made foolish decisions, and the business faltered. The last generation, Toni and her brother were artistically inclined and well-meaning but had no desire or the selfless duty ("dharma" in the Indian concept) to continue growing the business. They were content to live off the fruits of the previous generations. This is what I witnessed today with Hwe Li's situation. I also reflected on my own life: in America, each generation is expected to do better than the previous one. Would I do better than my father? Looking at my current life, I felt that responsibility weighing heavily on me, but as Scarlett infamously quipped: "Tomorrow is another day".

Chapter Twenty-Five: Celebrating Life and Honoring Death

"Fire and Rain": James Taylor

Malaysia is a potpourri of peoples and religions. The predominant religion of the ethnic Malays is Islam. When I was in Kuala Lumpur, I visited the new central mosque - all steel, glass, and marble with a futuristic call-to-worship mazarine. The interior was airy, bright, and clean, with corridors of gleaming marble surrounding a large marble water pool with a spouting plume of water in the center.

The worship hall was carpeted and striped with long sheets of white Muslin cotton, where the faithful sat, listening to lessons from the Koran while making their adulations to Allah. The mosque gave an aura of solemn austerity; there was nothing to distract you from your communication with Allah.

While exploring the back alleys of Malacca, I came across a small neighborhood mosque. The exterior was a weathered, whitewashed stucco; you could easily miss it if it weren't for the steady procession of the faithful leaving and going into the edifice. I ventured inside the dark, low-ceiling prayer hall. The old carpet in the hall was worn and moth-eaten, and the drone of the Iman was barely audible. I walked out to the small courtyard adjoining the mosque and was immediately transported to a wonderland. In the center of the courtyard was a 19th-century wrought iron and glass canopy fountain, surrounded by lush tropical vegetation of palm and banana trees. The flowing fountain was bathed in defused tropical light from the stained-glass canopy and for the first time, I truly understood what a modern oasis is - a place that offered succor from the noise and bustle of the city. I sat contemplating this magical water garden, freeing my mind the same way I'd tried at Ryongi-Yu in Kyoto. Here instead of rocks and patterned raked sand, you had water cascading almost musically from the simple cement fountain. The flowing water formed concentric circles; truly, this is the Paradise that Mohammed promised his followers. Here you could freely talk to Allah on His home turf. Your mind was lost in the waters of life: earth, life, and death were reflected and refracted in the calming, quietly gurgling pool.

A Magical Mosque Pool In Malacca (author's photo)

I thought of my own church back home in New Jersey. A simple white rectangular box on the outside, like the New England village square churches, but inside were high multi-paneled plain glass windows, dark polished wooden pews and floors, and a single large plain oak Cross over the altar. God is Living Light. This is His home, pervading pantheistical throughout the sanctuary, enveloping it with His Loving Presence.

In college, I read Alfred Kazin's "A Walker in the City" memoir of growing up in Brownsville, Brooklyn, when that neighborhood was all lower working-class Jews in the 1930s. As a young boy, he ventured into a small Protestant church, a lone living remnant of what Brownsville was like before the Jews: working-class Protestant and Catholic immigrants who had lived in the already crumbling walk-up tenements and deserted the neighborhood when these new foreigners came in droves. The wooden church on the outside was peeling white paint; inside there was a plain white interior, with worn wooden pews, frayed runner carpet, and an iron cross over the altar.

Young Alfred thought this church was strange and forbidding; how could God feel at home in this simple, empty, unadorned space. There was no mystery, no welcoming candle lights, no sumptuously decorated altar with the sacred Torah encased in a glittering gold case. Surely Yahweh needs to be welcomed majestically with incense, candles, and polished wood like the fabled Temple of Solomon in the Bible.

The Chinese dominate the local economy, running small businesses, banks, and housing in the small towns. They also assisted the British in administering the colonial government. The Chinese are called the Straits Chinese (from the Straits of the Malay Peninsula, jutting out into the Indian Ocean). The Straits Chinese have their own language: a mixture of mainland Chinese, Malay, and English languages. Many have also inter-married with the local Malay women. They built beautifully decorated temples and founded religious and fraternal organizations to fund these temples.

I was privileged to witness a typical Chinese worship service in a small coastal Malaysian town. The garishly colored and decorated exterior belies a simple interior: a dark, smoky, large single room filled with incense and candles. The service alternated between chants of the priests, punctuated by the shrill blasts of cacophonous music and clashing cymbals from the temple orchestra. The altar was full of burning candles, with silk scrolls on the wall behind and small figurines of dragons and ancestor photographs on the altar.

Interior of a Chinese temple in Malaysia (author's photograph)

The Chinese are in a precarious position in Malaysia today. The central Malay Islamic government is envious and fearful of the powerful Chinese minority. They passed drastic laws, such as limiting the number of Chinese admitted to State Universities to draconian taxes imposed on Chinese businesses. Mandating Malay as the official language drove thousands of Chinese immigrants to Singapore. All over Southeast Asia, the overseas Chinese are on the defensive. Store names must be in the majority race language. Each business must have a quota of ethnic native workers, and larger successful companies are often forced to sell out to the government at ridiculously low prices. The Chinese, with their hard-working and industriousness nature made them wealthy and indispensable to the reigning colonial powers. Now that the colonials have left, they are persecuted by the Malay, Indonesian, and Filipino ethnic ruling classes for their hard-won wealth.

The Hindus from South India started as laborers in the rubber plantations and now perform working-class jobs in the cities and run Indian stores and restaurants. Many have inter-married with Malay women, but the cohesive glue that keeps this group together is their Hindu religion. They celebrate all of Mother India's religious festivals, and their daily lives revolve around temple devotion and activities.

The way of death is totally different also. The Malays have simple ceremonies honoring their dead; a typical graveyard is just small wooden stakes with an austere photo, the name, and dates of life and death.

The Chinese go out with a bang! I took a photograph of a Chinese funeral van. This was just a flower-bedecked, colorfully painted flatbed truck, which holds the casket and slowly proceeds to the graveyard, followed by loud musicians, relatives, and friends walking behind. The Chinese have elaborate mausoleums, which are usually bedecked with flowers from relatives and friends.

Our closest ritual to this is the New Orleans Jazz Band that blares out "St. James' Infirmary" as they follow the casket to the graveyard, along with a procession of mourners, close relatives, and curious bystanders. In New Orleans, the gravesites are huge ostentatious mausoleums with weather-eroding cement angels, blackened by the soot of the city.

The Hindus cremate their dead and, unlike in India, where the ashes are thrown into sacred rivers, the Tamils here scatter them to the winds.

Chapter Twenty-Six: Malay Christians (Kristangs)

A group of Kristang people performing a traditional dance in Malacca, Malaysia.

Malacca is a multi-layered city, one where the layers of previous conquerors are still visible through buildings, churches, and people. When the Portuguese arrived there (early 16th century), it was a prosperous Muslim kingdom. The Portuguese goals were getting spices and converting the inhabitants to the Catholic God. The spices are still in abundance, and the conversions to Christianity have held up for over four hundred years. They built their forts and churches and inter-married with the native Malay population. To this day, there are still descendants of this mestizo race, numbering around 40,000 people that speak Portuguese, worship in Portuguese churches, and eat Portuguese cuisine. They are called "Kristang" in the Malay language from the Portuguese "Cristao".

I sought out these survivors and found a small village where they lived. This place is called St. John's village, and the people are mostly fishermen and small restaurant owners. They have their own church, with services in Portuguese, and every house has a small shrine with a crucifix and saints.

I went to a small restaurant and had a delicious meal of fresh fish "a la Portuguese", potatoes and local home-brewed red wine. I got a chance to speak with the owner of this restaurant and he told me that business was booming. Tourists were just discovering this area and now his business is about half and half: locals and tourists. I asked him about the community and what opportunities there were for the young people. He confessed that outside of restaurants and fishing there were really no job opportunities available for the young people. His own son Rodrigo was working overseas in Saudi Arabia and sent back money which enabled him to expand his restaurant. He also told me that he has not had any trouble with the local authorities because of his religion. However, he did tell me that the young men had to marry within their own Christian community since the authorities would not permit conversions of Muslim women to the Catholic faith.

Also, the Malay Christians are mostly fishermen, and they are too poor to be a threat to the local Muslims like the enterprising Chinese are. Lastly, since the British controlled Malaya for over one hundred years, their unique status was protected by the British, who enforced tolerance amongst all the multicultural and multi-religious inhabitants.

The real question is, how will these Christians survive in a xenophobic Muslim state? Even if they do, will they be satisfied with their lower economic status, especially when the rest of Malaysia is wholeheartedly embracing the ideals and "glamor" of western capitalism?

Chapter Twenty-Seven: Let The Good Times Roll

"Let the Good Times Roll": Louis Jordan and his Tympany Five 1946

Following the shrine through the streets of Malacca (author's photo)

I was wandering the streets of Malacca when I stumbled upon a Tamil Temple Festival. Temple festivals are colorful extravaganzas, where a "shrine" (statue) of the deity is paraded around the streets on a huge wooden chariot. This procession is accompanied by musicians, dancers, pilgrims, and devotees. This moveable shrine was pulled and pushed by ropes along the streets by the faithful followers.

Priests rode on the top of the wagon, giving blessings; little children accompanied, throwing flowers at the crowd. There was food, drink, and general merriment, and the smell of incense permeated the streets. This festival went on long into the night, and the shrine was elaborately lit by thousands of electric light bulbs powered by a generator in a truck that followed behind the shrine chariot.

Festivals usually commemorate an important day in the life of the deity, such as this one: the marriage of Siva and Parvati. Special meals are prepared and fed to the shrine deity. As it moves slowly through the streets, the devotees crowd the chariot, to try to "touch" the flower-garlanded gods, who they believe will bring them good fortune in the future. Periodically the chariot halts, and there are impromptu performances of temple dancers accompanied by blaring musicians. It was great fun, and I'm sure that Siva and Parvati enjoyed their bridal sendoff, not to mention the nuptial bliss that night once the crowd left.

Since the Middle Ages in Europe, especially in France and Italy, there are similar shrine festivals, where the Virgin or Patron Saint of the Church is carried through the streets, with priests blessing the crowd and children throwing flowers to the devotees. There too, the devotees throng to touch the sacred image for good luck and good fortune.

In New York City, the most popular church festival is in Little Italy on Mulberry Street: The Feast of St. Gennaro. Here the emphasis isn't on religion but on food and drink, street games, and Frank Sinatra music. The festival celebrates the Italian heritage of the festival goers while eating a calzone and wearing a "Kiss me, I'm Italian" button (the latter never really worked for me, but it did earn me a slap).

St. Gennaro was a Christian martyr who died for his faith in 305 A.D. He is the Patron Saint of Naples, and his "miracle" is that there are two glass vials of his dried blood in the cathedral, which liquefy three times a year, thanks to the pious prayers of the faithful. However, you don't need to know this to have a "bloody good time", playing and eating Italian at the festival. There is a similar, but smaller feast in North Brooklyn, sponsored by Our Lady of Mt. Carmel Church. Here each year, the church constructs a huge wooden tower on a wheeled cart, decorated with plaster images of the Virgin and bedecked with flowers. Again, you have the Priests riding and blessing and children throwing flowers; all pulled by muscular Italian studs, through the crowded Brooklyn streets. Here you have the same food, smaller parade floats, and "dancing in the streets" to schmaltzy Italian music. I included a photograph of the Brooklyn feast; for one day in the year, you can be an Italian in grand style, and you don't have to put a bloody horse's head in someone's bed either.

Mount Carmel shrine parading through the streets of Brooklyn (author's photo)

Chapter Twenty-Eight: And Now For Something Really Different

"Lola": The Kinks

Transgenders in Malaysia were known as sida-sida in the 18th century, combining male and female properties. They had great spiritual power; many were shamans, and others served as eunuchs, protecting women of the Muslim royal courts. Similarly, in Indonesia, the Bugis people believe that once a human being becomes a man or a woman, they are cut off from God but a transgender combined man and woman (called a bissu), and they alone can mediate between humans and gods through blessings. However, before a blessing can be performed, the bissu must perform a ritual self-stabbing (ma'giri) to prove immunity to pain and injury. If a bissu attempts to stab himself and the kris (sword) does not penetrate the skin, it shows that he is possessed by powerful spirits, and he can now enact the blessing of the gods.

When the British took possession of Malaya, they outlawed homosexuality. With British and later Malaysian rule, the local rajah principalities had little power, and sida-sida were no longer needed. Malaysia kept the homosexuality ban in place, while in Indonesia, private homosexual relationships are legal.

Aceh, a transvestite in Malacca (author's photograph)

The transvestites that I saw in the cafes of Malacca were taking a huge risk by openly soliciting in an increasingly xenophobic, orthodox Muslim state. I started photographing them when one approached me, asking if I wanted to buy her a drink. I agreed and sat down at a table with her and three transgender friends. They all spoke some English, introduced themselves, and asked me where I came from.

As we were talking, I found myself strangely attracted to one of the groups, Aceh, a quiet, sensitive-looking person with a hauntingly appealing demeanor. She was tall, light-skinned, with a narrow face, limpid mahogany eyes, a finely chiseled nose, pouted lips, and long straight jet-black hair; she was one of the most gorgeous persons that I had ever met.

This attraction was especially weird and amazing because of my failed homosexual encounter with the bear-like chaplain in Korea. Here was an image of a girl who made me rethink my sexuality but also anxiously increased my paranoia. If I were caught with her, I would be thrown in jail. I heard grim stories about Westerner drug smugglers spending years in a hellhole, where you would be sexually violated at will and beaten by sadistic guards. I told Aceh of my nervousness, and she nonchalantly replied, "We arrange hotel; no police, no worry." Right then, I was thinking with my glands and not my head. I threw caution to the wind, negotiated a price, paid her, and walked into the darkness, holding hands. I was still paranoid, looking over my shoulder every few seconds, making sure we weren't being followed by the police.

We entered this "fleabag" hotel with no lobby, just a grimy plexiglass shield right at the entryway. Behind a cutout slot sat the balding, middle-aged Chinese proprietor, who knew Aceh, gave her a key with a smile and me a sarcastic shrug. The room was standard traveler's fare – a double bed, small table, battered wooden wardrobe, and a single dangling ceiling light bulb, with the bathroom outside in the hallway.

Aceh: "Don't worry, Flash Gordon. I, Princess Aura from the planet Mongo, will protect you from Ming the Merciless!"

(Aside, in the Malay language) "I've done role-playing with clients before, but this has to take the cake! We no sooner get into the room then he makes me put on this cheap plastic tiara and gives me this odd-shaped water pistol and tells me that I am supposed to be Princess Aura from the planet Mongo and that he is Flash Gordon, trying to save the Earth from this evil emperor called Ming the Merciless. This Ming has a death ray a death ray aimed at the Earth. At first, I thought he was paranoid about the police coming in, but no, he changes into a grey leotard uniform with a large neck vestment and a huge metal belt buckle, both studded with rhinestones and metal studs. On his uniform was a yellow lightning bolt and his monogram Flash Gordon, and he kept repeating that I needed to protect him from Ming. He starts prancing around the room, paranoid that Ming is going to find him, checking the windows every few seconds for Ming's soldiers. He must be on a far-out acid trip, but since he's paying, I'll go along with the charade."

I was at a loss, not sure what I was supposed to do, let alone what I was actually feeling. Aceh went to the hallway bathroom, and I was having second doubts. Was I really attracted to this person, or was it just another box to check off, like trying opium in a seedy Chinese den; did I really need to experience every forbidden fruit? Here I was in a filthy room with a strange "Botticelli beautiful" person; my curiosity over my confused sexuality even overpowered my desires.

Aceh returned in a kimono robe and, sensing my hesitation, spoke softly, "This first time, you?"

"Yes," I stammered confusedly.

"No problem – I take care you," she spoke assuredly. With that said, she came over and started to undress me until I was completely naked; she led me to the bed.

She disrobed in the darkness; we were lying naked and silently side by side. She reached over and gave me a long-wet kiss. Her mouth was sweet, the way your lips taste when you smoke a kretek (clove) cigarette. I returned her kiss, and soon we were embracing, a passionate jigsaw tangle of arms and legs. She moved on top of me, her body smooth and lilt. She started kissing my face and worked her way down to my penis. My tension was gone, tingling pleasurably at her deft moves.

Soon to my surprise, I was getting hard, her tongue caressing my crown and then gently moving to my balls, massaging them with her rasping, dart thrusting tongue. She enveloped my penis, moving in a slow, measured cadence. I clasped her head, but when the pleasure overwhelmed me, I lay back while she continued her rhythm. I came with a prolonged spurt, but she continued sucking until I fell limp. Afterward, she moved up and kissed me, my sperm mingling with our wet kisses. We were both sated and silent, cradling her in my arms. After a while, I asked her about her life.

"I different, no like football (soccer) – I play with girls - dress in woman sarong – have fight father – he tell me go – I seventeen -I know no one, cry – what I do? I live under bridge Telekun, suck old Chinese men for money. One time nightclub, I met Sava – she kind – take me her room – we make love – she care for me – buy me clothes, makeup – teach me how to give love joy. Now I work her – give her part my money – I happy."

I lay there listening; she was pouring out her life, and I felt like a lecher, taking advantage of her innocence. But I could not resist beauty – whether it is a natural wonder of nature or the face of an angelic person lying next to me. Beauty is so fragile and fleeting, you must embrace it wholeheartedly. Only by surrendering completely to its spell can you truly feel alive!

As I left her, I thought of Gustavo von Achenbach and his unrequited obsessive love for the beautiful youth Tadzio in Thomas Mann's "Death in Venice". I had abandoned my sexual taboos, embraced incarnated beauty, and lost myself completely in her arms. Yet walking on the main boulevard, I was just glad they didn't have canals and gondolas in Malacca.

Singapore

Singapore in 1823 by LT. Phillip Jackson

Chapter Twenty-Nine: The Freak Takes a Dare

"Running Up That Hill (Make a Deal with God)": Kate Bush

Malacca is a dream city, a Lotus Land which keeps you in its enthrallment with the wonders and beauty, but there was another siren call: this one sang of tropical beaches, lush greenery, magic mushrooms, and beautiful freaks. Bali was beckoning me, but I had to go through Singapore first to get to Bali, and that might be a problem. I was still a stone head freak- long matted hair, beard, dressed in baggy Chinese fisherman's trousers, flowery shirt, and worn sandals. Every one of my freak friends told me that I would have a hard time getting into strait-laced Singapore with the way I looked. And if I tried to bring in dope, I would be arrested for a long jail term. Being a stupid, stone head freak, I accepted the challenge. I shaved my beard, got a crew cut, and put on a blue pinstripe dress shirt and a freshly laundered pair of blue jeans. At the bottom of my duffle bag, I placed a small 2" square of hash.

I got off the bus at the Malaysia/Singapore border with three other freaks who looked exactly like I did one day ago. These freaks were strip-searched, and their belongings were strewn across the customs table. When it came to my turn, the customs official politely asked my reason for visiting Singapore. I calmly told him tourism, and after a perfunctory inspection of my bag, he stamped my passport. I had foolishly tempted fate and got away with it. I found a travelers' hotel and settled in to explore the city-state.

The hotel in Singapore was cheap and clean. There were signs in the lobby stating, "No smoking in your room. Violators will be removed, and the police notified". This was quite different from the freak hotels in Bangkok, where the hash smoke was so thick that it was like wading through mustard gas in the trenches of World War One. The travelers here were serious and certainly not freaks. I had decided to go "Cold Turkey" and didn't even touch my smuggled hash. In fact, I even sold it at a profit to a dope-hungry freak that was obviously going through signs of withdrawal. I hung out with three other travelers: Don, a Filipino American from California, and Margaret and Susie from Australia. Don had been visiting relatives in the Philippines and was taking in the sights before returning home. Margaret, a nurse from a one-horse bush town in outback Australia, was headed to Great Britain for a new life and increased opportunities in the

Motherland. Susie, a Sydney girl, was despondent after being dumped by her American boyfriend and was headed to a boring job back home. We ate dinner together every night, sampling the extraordinary variety of Chinese food. Whereas Hong Kong was primarily Cantonese cooking, here you had the fiery Szechuan pork, delicately favored Hakkanese shrimp and a barbecue chicken with a black bean sauce from Fukien that would give a Texas barbecue a run for the money.

Tiger Balm Gardens

Surreal exhibit in the Tiger Balm Garden

One morning after breakfast, we decided to go *en masse* to see the sights. I had already visited the busy port, photographing Malay and Chinese workers offloading cargo against a backdrop of crumbling one-story colonial warehouses. I suggested having a Singapore sling at the last bastion of British colonial power, the white-columned Raffles Hotel, but that was nixed by the rest of the group. So, we decided to go where the local Chinese go on weekend outings: The Tiger Balm Gardens. I expected lush tropical vistas and perhaps some Disneyland rides, but the reality was so much worse.

Tiger Balm Gardens was founded as a fantasy concoction to entertain and promote Tiger Balm (a sweetly scented gel rub, similar to Vicks Vapor Rub, without the smelly camphor odor); however, the Chinese believe it cures everything from muscle aches to colds and even arthritis.

I can honestly say that I have never seen such a collection of kitsch in one place in my entire life (it even tops one girl's bedroom I stayed in; she had over a hundred stuffed dolls, teddy bears, and unicorns lying everywhere). Here there are dozens of fat, bare-chested, smiling plaster Buddhas in all sizes, naked pinup girls, some with a luscious body and head of a ram (see above), fantastic representations of sea monsters and dragons, and strangest of all, plaster figures being sawed in half, others with intestines being pulled out of stone-faced victims and other bizarre depictions. I have no idea of what they were trying to convey to us unless they believed Tiger Balm could cure being sawed in half (now, if they were selling crazy glue, it might make better sense). This array of surreal images went on forever, and I kept thinking: "Where is my dope when I really need it?" However, we had fun posing for pictures in the grips of the sea monsters and laughing at the locals as they toured the park. Margaret was especially brave: she threw herself into the tentacles of a huge cement sea octopus without a single scream. Needless to say, we all headed for the closest restaurant and laughed about our great adventure over many cold beers.

At night we sat in the hotel lobby and talked about our travels and where we were headed next. Don wanted to see Bangkok, and I gave him some good dope (without the high) on places to stay and sites to see. Margaret was economizing and trying to find the cheapest airfare from Singapore direct to London. Susie, still forlorn, eventually wanted to get to Australia but was in no hurry. I was going to Indonesia and looked forward to Bali, but this was a great crew of travelers, and I wanted to do something with them.

I was leafing through my trusty, well-worn Golden guidebook, and Borneo stood out as an attractive side trip. Two weeks in the wild jungles, living in longhouses with native headhunting Iban tribespeople. It took me a few hours of persuasion and lots of beer to convince them to come along with me. Finally, they all agreed if I got the boat scheduled. We christened ourselves the Scott Expedition, named after the doomed British Antarctic explorers, who all died in their attempt to be the first to reach the South Pole for God, King and country. Incidentally, it was one of the people on my mother's side of the family, the Norwegian Roland Amundsen, who beat the British at their own game and became the first man to reach the South Pole. "I claim the South Pole for Norway. God, what a forsaken place! I'll have to rename it; otherwise, no one will come here. Let's see: "New Vineland" has a nice tropical vibe. I could even dress the penguins in Hawaiian shirts and shorts with Ray-Ban sunglasses."

We even adopted nicknames: Don, with his goatee beard, fine features, and dark complexion, was the Sheik. Margaret, because of her bravery in the face of the Tiger Balm cement sea monster, was "Fearless Heroine". Susie, who was always lagging behind wherever we went, was "Straggling Susie". I, because of my clean-cut image and thorough knowledge of map reading, was Boy Scout. (To be continued)

Chapter Thirty: Stamford Raffles: The Founder of Singapore

"Miracles" and "We Built This City": Jefferson Starship

"Miracles": "If only you believe like I believe, we'd get by" This symbolized Raffle's dream for a great International city and the negotiations and patience to see that dream through.

"We Built This City" symbolizes Raffle's hard work and administrative skills in building a great city out of a strip of barren land.

Stamford Raffles by George Francis Joseph 1817

Stamford Raffles was like many other bright and ambitious but poor Englishmen who heeded the call "Go East Young Man", starting as a clerk in the British East India Company in Calcutta (which at the turn of the eighteenth century controlled almost all of India).

He rose quickly in the ranks, and by the time of the Napoleonic Wars, he held a high position in the company. Napoleon had conquered the Netherlands making it a vassal state and thus an enemy of Great Britain. The British, based in Malacca, Malaya, were determined to conquer the Dutch Indies (Indonesia) and grab the lucrative spice trade for themselves. The British Navy defeated a joint French-Dutch force and took over the Dutch colony. For his war service, Raffles was appointed lieutenant governor (Johnny-on-the-Spot or, as the British would say, "Jonathon-at-the-Bat). He served in this position from 1811-1816 until the British handed back the Dutch Indies to the Netherlands after Napoleon's final defeat.

During his tenure of office, he reformed the civil service, and worked with the local rulers to improve living conditions and stop the exploitation of workers, which the Dutch were notorious for doing. He studied the native peoples' customs and religion, collected native ceremonial artifacts, and wrote a scholarly "History of Java". He befriended the local Javanese Rajahs, fully respecting their religious freedom and practices to ensure there would not be any revolts against British rule.

Rafflesia Arnoldi, the corpse flower (so called because it smells like a decaying corpse) or the Giant Padma, is a species of flowering plant in the parasitic genus Rafflesia. It is noted for producing the largest individual flower on Earth.

It is interesting to note that the creature in the movie "Alien" bears a remarkable similarity to the Rafflesia "corpse flower" when it is first "hatching".

Raffles was passionately interested in the exotic flora of the Dutch East Indies and led expeditions to discover and collect flower and plant specimens. On one expedition in Sumatra, his team discovered the corpse flower (Giant Padma), which produces the largest individual flower on Earth, and this flower was named Rafflesia in honor of Stamford Raffles.

Raffles "rediscovered" Borobudur and other ancient Buddhist Shrines, preserving, repairing, and cataloging them.

Borobudur in 1872 before restoration

While in the capital Batavia (now Jakarta), he realized the vast potential of that city to be the gateway to China and Japan. The Dutch already had a monopoly on the Japanese trade in the port of Nagasaki after the Portuguese were expelled for proselytizing the Catholic faith. The Dutch were looking to expand their trade to mainland China. Raffles was determined to beat the Dutch and capture this lucrative trade for the British East India Company. However, he needed a city that could match Batavia's advantages. Malacca, the current headquarters of the company, didn't have a deep-water port, so he determined to build one from scratch.

Raffles found a suitable location at the bottom of the Malay Archipelago with a prime location for shipping lanes and a beautiful natural deep-water harbor. He then spent years wooing the local Malay rulers to sell him this barren, uninhabited piece of land. Finally, the local Rajahs agreed to sell, and Raffles paid the two Rajahs about 5000 English pounds for this land ("I don't know Stamford, the Dutch only paid $24 for all of Manhattoes Island, and now we have to shell out 5000 guineas for this uninhabited wasteland. Are you sure we can't get a better deal?").

Now that he had the land, Raffles set about planning the town, which he called Singapore: building up the port, putting up administrative buildings, and most importantly, making it a Port-of-Call for ships of all nations. He drafted Singapore's first constitution: forbidding slavery, opium, gambling, and public drunkenness, as well as guaranteeing total religious freedom for all the inhabitants. He didn't neglect the native Malays, permitting their madrassas (schools) and mosques, and he even started a college exclusively for the native population. Under his strict but just rule, the city quickly prospered. Within five years of its founding, the city had over 5000 inhabitants: native Malays, English administrators, missionaries, merchants, and sailors from all over the world. In the early nineteenth century, Singapore continued growing; the Chinese came in droves to operate the port and start small businesses. Tamils from South India came to work the rubber plantations in nearby Malaya. Merchants from all countries gave the city a cosmopolitan feeling like the early days of New Amsterdam. Raffles' vision came true: Singapore captured the Southeast Asian trade lines and was the starting point for British and other nations' entry into the Canton area of China, surpassing both Portuguese Macau and the Dutch Batavia.

Raffles' long stay in the humid tropics took a heavy toll on his personal life: he lost his first wife and four children to Asiatic fevers and typhus. He returned to England and was knighted for his service.

Raffles set the tone of a strict but benevolent ruler of this city. He was followed one hundred and fifty years later by another strict disciplinarian that saved Singapore upon independence from Malaysia and brought it to new heights of prosperity: Lee Kwan Yew.

Chapter Thirty-One: Lee Kwan Yew

"Superman": R.E.M.

Lee Kwan Yew

Singapore was originally part of Malaysia and had the same three predominant races of Chinese, Malays, and Tamil Indians, with small minorities of Western businessmen and Eurasians, but the overwhelming majority of the inhabitants were Chinese. When the majority of Malays in Malaysia started persecuting the Chinese with exorbitant taxes and restrictions, the Chinese reacted by forming their own Chinese party (People's Action Party) and winning all the seats from Singapore in the national assembly. The Malay leadership feared that the Chinese would soon control the national assembly and mustered the votes to expel Singapore from Malaysia.

Lee was the head of the People's Action Party (PAP). He had fought unsuccessfully to keep Singapore within Malaysia. However, when Malaysia kicked out Singapore, Lee retreated to his house and was not heard from for two weeks. He was not bemoaning his situation; instead, he emerged with a master plan to save the city. He immediately sought UN recognition and established treaties with all his independent neighbors to bolster this newly founded independence. He developed a new constitution, enshrining the dual principles of meritocracy and multi-racism. He sent out trade representatives to lure American and European companies with huge tax breaks. Lee had a highly educated and trained workforce and coupled with a highly efficient and corruption-free bureaucracy; Singapore was able to get multinational corporations to do business there. He also rebuilt his port infrastructure to make Singapore a leading hub of international shipments. With new money flowing in, Lee was able to give low-interest loans to small businesses, rebuild the slums, and encourage tourism. Within a few short years, Singapore became a thriving success, with one of the highest living standards in Asia. Unlike many countries in Asia, the wealth was shared by ordinary citizens. The excellent schools and the enshrined principle of meritocracy ensured that even the poorest could have a decent standard of living, if you are willing to work for it.

As I admired Lee's accomplishments, I reflected on New York City. In the late 1960s, Norman Mailer, the novelist, ran for mayor on the platform of making NYC the 51st state. Why couldn't NYC be a successful city-state like Singapore?

New York City is the financial center of the world, the center of corporate America, home to dozens of top universities, the nation's media center (newspapers, television, radio, book, and magazine), the nation's cultural center (art, dance, orchestras, museums, Broadway) and a major international tourist attraction, visited by millions yearly.

Then I looked at the differences. New York City has over one million people on welfare (1 out of every 8 New Yorkers), close to half a million drug addicts, rampant crime from the mafia to street and subway robberies and murders, exorbitant utility rates, and a massive tax burden that is driving businesses and residents out of the city. Even more glaring is the failure of the public educational system, substandard schools not being able to provide literate and suitable workers to attract industries to relocate here. NYC has the greatest hospitals in the country, but the average New Yorker cannot afford basic health insurance and preventive medical care. NYC has huge slums, dirty streets, unbelievable auto congestion, unsafe subways, and bad air quality. Our shipping ports are obsolete - all the import/export traffic has moved to New Jersey, and our bridges, tunnels, and roadways are in terrible shape. New York City is heavily funded by New York State: without these funds, the City would go bankrupt overnight. Crime and poor schools have driven out the middle-class, who were replaced with welfare families, which decimated the tax revenue needed to keep the city running.

There is also one major difference that stands out: Lee was able to accomplish all his improvements because he was a "benevolent dictator" that engineered major economic and social changes without any opposition. He prohibited large-scale protests and controlled the media. This could never happen in New York. To voice your opposition and protest publicly are guaranteed in our Constitution, and there are protests about everything in NYC daily.

Robert Moses

The one man that came closest to Lee's power was Robert Moses. He was an enigmatic bureaucrat that did more to change the landscape of New York than any man ever did in the history of the City. He ramrodded the building of bridges, superhighways, parks, and Jones Beach. He answered to neither the mayor nor the Governor of New York and had a public relations office that made him the media's white knight hero. In the beginning, he gave the people what they wanted: he built highways and bridges to the newly formed suburbs on Long Island that needed highways for the residents to commute to work in the city. He gave them recreation: parks and Jones Beach; he worked with the suburban developers to provide schools, hospitals, and shopping centers for these new suburban towns on Long Island. He financed many of his projects by using the revenue from tolls on the bridges, which he controlled. This will be his lasting legacy.

Now comes the villainous side of his vision. He believed that the wave of the future was the automobile. To fulfill this "master plan", he destroyed whole neighborhoods in the Bronx, evicted hundreds of thousands of people, and built his Cross Bronx Expressway, a superhighway in the heart of the city. He had no respect for the fabric of a city, the small neighborhood shops, where you buy your food and clothes, exchange greetings with your neighbors, walk your dog, and feel the energy, pulse, and smell of the human-scale streets. The most livable cities are the cities you can walk around in, discovering small boutiques, exciting clubs, specialty bookstores, exotic restaurants, and myriad other activities. Unfortunately, his vision of the city, emphasizing massive faceless Bauhaus slabs of public housing crisscrossed by superhighways and neglect of public transport influenced a whole generation of urban planners all over the country. These huge housing projects became instant ghettos of crime, drugs, and gangs. Once you destroy a livable and safe city environment, you have destroyed the reason for living in the city, and you leave. The superhighways facilitated this flight, leaving behind the poor and elderly, preyed upon by addicts and criminals.

Finally, Gov. Rockefeller stopped him before he could destroy cast iron Soho, Little Italy and most of Chinatown for a ten-lane expressway to New Jersey (Native New Yorkers called this a "Highway to Nowhere" - it's strange that Congress didn't fund it, this is what they do best) and saved the unique qualities of America's greatest city. So far, Singapore is still a vibrant walking city. Lee is still wildly popular here because he is giving his citizens a rising standard of living, great education, crime-free, cheap public transportation, clean streets, and the sense that the future will bring more opportunities and wealth for everyone.

Chapter Thirty-Two: The Grand Tradition: A Tale of Three Raj Hotels

"You can check out anytime, but you can never leave"

"Hotel California": Eagles

The British Empire (The Raj) in the Far East reached its grandiose pinnacle in the years 1880-1929. This was also the heyday of Edwardian and Victorian tourists doing the Grand Tour of Asia.

During the years of steam-trunk travel, Victorian ladies viewed the "exotic" Orient with all of their creature comforts intact ("Yes, I would love to see the temples at sunset, but it is almost time for Tea, and this tropical sun is raising havoc with my delicate complexion"). Rubber Plantation owners and government officials used these bastions of luxury to wind down after their daily duties were completed. Explorers and writers used them as a starting point for jungle adventures, both real and fictional. ("Yes, there I was in the bush, staring down the eyes of a huge, snarling Bengal tiger, not more than five feet away- just as it leaped at me, I dispatched him with my trusted Browning- made a rather lovely rug in my Kensington drawing room"). The fate of the empire was decided in its wood panel encrusted smoking rooms and polished bar rooms ("You know, I was telling Cecil, 'You must do something about the natives in your little fiefdom in Africa'").

The Sarkis Brothers 1900

"And the winner of the best mustache goes to the brother on the lower right."

Three enterprising brothers, the Sarkis built all three hotels and established, once and for all, what a tropical luxury hotel should look like: a white-painted mansion with imposing Grecian columns, surrounded by huge palm trees, manicured green lawns, spouting fountains, and beds of exotic flowers. Inside were white, high-ceiling, airy reception rooms, immaculately polished wood floors, whirling ceiling fans, and ornate Victorian chandeliers overhead. As you entered the foyer, there were potted palms, surrounding leather club chairs, set in sweeping verandas overlooking the ocean or a pastoral river. The individual rooms were spacious, with breezy balconies, four-poster beds with lacy mosquito netting, mahogany desks, plush upholstered furniture and lace curtains, fluttering in the ocean breeze. Each hotel had its mandatory huge Sikh doorman, with a colorful red Beefeater waistcoat, intricately folded turban, and flowing black beard, accompanied, of course, by the mandatory ornately curved dagger. Even today, this is the "platonic ideal" of a luxury Oriental hotel.

The Sarkis brothers were Armenians born in Isfahan, Persia. Their first hotel was the Eastern hotel in Georgetown, Penang, in 1854, which later became the famous Eastern & Oriental hotel. The brothers were the Hiltons of the 19th and early 20th century and were immensely wealthy. However, the grand era of Victorian travel ended with World War One. Then came the worldwide depression in 1930 which caused severe losses for the brothers, including the bankruptcy of the Raffles hotel. In the 1930s, they lost all of their hotels, and the last brother died penniless shortly afterwards.

Eastern & Oriental Hotel, Penang, Malaysia

The first of these Raj hotels was the Eastern & Oriental (E&O) (1885) in Penang, Malaysia. Penang is a colonial gem of small colorful houses, imposing brightly painted white government buildings, churches, and lively streets filled with small cafes and restaurants serving Chinese, Malay, and Indian cuisine.

I took an attractive English tourist for "high tea" at the E&O: fancy sterling silver tea setting, Earl Gray Tea, and adorable little sconces with jam and honey. The service and delicacies were superb; the "dog and pony show", however, failed to bed the girl, "Will that be one or two lumps, sir?"

Raffles Hotel, Singapore

The crown jewel of the three hotels was the Raffles of Singapore (1887). Its "long bar" was the watering hole for Kipling, Somerset Maugham, penniless European nobility, movie stars, and writers, Ernest Hemingway among them. The Raffles even invented its own drink: the Singapore Sling, a murky concoction of gin, brandy, orange liqueur, lime, bitters and grenadine, which became world famous. (When I was in New York, trying to impress Catholic college girls with my "worldly knowledge", I always ordered them Singapore slings {and usually had the same luck in the bedding department as I had with high tea at the E&O in Georgetown}). I visited the Raffles, where I drank a "Sling" sitting on the veranda in a white wicker chair, smoking a fat Churchill blunt, overlooking the spacious verdant garden and dramatic water views (somehow, "We'll fight them on the beaches" took on an entirely different meaning).

The Strand Rangoon

The last Grand Hotel was the Strand in Rangoon, Burma. This has now fallen into disrepair, but like an aging Victorian Grand Dame, she still retains a sense of decaying gentility. I stayed one night in the Strand after my plane crash in Burma. As I described in my first book, "Soldier to Sojourner", the hotel was a former shadow of itself and in sore need of renovation. Furthermore, due to the isolationist military regime and the lack of tourists, the renovation that had been started has stopped and the hotel is presently closed.

The E & O and the Raffles hotels are now owned by International Hoteliers, and the Raj is no longer. But at that time, this was "the place" to stay and be seen.

Borneo

Longhouse we stayed in Borneo

Chapter Thirty-Three: A Personal Fiefdom

"Everybody Wants to Rule the World": Tears for Fears

Portrait of James Brooke 1847 by Francis Grant

Borneo, the name conjures up visions of the fearless American hunter, Frank Buck, capturing snaring tigers while fighting off headhunters or the famous two-headed Lady from the jungles of Borneo, the main fun house attraction in small town carnivals.

I found a small freighter that carried machinery, dry goods, and Japanese electronics and was outfitted with separate, small cabins with bunk beds. The trip would take two days, and our destination was Kuching, the capital of the Malaysian state of Sarawak.

While I was picking up the boat tickets for Borneo, I met an older British expatriate, Nigel. He'd been in Singapore for over thirty years, arriving with the British Army that liberated the city from the Japanese in 1945. He originally worked for the British colonial government. but lost this job when Malaysia became independent in 1963. He survived by doing odd jobs, like helping foreigners and businessmen steer through the bureaucratic maze of Malaysian regulations for shipping exports or clearing and releasing imported goods. Nigel was quite a character; he drank a little too much but had a wealth of knowledge about Southeast Asia. I told him I was going to go to Borneo, and for the price of a few beers, he told me about a crazy English adventurer and his descendants that ruled Malaysian Borneo as their personal fiefdom.

This adventurer, James Brooke, like many young and poor Englishmen, went to India for fame and fortune. He served in the British Army, was wounded, resigned his officer commission, and returned to England.

Shortly afterward, young James received a sizable inheritance; he spent it all on a large, well-armed schooner, complete with a small private army, and sailed for Borneo. His intentions were to open the country to trading with the British East India Trading Company. He arrived in the middle of the civil war and was instrumental in restoring the Sultan of Brunei to his throne. The grateful Sultan gave him the governorship of Malaysian Borneo called Sarawak. At that time (the 1830s), the eastern third of Borneo was under the Sultanate of Brunei, and the western two-thirds were under the Dutch colonial administration.

However, Brooke didn't stop there; with his little army and indefatigable schooner, he cleared the Borneo coast of Chinese pirates. Again, the grateful Sultan of Brunei now rewarded him with the title of Rajah, absolute ruler of Sarawak.

Now it gets interesting: instead of exploiting the population or taxing his subject exorbitantly, he became the "Great White Father", protecting his children. The Brooke family were benevolent dictators who respected the native Iban people and their culture and prevented outside interference, including Christian missionaries, from destroying the Iban way of life. He wrote laws, started a civil service, and built municipal courts and government buildings. His private army enforced laws, stopping internecine Dayak conflicts and forbidding headhunting. To finance all these programs, he granted licenses to foreign companies to start trading venues and a mining company. All these companies used imported foreign workers, and the revenues from these ventures were enough to support the bare bones governing bureaucracy and keep the country running.

James was succeeded by his nephew Charles, who had the same paternalistic philosophy. Charles loved these people, even learning a Dayak language and living for a period in their village longhouse. He built hospitals and ports and started a native "Dayak" police force.

The third generation Brooke, Vyner, ended absolute rule, established a native governing council (Negri), and, after WWII, ceded the fiefdom to Great Britain, against the wishes of the Negri Council, who wanted to remain under Brooke's rule. Britain later gave it to Malaysia when it became independent in 1963.

For over one hundred years, the Brookes ruled Sarawak. While other colonial powers in Asia exploited the native population for spices, gold, and rubber, the Brookes benevolently left the Dayaks alone. This contrasts sharply with the large-scale destruction of the Iban way of life in the Indonesian portion of Borneo (Kalimantan), where farmers and loggers are displacing traditional Iban communities, and there is an extensive Islamization program to convert the Ibans away from their old animistic religious beliefs.

Nigel thought the Brookes were benevolent rulers who preserved a unique culture. I agreed and looked forward to experiencing the Dayak longhouse for myself on my upcoming trip.

Chapter Thirty-Four: Frank Buck the American Myth of the Self-Made Man

"Heroes": David Bowie

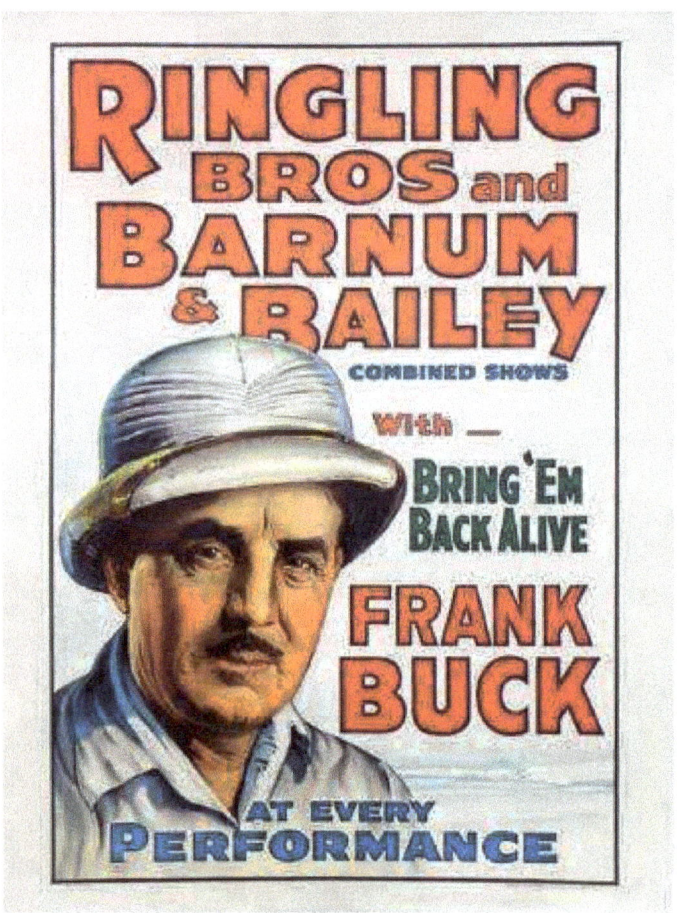

Circus Poster featuring Frank Buck 1938

On the ocean ship bound for Borneo, I tried to imagine what this primeval jungle land would be. Would it be the wild, mysterious and dangerous land that had been engraved in my mind by reading Frank Buck?

The first time I read "Frank Buck" was the "Classics Illustrated" comic book when I was about nine years old. This comic showed me a real-life hero, not a fantastic creation like Superman, but a real genuine person. I remember him fighting a huge king cobra, using only his jacket to pin down the poisonous viper. Most of his adventures took place in Malaya-Borneo, where I was now bound with the Scott Expedition.

Frank Buck was a self-made American man. He dropped out of school in the seventh grade and lived by his wits; he was a cowboy, gambler, hunter, and wild animal collector. In his life, he brought back alive 49 elephants, 60 tigers, hundreds of snakes, thousands of rare birds, and 52 orangutans (incidentally, in Marco Polo's homeward journey back to Italy, he sailed passed the Indonesian islands, where he saw "orange men", these "men" were orangutans). All of the animals he captured were sent to zoos and circuses.

What is fascinating about Frank Buck is that he created his own myth; for every schoolboy like myself, he was the "Great White Hunter". He exploited this myth, starring in seven motion pictures, where he staged "fight-to-the-death" scenes with savage animals. He started a roadside jungle show with performing animals and daring feats, which was one of the most popular attractions at the New York World's Fair in 1939. He was even a headliner in the Ringling Brothers' Circus, coming on stage in jungle costume and riding a huge elephant. Not only did he believe the myth, but he popularized it, bringing the exotic into the average American family home.

Americans want their heroes "larger-than-life". A man who leaves everyday life behind and heads out to the new territories, whether it is the west or a jungle. He then remakes himself into the fanciful myth we all so much admire. In our time, the most famous mythic hero is Ernest Hemingway. Many people believe he is the actual embodiment of his fictional novels. He is the "man of action" who lives his life to the fullest. All of his fiction is a projection of the man "Hemingway", and he sold that myth to us to become a famous novelist. Time after time, what appeals to us

Americans is a down-to-earth, common man who rises above his circumstances to become a hero.

I reflected on my own circumstances. I could have played it safe. I served my country and could have chosen to get on with life: a wife, kids, and a house in the suburbs. Instead, I left it all behind and headed out to the "new territories". I see myself as making my own destiny, remaking myself in a particularly American way. Instead of savage, wild beasts, I am discovering new religions, philosophies, and ways of thinking and living that are totally alien to my upbringing. I am searching for the answers to questions that will define who I am as a person. In this process, I am creating and believing in my own myth: the passionate seeker, a modern-day Siddhartha, using drugs, sex, and even religions as guideposts in my quest for the self-made myth of the seeker. Step right up, keep reading, and you will experience "The Greatest Show in the World"! (If the above sounds like a guy who is really full of himself, then I'll give you a quote from Joseph Heller's "Catch -22", which is a more nuanced picture of my personality: "Some people are born mediocre, some people achieve mediocrity, and some people have mediocrity thrust upon them.")

Chapter Thirty-Five: Borneo: Into the Heart of Lightness

"Your Mission, Agent Gordon, should you accept, is to bring the Scott Expedition Back Alive and Safe from the jungles, headhunters and wild animals of Borneo (loud theme music plays in the background)", Peter Graves solemnly speaks in the television show "Mission Impossible".

The Scott Expedition: The Sheik, Fearless Heroine and Strangling Susie

The "Boy Scout"

(Author at 10 years of age)

We finally arrived in Borneo. Kuching, being just a nondescript Chinese town, was a disappointment, and we were determined to get to the jungles as soon as possible. We got two rooms, one for the gals and one for the guys; over dinner in a Chinese restaurant, we asked ourselves, "Where do we go now?" All good expeditions have a goal and a plan to achieve that goal. Other than exploring the Antarctic, which did not seem feasible (we only had summer clothes and sandals, and we were really off course for that), we had no plan. Luckily, at a nearby table was an American Peace Corps volunteer, Bob Tilden, who overheard our dilemma and suggested we go to the Ethnology Museum in town; they could help us with information for a plan.

Shrunken Head

In the morning, we went to the museum, which was founded by an American anthropologist, Tom Conlin. The museum was fascinating: there were examples of shrunken heads from former headhunters and beautiful examples of the Iban's distinctive weaving called IKAT.

The Process of IKAT

I was fascinated by the intricacies of this beautiful fabric I viewed in the museum. The curator explained how it was made. IKAT cloth is made by applying a resist (a wax that resists dye coloring). Resist dyeing is a traditional method of dying textiles with patterns. IKAT uses wax, which prevents the colored dye from reaching all the fabric. IKAT does not use a tool to "scratch out" a design like in batik. The design is the individual thread or bundles of yarn bound tightly together to form the individual design, which is then dyed. To achieve multi-colors and intricate patterns, the bundles are unwrapped, the original wax washed off in hot water. The bundles are rebound in an altered way to complete the original design scheme or create a new design and can be dyed in the same or new colored dye. You can repeat this process many times to create multicolored, complicated patterns. After all this is completed, the bindings are then removed, and the dyed yarns are woven into cloth. The wonderful thing about IKAT is that the completed weave is identical, front and back, because the design is in the yarn, not on the exterior of the finished weave, like batik.

One characteristic that you notice immediately is the "blurriness" appearance of the cloth. This is because the weaver has great difficulty in matching the different dyed, designed threads (line them up to form a perfect pattern). This is especially true in multicolored, intricately patterned designs. The less the "blur", the better the weaver. However, blurred weaves are still very valuable, and this is mostly what you see in textile museums in the States.

What is also interesting is the meaning of IKAT in the Indonesian language: it has a double meaning. It can be a noun, "thread", or a verb "to bind" (the process of creating IKAT). Thus, the word IKAT describes the whole process from thread to woven cloth.

Indonesian Ikat funeral shroud 1910

The staff was very helpful, and we set up a plan to visit a Land Dayak (Iban) and a Sea Dayak village. The curator told us to take provisions like canned food, biscuits, toilet paper (of course, this was an essential item), and salt. I thought, why salt? Would we trade salt for lodging or, better yet, salt in trade for native women?

After stocking up on provisions (no OREO cookies, damn!), we boarded a dilapidated, overcrowded bus to a stop near our destination. Bus stops are marked in kilometers from Kuching. We got off at the 78th KM stop and started walking on a dirt track, which led us into the jungle for a "Kleine Spatzergung im das Gruner Wald" (a "Little Walk in the Green Forest"), keeping a watch out for the wicked witch. I suggested leaving biscuit breadcrumbs, so we could find our way back, but that was nixed by the rest of the group.

We walked for about two hours, getting sunburnt and sweating through our clothes. Finally, we reached the outskirts of a village. We were greeted by a swarm of Iban kids, and they escorted us to the headman of the village. He spoke no English, but one of the villagers spoke some English, and we told him we would like to stay in the village for the night. They found us lodging, a large storage hut, where we put our belongings. We followed the children around, and they led us to a small stream, where they jumped in. It looked so inviting; we went back and changed. We joined the kids and started swimming in the cold but refreshing water. This was a small farming community, not a longhouse settlement. The farmers raised rice, sago, and of course, coconuts. Everywhere we went, we were surrounded by kids, but when I tried to photograph them, they were gone. The young men in the village frequently work in Kuching to supplement their income. One was working with the Malaysian army and another taught school there.

This was a simple life here, and our group was the first westerners to stay in the village. The headman gave us a kerosene hurricane lantern, and we feasted on canned beef and a bottle of rice wine, all the comforts of home. We left in the morning for our return to Kuching.

The next day, we got a map from the museum, bought more provisions, and boarded another bus in the opposite direction for a Land Dayak longhouse. This time we rode for about two hours and got off for another dirt road. We walked for about two hours, sweating and getting scratched and cut by the vegetation of the jungle trail. I re-checked the museum map, told them we were on the right path, and we trudged on. The rest of the group was very supportive: "Are we there yet?", "Let's stop to eat!" and "You couldn't find your ass from a hole in the ground!" At dusk, we stumbled upon a small grass thatched hut. An old farmer and his wife greeted us and offered to let us stay the night. It seems my army map reading skills left something to be desired: we had overshot our destination by about five miles. However, the farmer and his wife were very friendly, giving us cooked rice to go with our canned meat. We literally sang for our supper, singing folk songs for them and taking their pictures. They gave us straw mats, and we slept peacefully under the stars.

The next day we walked for about two hours and saw the longhouse community.

A typical longhouse in Borneo (author's photograph)

The Longhouse

The longhouse is exactly that, hundreds of feet long, traditionally constructed of thatch on the exterior and palm fronds for the roof, although many have sheets of corrugated tin for the roof and sometimes for part or all of the facade. There is a shaded roof - an overhang verandah that runs the length of the house. The house sits on silts and is accessed by crude notched-wood ladders. Many times, you hear of a 30 or 40-door longhouse. This means that the house is divided into 30 or 40 separate rooms, each room is an individual living space for a family, and each door to the separate space is accessed through the verandah. The entire longhouse has wood floors, and the interior walls are thatch or tin in some cases. The lintel and post-construction support the roof; all longhouses are one-story. These partitioned rooms are on one side of the house, and the rest of the space in the longhouse is a common space for meetings, gatherings, or just a place for the inhabitants and dogs to hang out. Many large villages have more than one longhouse, like the rich Sea Dayak village which we visited, while smaller villages have just one, like the Land Dayak house we stayed in. When the village gets a new family, for example, a son gets married and brings his wife, the village builds an addition to the building, making the longhouse even longer. The longhouse has no bathrooms or running water. The outhouses are away from the building, and in the longhouses we stayed in, the cooking was done outdoors. Many longhouses have gas generators for limited electricity, usually for the common space areas. This living style is unique but also threatened by the lure of the cities, especially for young people, for making more money there than they can earn in the longhouse farming villages. Even more enticing is the modern western lifestyle that promises young Iban families the comforts we take for granted, like electricity, individual kitchens, indoor toilets, and separate bedrooms for parents and children.

The village consisted of a series of long thatched roof houses, sitting on stilts and accessed by ladders. The longest building is the longhouse, where all the village lives together. Amazingly, we were approached by villagers who spoke some English. Later, we found out there had been an American anthropologist who had lived in the village for two years with his wife and kids, studying the Iban lifestyle.

The people were very outgoing, offering us their food and even cooking our canned goods. We wandered around the community, watching the men climb up the coconut trees and the whole process of processing the husk, which they sold. They farmed rice and sago and seemed very content. We guys slept on straw mats outside on the verandah while the gals slept inside. We passed the time, swimming in the stream and speaking with the villagers about their way of life.

On our second day there, the peaceful calm was shattered: a unit of the Malaysian army stopped in the village, questioning the young men about the communists. These communist rebels were responsible for ambushing an army patrol, killing 15 soldiers a few weeks ago. After about two hours, they left, but the villagers were very frightened of the army.

That night I had a surrealistic experience: I went out in the dark, climbing down the ladder to take a crap. I had to fight off a 100-pound pig that gobbled up my crap before I had even finished and wanted more. (I passed on the pork that they gave us the next day).

We left the village the next afternoon, heading back to the main road for the Kuching bus. We were getting sunburnt again, our sandaled feet scratched by the underbrush and soaked, fording streams and wetlands. I suddenly felt a tingling on my ankles and feet; I looked down, and there must have been a dozen white worms hanging on my skin. I screamed and bent over to start pulling them out. But "Fearless Heroine" stopped me, calmly saying, "Get out the salt we have been carrying." I reached into my duffel bag and pulled out the box (iodized, no less). She poured liberal amounts in her hands and padded the worm heads on my skin. One by one, they fell off, leaving only bloody blotches. "These are leeches, and salt is the only way to get rid of the whole leech; pulling them off leaves a part of them in your skin, and that causes infections and swelling." When they were all off, I profusely thanked her and gave her a big hug. From that moment on, I was constantly looking down, checking my feet and legs. Even with this setback, we caught the Kuching bus.

We again stocked up on provisions (salt, even before toilet paper!) and headed up the coast to visit the Sea Dayaks. We got a late start and decided that we would stay in the beach town of Sematan for a well-deserved R&R. We found a cheap, clean beachfront hotel. The water was cold, but there was no riptide, and the beach had soft golden sand. The girls looked great in their swimsuits, and everyone enjoyed body surfing and swimming.

After dinner, I went out alone, it was late dusk, and I was walking barefoot in the wet sand. The tide was out; the sea had retreated out about a ¼ kilometer; you still could hear the surf breaking in the distance. There was a mist coming up, and as I turned, the last rays of the setting sun fell into the jagged black jungle. Man alone, confronting the raw, vital power of nature. I felt overwhelmed by the beauty and ran back to get a beach towel and bring the expedition to experience this epiphany. The Sheik and Straggling Susie were playing cards and weren't interested. And Fearless Heroine was, well, Fearless Heroine. The Ice Princess had melted a little while we lay in the warm sand that afternoon. We had been alone for the first time and spoke openly about our dreams and ambitions.

She had nice breasts and shapely-sculptured legs; her face was narrow, with full lips and an aquiline nose that crinkled when she was pissed off, which was quite often, especially at me. On the beach, she was relaxed, and I wanted to kiss her there but was afraid it would break the fragile trust we had just developed. At dinner, we reverted to our old selves, sharing funny stories but reserved in our feelings.

I grabbed Fearless Heroine by the hand and almost forcibly dragged her out of the room. When we got to the beach, the sun was gone, but the sound of distant breakers and low-lying mist was as captivating as before. "What do you feel now?" She was silent for a moment and then said, "Calmness."

"Yes, you brought that with you." I held her and gently kissed her. She kissed me back with a forcefulness that caused me to sway backward. We were standing in the wet sand, hungrily kissing. I released her and grabbed the towel, and we walked hand in hand down the beach to where the jungle meets the sea. We walked into the grassy part and spread the towel. We laid down on the towel; I was kissing her and gently fondling her. I started to undress. She looked up and suddenly asked, "Do you have protection?"

I was taken aback but recovered quickly, "Of course, that's why I'm the Boy Scout." She laughed, and we undressed and lay together, touching and kissing each other. Even in the darkness, our naked bodies shone luminously white. After a few moments of intense foreplay, I was fully erect. I found my pants and pulled out my last rubber from my wallet.

I slipped it on with a snap and pulled her over me, easing my penis in her. We moved slowly at first, savoring our desire, then thrusting quickly until we hit our crescendo and moving slowly up and down to maximize our pleasure. We separated and held each other closely without speaking. We dressed and walked back; we both knew we couldn't tell the others. We came into the room laughing and telling them about the nighttime beach. We had a beer and played a 4-hand casino card game before retreating to our boys' club room.

We left our beach after three days of sun and surf and took a bus to the Sea Dayak village. After another two-hour bus trip, we got off and walked for about an hour until we reached the village. When we first arrived at the longhouses, we didn't think the Ibans here were very friendly, but after befriending a few of the local young men, things got lively. They brought out a jug of fermented coconut toddy, and soon we were all floating high and laughing at everything.

The Chief Headman was an interesting figure: he had long earlobes, as you see in depictions of the Buddha, only he wore large metal earrings, but he didn't speak English. He did give us a delicious dinner, but afterward, the real fun began. He had a generator-operated record player and put on a Jim Reeves record. Reeves is an American country singer that is a national hero here and is considered the best singer in Malaysia and even in Indonesia. They brought out other records, and Sue and I started dancing. Soon we got a few of the older village boys to dance, and after multiple coaxing, a few of the young girls started to dance, and they had an innate sense of rhythm. Even the headman got into the spirit, doing a fairly decent twist dance. However, his eldest daughter thought it did not become a headman to be dancing, and she pulled him off the floor. The rest of us continued dancing until we were exhausted, and then we all slept together in the chief's longhouse room.

In the morning, we walked around the village and were very impressed. They had many pigs and chickens, but more importantly, two large hand-operated weaving machines, where they wove IKAT fabric. They bought the cotton yarn in bulk and the resist wax in the nearby town, but everything else was done in the village. They even had large wooden tubs filled with colored dyes. We observed the entire IKAT process, and it was fascinating to watch the weaver work. They sold the IKAT for good money in town, and this was a way they could keep their way of life viable. That night they killed a chicken for us, and we had another delicious meal. They served it to us with rice wine and, afterward, gave us arak (a fermented alcoholic drink similar to mescal). The Sheik got sick and rushed out to throw up, but the rest of us just got high and giddy. The next day, I had a hangover, and we spent the day swimming in the river and watching the people farming and picking coconuts.

In the afternoon, we met an Indonesian Iban named Nasim, who invited us to his longhouse across the border in Indonesia. It was a half-hour walk through the jungle without any visible road. His village was also very rich: they had lots of livestock, a few sewing machines, and presses to process raw rubber, which they collected in the jungle. They treated us to a delicious chicken meal and afterward brought us to a room where they had a generator, which operated a film projector. They put on an educational film in Indonesian about how to improve farm yields and raise new farm crops. After this was over, we went to a larger room where they also had generator-operated electricity, and they hooked up a record player, and we started dancing, at least our girls did. The music was Indonesian pop, and here the Iban young men were not shy and kept Margret and Sue swirling for hours. There were Iban girls who danced with each other, but when we asked them to dance, they ran away as if we had the plague. This merriment went on until the early morning. Finally, Nasim showed us a space in the common area where we could sleep. In the morning, he walked us back to our original longhouse. These Indonesian Ibans live an easy-working life, bathing three times a day in the nearby river, and working at their own pace. They hunt and fish, and some young people work in the nearby town. But when they see life in the towns, they leave the longhouses for a town apartment and save up for motorbikes and store-bought clothes.

It was time to leave our longhouse since we had to return to Kuching for our return vessel departure. We thanked the chief headman and walked out for the bus back to Kuching.

Chapter Thirty-Six: Ice Princess to Primeval Eve

"Close to You": The Carpenters

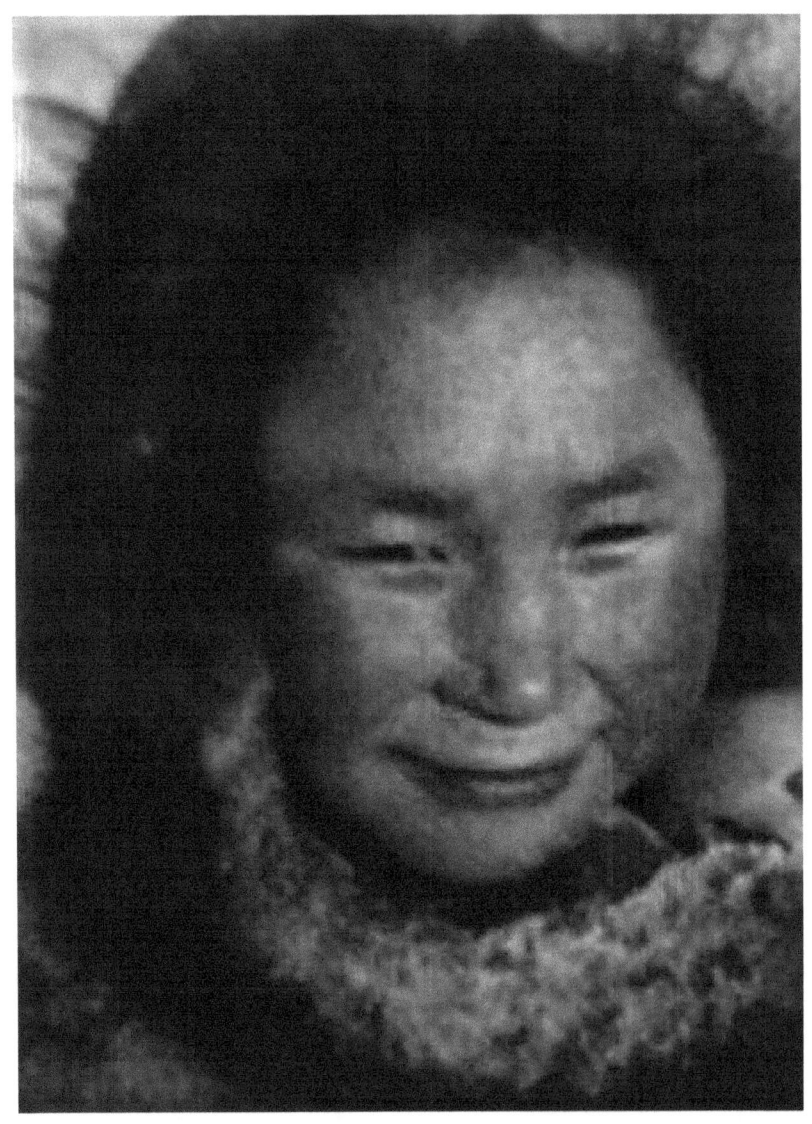

Nyla, wife of Nanook of the North

THE ARCHETYPICAL ICE PRINCESS

TO

PRIMEVAL EVE

Eve by Gislebertus 1130 A.D. Autun Cathedral France

We got back to Kuching late in the day to find our boat had left a day early, and we were stranded for four more days until we could get another boat to Singapore. Luckily, we ran into Bob Tilden again. He was the Peace Corps volunteer who had steered us to the museum. When he heard of our plight, he graciously offered to put us up in his house. Bob lived alone, in comfort, in a new house located in a middle-class Chinese suburb of Kuching.

Bob was an agricultural expert who worked with the local farmers to improve production yields and introduce new crops, particularly the sweet potato, which was higher in nutritional value than the traditionally farmed sago. We had the run of Bob's house; he had a stereo and lots of American pop music cassettes and a film projector with a bunch of agriculture education films, similar to Nasim's, but these were in English. He even let me use his 100cc Honda motorbike while he was at work. I used it to take the expedition on sightseeing tours around town.

I saved the last tour for Margaret. We stopped at a Chinese grocery, and I bought rice wine, biscuits, and fresh lychees (and a package of Chinese prophylactics) and headed out in the afternoon for parts unknown. About 20 km out, we turned onto a dirt road and found a grassy cul-de-sac away from the trail. We unpacked our American-style picnic lunch and sat on the blanket, swigging rice wine and eating biscuits and lychees. After we were sated, I kissed her, and we undressed. We lay back naked, and I told her we were in the original Garden of Eden, the first man and woman, and there was no serpent in sight. We lay there motionless, silently reveling in the beauty of the jungle and our own bodies. After a few moments, we started kissing and touching each other. Soon I was erect, and I fumbled in my pants for a rubber; I'm sure the package lettering in Chinese stated: "Open Other End" because it took forever to get it open, now where are we? Oh, yeah! I slipped on the rubber and came over her, easing my clothed penis into her vagina. I now knew her body, and we moved smoothly in sync. We thrust back and forth, hearing her moan quietly. I climaxed in organistic joy and continued my thrusts until I was spent. We lay side by side; she nestled in my arms.

We awoke as the last rays of daylight were dissolving into darkness. An old song with a similar situation ran through my mind, "Wake up, Little Susie" by the Everly Brothers, about a couple that goes to a drive-in movie, falls asleep, and they rush to get home, so their parents won't think they were doing a little hankey-pankey. We quickly got dressed, packed our lunch, and headed out. When we got back to Bob's place, it was totally dark. Everyone thought something had happened to us; I lied, saying we ran out of gas and had to walk a couple of miles for a petrol can of gas. They all looked at us incredulously, and I thought to myself, "And if you believe this bullshit, I have a bridge in Brooklyn to sell you really cheap."

The next day we all hung out, playing cards and listening to the music cassettes. We were leaving tomorrow morning, and we treated Bob to a meal at his favorite Chinese restaurant for his gracious hospitality. The boat actually left on schedule, and we had two days to say our goodbyes to each other. Don was going back to California to start a job in a new field, computer programming. Sue was going back to the Promised Land with the kangaroos and koalas. I got to talk to Margret privately on the return voyage. We had remained silent about our affair (Loose Lips Sink Ships), and we talked about her new life ahead. Swinging London was a big step up from the dusty one-horse town she came from. "Are you a little scared?"

"A little, but I have references for a job from the hospital back home, and if I need more training, I'll do home care until I get the certificates." She seemed confident, the "Fearless Heroine" persona that we all knew.

I told her, "I just want to thank you for your time. I could really be at ease with you, not afraid to open myself to you, and hope you have the same feelings. I will miss you."

"You really changed from the obnoxious loudmouth, know-it-all that you were when we first met. Don't change; I want to remember you the way you are now."

"I hope I can live up to your expectations. After all, you can tell by my outfit that I am a Boy Scout."

I felt like the odd man out, everyone heading for a job or new life; I was the guy in the song "King of the Road" by Roger Miller, going nowhere, a bum with no ambition or direction in my life.

We said our farewells, and I stayed in the port, booking the first vessel to Indonesia, which would leave early tomorrow morning.

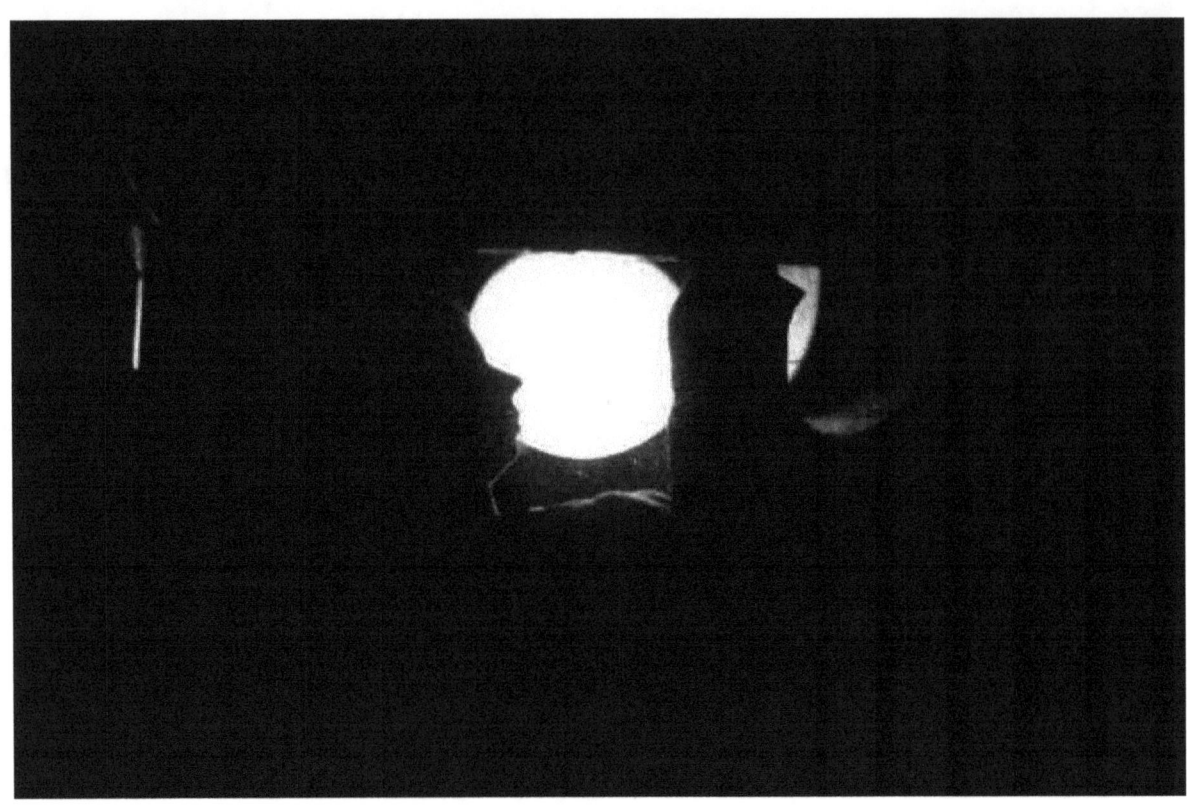

"Fearless Heroine" in route to Borneo (author's photo)

Indonesia

Dutch East Indies Travel Poster of the 1930s

Chapter Thirty-Seven: Indonesia Entry

"On the Good Ship Lollipop" Shirley Temple (1934)

I was still a little depressed, thinking of Margret and our time in Borneo as I boarded the ship that would take me to Sumatra, my first destination in Indonesia. I was traveling steerage and set off alone, but I met several travelers on board. The most memorable experience of this trip was the food. I bought a meal of rice and chicken. When I started to eat, I noticed the rice moving. There were little white maggots squirming in my platter; that was the end of my appetite (get it while it's hot, not while it's moving!)

We docked in Palembang, Sumatra, and spent the whole day waiting to disembark while Indonesian Customs officials searched for contraband. They found stacks of china, Chinese records, and silks. However, they didn't find the pallets of contraband cigarettes, which had been off-loaded to a smaller boat outside of the harbor before we docked.

Finally, they let us off, and we all had to go to the Police Station to get our Visas stamped. Of course, we arrived after the Immigration Officer had left for the day, and we all had to sleep on the floor until he arrived in the morning.

After traveling in Asia for eight months, you get used to the public toilets, which are basically smelly holes in the floor. To take a crap, you must bend down, squatting, while you hold your knees and pants and do your business (you always have to travel with toilet paper or, in a pinch, a thick paperback book; "War and Peace" is excellent for this function). There was an American traveler, Kip, who had just gotten off the plane in Singapore from the States, and this was his first experience with Asian toilets. He dutifully left with his roll of toilet paper and about ten minutes later came back smelling like an untreated outhouse. "I'm not that good a trick artist": he had fallen into the hole and got covered with the contents. We laughed ourselves silly, but we made him go to the far corner of the room.

Finally, in the morning, all of us half asleep, we got our passports stamped, and we caught an all-day long train to the Java ferry.

The ferry was an all-night trip, and we slept on the deck, or at least tried to. We were kept up all night because they were blaring loud Indonesian pop music. It was crowded with women openly breastfeeding, kids running and screaming everywhere, and men sleeping, covered with newspapers. You couldn't move around from your little confined space. Thoroughly exhausted, we groggily awoke to the sight of green hills, dozens of small fishing boats, and a chaotic port scene of porters shouting as they loaded and off-loaded cargo.

I had befriended a Swiss traveler, Bert, and we took a pedicab to the youth hostel after disembarking our vessel. At the hostel, I ran into Marc Clague, the French stoner I had roomed with in Bangkok. He told me that he had spent a month in jail in Bangkok for hash possession and now couldn't return there. Luckily, he had received his Australian work permit and was slowly (meaning stoned) making his way there.

This was the first time I had a chance to sample a variety of Indonesian food. The first thing you notice in the marketplace is the overwhelming sickly-sweet smell of cloves. This comes from the cigarettes called kretek, which is part tobacco and part cloves. Everyone in the market, the merchants and the customers, had a kretek cigarette dangling from their mouths.

Indonesian stall food is distinguished by the use of peanut flavoring. The Indonesians cook with peanut oil and make a peanut sauce that they bast on their chicken satays. The flavor is unique and not overly sweet, like the "Skippy" peanut butter sandwiches you used to have for lunch at home.

The Dutch taught the Indonesians how to brew beer, and the local brand "Bintang" tastes very much like Heineken and is widely popular in the country.

For dessert, Indonesia has the most variety of exotic fruits in the entire world: mangos, rambutans, litchis, mangosteens, soursop, star fruit, coconut, pineapple, custard apple, and the stinky fruit that I will describe later with much fanfare, drum roll and full orchestra called durian.

Chapter Thirty-Eight: Old Batavia

"Amsterdam": Scott Walker

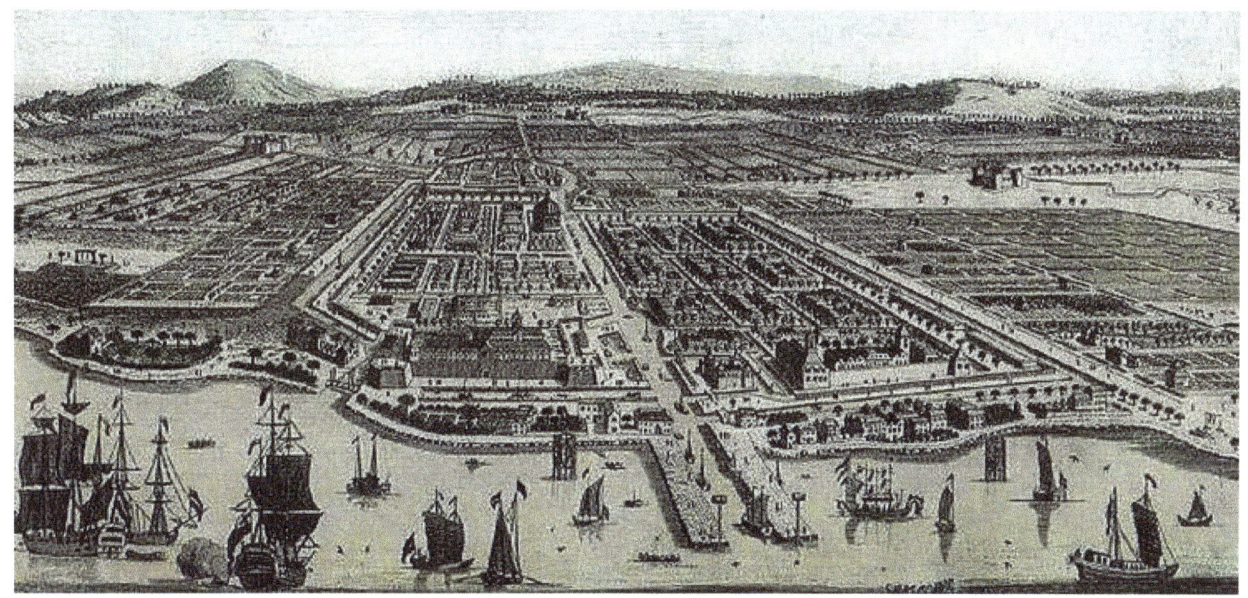

Old Batavia in the 18th century

I spent the day wondering about the old Dutch city of Batavia (the old central core of modern Jakarta). Walking these cobblestone streets, you could really see how the city was laid out; a central fortress (now gone), public squares with huge Dutch-style government buildings, banks, and museums. There were blocks of gabled houses separated by fetid canals. The old guild houses and gabled warehouses were crumbling away in the humid tropic weather. There was even an old-style Dutch drawbridge appearing just like a print from a Rembrandt drawing (if you left out the overgrown vines and palms).

I visited the Jakarta History Museum, located in one of those huge Dutch open squares now crowded with Indonesian families and young lovers. The building could have been transported directly from Amsterdam. Inside the museum were artifacts, maps, and furniture from the Dutch days proudly on display. There was one huge baroque bookcase (see below) with a delicate lattice top surmounted by the crest of the city Batavia and two magistrates representing justice: all intricately and exquisitely carved by skilled Javanese woodworkers for the Dutch colonial government. This is one of the most beautiful pieces of furniture I have ever seen. It was heavily lacquered, filled with old leather-bound books and ledgers, gleaming dark-red mahogany, bathed in the sunlight coming through the tall clear glass windows of the old baroque City Hall, now the History Museum.

Afterward, I explored the nearby streets, visiting shops and cafes carved out of old gabled warehouses. As I drank a chai in a small café, which was the ground floor of an old warehouse, I marveled that after four and a half centuries there was still a small central-core Dutch city in this sprawling, chaotic metropolis.

Indonesian-made sculptured bookcase from the collection of the Jakarta History Museum 18th century (photo by Brian Giesen (Flickr, U. S. license: Creative Commons 2.0).

This brought to mind New York City, and I imagined what would have happened if the British had not taken over and it remained New Amsterdam.

New Amsterdam in the 17th century

Both Batavia and New Amsterdam were founded in the seventeenth century by private Dutch mercantile companies. Would New Amsterdam still be a miniature copy of the old Amsterdam like Batavia? New Amsterdam, unlike Batavia, is a perfect place for concentric canals which would stretch from the Hudson River to the East River, daily flushing out the sewage and other fetid materials. Instead of Times Square, you'd have AmsterLand downtown with the bars, dance halls, drug cafes, and wooden clog shops in one central location, all surrounded by the original

Dutch wall (now Wall Street). On Bowling Green, this "wonderland" would also have amusements, carnival rides, and a huge windmill ride, where riders go round and round on the giant blades ("Who's that guy dressed in armor like a medieval knight on a sagging steed, welding a long lance and charging at the windmill?" "Oh him, that's Tom, he's just the Windmill ride operator; on his time off, he dresses up as a knight and practices tournament jousting for a better job with the 'Renaissance Fair' over in Jersey") and fast-food eateries: raw herring on a pumpernickel slice of bread and French fries doused in mayonnaise, all washed down with a Heineken. However, knowing the Dutch, there would be an admission charge getting into this Amsterland, but in true Dutch fashion: "Whatever happens in AmsterLand, Stays in AmsterLand."

Amsterdam's red-light district (photo by GIO May 2020, UNSPLASH photo)

If Rip van Winkle were to wake up in this 20th-century fantasy AmsterLand, he would be reassured by the facades of newly built guild houses, gabled warehouses, windmills, old-style Dutch drawbridges, and boats plying the canals. He would feel right at home, seeing the Williamsburg-style actors in period dress raising tulips, bowling outdoors in Bowling Green, and being greeted by Peter Stuyvesant with a fake wooden peg leg. He'd be amazed by the dress of the tourists, deafened by the loud Rock & Roll blaring from every shop, and afraid of being run over by the swarms of bicycles in the streets ("A lot has changed", he thought, "since I last visited New Amsterdam ten years ago. I really must get out more!"). However, he might be taken aback at the scantily clad lovely ladies sitting in their neon-lit windows, beaconing him, "Hey Gramps, looking for a good time?" But since he's Dutch, he'll just shrug his shoulders and ruefully accept that his fellow Dutch countrymen will do anything for a guilder.

Chapter Thirty-Nine: Jakarta Stadium

The Russian built Jakarta stadium

BREAD AND CIRCUS

Katie Casey was baseball mad,

Had the fever and had it bad.

Just to root for the hometown crew,

Ev'ry sou[1]

Katie blew.

On a Saturday, her young beau

Called to see if she'd like to go

To see a show, but Miss Kate said, "No,

I'll tell you what you can do:"

Chorus

Take me out to the ball game,

Take me out with the crowd;

Buy me some peanuts and Cracker Jack,

I don't care if I never get back.

Let me root, root, root for the home team,

If they don't win, it's a shame.

For it's one, two, three strikes, you're out,

At the old ball game.

Katie Casey saw all the games,

Knew the players by their first names.

Told the umpire he was wrong,

All along,

Good and strong.

When the score was just two to two,

Katie Casey knew what to do,

Just to cheer up the boys she knew,

She made the gang sing this song:

"Take Me Out to the Ball Game" is a 1908 Tin Pan Alley song by Jack Norworth and Albert Von Tilzer

While I was staying at the youth hostel, a fellow freak from Switzerland, Bert, whom I had traveled with since Sumatra, asked me to go with him to a soccer game. He said that the Santos Brazil team was playing the Indonesian national team and that there was a chance to see the greatest soccer player ever, Pele.

Having lived in West Germany, where soccer players are mini-gods and unlike in America, are avidly watched by males and females alike. I remember going on a date where my German girlfriend insisted that we watch the German Bavarian team before we did anything else (soccer now, sex later!). Pele and Brazil dominated the World Cup, so it was off to the races.

The large stadium was built by Communist Russia as an expression of friendship between the two countries.

The game was exciting, and the crowd went wild every time the national team scored (alas, there were no hotdogs, but they did have beer.) Brazil won the match, but the crowd still loved Pele. He was one of them: a poor kid from the slums who made it big. Soccer is very popular here, and every alley and field have kids in make-to soccer games.

However, when I traveled around Jakarta, I saw the extreme poverty, the stinking canals, lack of public health and education. I now saw the Stadium as the modern equivalent of the Roman Colosseum. This was Sukarno's Circus to appease the masses and keep them quiet.

The money to build this huge stadium could have been better spent on clean water projects, improved bus systems, and rebuilding the electric grid for the city. But before I get "holier than thou", I thought of America: the huge waste of money and lives in Vietnam. We could have rebuilt our own crumbling cities, fixed our education system, and created jobs for our poor. No, we pissed it away in the jungle based on an outdated political philosophy, the domino theory: if we don't stop communism in Vietnam, it will spread all over southeast Asia and beyond.

Indonesia needed a new political system, but it wouldn't be communism. The abortive communist coup in 1965 cost over half a million dead, and the average Indonesian is very anti-communist, including the students.

So, what's to be done? I didn't have the answer, but maybe "little victories" in the battle against poverty was a partial answer.

There are very many diseases in this country: one-eyed people, skin diseases, and many cripples and one-legged people. These unfortunate people were like the maimed and grotesque German soldiers returning from World War I: insane, crazed, wandering men with faces half blown off, one-eyed and one-legged beggars as drawn by George Grosz in his book *Ecco Homo*.

Throughout Indonesia, you have health and dental clinics and hospitals run by the Pentecostal and Seventh Day Adventists. These efficient and caring facilities are doing what the national government doesn't have the resources to accomplish. These selfless health professionals are making a difference on a person-to-person basis. Again, I thought of Christ's words, "If you help the poorest, you are helping me."

My hometown, New York City, needed this same kind of neighborhood clinic: we have world-class hospitals, but millions of our citizens do not have access to basic health care. Why? Crime is the main cause. We cannot ask our health professionals to risk their lives coming and going into dangerous ghettos when we cannot ensure their safety. What we could do is set up mobile clinics that could service these disadvantaged areas. This could be a joint city/private hospital partnership, where doctors and nurses could fulfill their residency requirements, treating patients in specially outfitted 18-wheelers with guaranteed police presence. The federal government could assist in supplying medical equipment and medicines at Medicare pricing and forgive prohibitive medical student debt for participating health professionals.

Pele in Sweden 1960

Chapter Forty: Kretek

Kretek: resin, nutmeg, cumin, clove, and tobacco hand wrapped in banana leaves and sold in pharmacies as a health product to cure asthma 1910

When I arrived in Indonesia, the first smell I inhaled in the marketplace was the overpowering aroma of cloves. The Indonesians combined cheap tobacco with shreds of clove to give a heavily scented smoke that sweetened your lips as you smoked it. The cloves crackled and popped as you smoked (No, they didn't taste like Rice Krispies, but the crackling pieces of clove popped out of the cigarette and burned little holes in my shirt and pants).

Back in the States, we cook ham with cloves to make it sweeter. The Chinese used it as a breath refresher; anyone having an audience with a high official had to chew a clove before he spoke to the official. I even heard it would mask alcohol breath, especially useful if you were taking that important job interview and wanted to impress the interviewer with your go-getter work ethic (however, it does not cure slurring speech or hiccups).

The Dutch introduced tobacco as a cash product in Indonesia, and the origin of kretek dates to 1880. The creator of kretek was an Indonesian Hji Djarmhati who suffered from chest pains and asthma. To relieve this pain, he rubbed his chest with clove oil. This helped, but he had the bright idea to mix clove buds, tree sap, and tobacco and get deeper relief by smoking this concoction. He was supposedly immediately cured, and the legend spread throughout the land that kretek could cure asthma. This was like the Woody Allen satiric comedy "Sleepers", where future doctors found that cigarettes and chocolate were actually good for you. These hand-rolled kreteks were then sold in drugstores as a cure for asthma (see illustration above).

While I was in Indonesia, everyone smoked, and the air was thick with the pungent clove aroma. The Indonesian government under the leftist Sukarno patriotically pushed the smoking of "native kretek" as opposed to capitalist "white cigarettes". The kretek industry is big business in Indonesia: there are over 500 companies producing this cigarette, employing approximately 10 million Indonesians in the making and selling of this clove cigarette.

There is a large cottage industry in Indonesia that makes kretek. Many are rolled in private homes, just like the immigrant tenement dwellers on the Lower East Side used to roll cigars on their kitchen tables. The companies supply the workers with all the ingredients, and then they are paid piecemeal for the hand-rolled product. All kretek are hand rolled without a filter, and each locality adds a special condiment to give a particularly distinctive flavor to their brand. Some kretek is rolled in banana or palm leaf to give an extra flavor.

I had my 15 seconds of fame when I came back to New York. I still had a pack of kretek cigarettes and started smoking them in a fashionable club called "Elaine's" on the Upper East Side. No less than the owner herself, Elaine, a big blond woman, came over and told me, "You can't smoke that stinking cigarette here and get out!" I was about to answer her with a paraphrase of Groucho's famous line that I wouldn't join any club that would have me, but the accompanying bouncer escorted me hurriedly out to the street.

I sometimes mixed kretek with hash to give a sweet mellow high. I really enjoyed them and tried all of the varieties of local brands, but my favorite was Gudang Garam, which left my lips tingling with sweetness. However, I really didn't need the sweet lips: the ladies of the night all said I was the "sweetest little thing".

Chapter Forty-One: Sukarno

"Those in possession of absolute power can not only prophesy and make their prophecies come true, but they can also lie and make their lies come true." Eric Hoffer

President Sukarno

The father of Indonesian independence was an ex-engineer named Sukarno, who founded the PNI, Indonesian National Party, in 1927. Sukarno was known for his fiery speeches and charismatic leadership. He was arrested by the Dutch and only freed by the invading Japanese. He collaborated with the Japanese in WW II in return for letting him set up a Home Guard militia. This militia became the nucleus of the revolutionary army. After WW II ended, the Dutch were determined to hold on to this lucrative colony at all costs. While researching this story, I found a disturbing little-known fact that the Dutch used U.S. Marshall Plan aid to fund their army to kill Indonesians to try to stop independence. When the U.S. discovered that their aid, meant to rebuild Dutch industry and their war-ravished cities, was being used for this war of attrition, they cut off the aid. Without this aid, the Dutch had few resources to carry on the struggle and quickly granted Indonesian independence.

Sukarno now inherited a country in chaos, where his first priority was to unite the various nationalities, religions, and social structures of the island nation. He was still fighting the Dutch over Kalimantan, the Dutch-controlled portion of Borneo and West Irian, the Dutch half of New Guinea, and subduing various rebel independence groups in the islands, far away from the central governing power of Java. The Dutch, like the French in Indochina, were shitty colonists: they were only concerned with the export wealth of the country for the benefit of the Netherlands and not the Indonesian people. Furthermore, the Dutch did little to build up the educational, social, health, and democratic systems needed for the country to be truly stable upon independence.

Sukarno had a vision that was unique among the developing countries recently freed from colonialism: He wanted to be totally unaligned, neither kowtowing to the West nor the Soviet Union. His government was founded on three principles: nationalism, Islam, and communism. In the late 1950s, he abolished parliamentary democracy for his vision of guided democracy, which was based on the old Indonesian concept of village rule, where problems are debated, and a consensus is reached. He courted both the United States and the Soviet Union to help him economically and militarily. New alliances were made with India, Ghana, and Cuba, trying to find a middle way that was not beholden to either of the superpowers. He looked to Red China as a model for developing the country without being dependent on outside influences. However, his economic policy spelled disaster for the country. He nationalized all of the Dutch and foreign western companies and put his cronies in charge. Industrial output fell by over 80%, and this was further exacerbated by his confiscation of native Chinese businesses and industry. He borrowed heavily from the World Bank, refusing to follow their austere guidelines to rein in inflation nor repaying the loans. In the early 60s, he withdrew from the United Nations, calling it a western capitalist organization that was just out to keep the third-world countries in servitude. His idea of keeping Indonesia independent was basically flawed economically: all the monies earned and borrowed went to building up the army to keep the country in line from the periodic revolts and the conflicts with the Dutch over Borneo and New Guinea.

The Indonesian people were jobless, uneducated, and had no social or health programs; Sukarno did nothing to alleviate this suffering. I had mentioned before the selfless work of the Seventh Day Adventists in establishing medical and dental clinics throughout the country. He alienated the U.S. and other Western powers with the nationalization of industry, and there was no income to make these much-needed social improvements. Toward the end of his regime he became a megalomaniac, declaring himself president for life in 1963 and totally aligning himself with the Indonesian Communist Party, the PKI. This angered the army and the Muslim clerics, who were huge landowners and saw the communists as a threat to their livelihood. In 1964 and 1965, there was hyperinflation of over 650% per year, which caused unbelievable suffering among the poorer classes.

Sukarno veered sharply to the left, accepting massive aid from the Soviet Union and imitating Red China's Red Guards with his plan to start a separate army of farmers and industrial workers to counter the influence and threat of the military.

In 1965 there was an attempted communist coup with five generals kidnapped and murdered. The rebels took over the radio station and the central government in Java, preaching alliance to the communists and Sukarno. This was quickly crushed by the army, led by an ambitious general, Suharto. The aftermath was bloody; over a half million communists were killed, destroying that party. Suharto took over the power, with Sukarno remaining under house arrest until he died in 1970.

General Suharto attending the funeral of the five slain kidnapped generals that started the 1965 Communist Uprising, in which General Suharto and the Indonesian Army crushed and deposed President Sukarno.

How will history judge Sukarno? He squandered Indonesian resources, installed his inept cronies in power, and neglected education, health services, and his people's welfare. Yet for twenty years, he kept this vast island country united and proud to be an Indonesian. His belief that Indonesia should go its separate way was unrealistic in a world increasingly controlled by the Superpowers both economically and militarily. He was a flawed individual but a patriot above all else, and this will be his lasting legacy.

Suharto is starting to rebuild internally and seeking allies and aid from the western countries but has kept the anti-Chinese persecutions and confiscations, making the Indonesian Chinese the scapegoat for the economic problems of the country.

I asked many educated and common people if they liked Sukarno and the current President, Suharto. Everyone said they were both great Presidents and national heroes, but Suharto was better because Sukarno favored the communists. And everyone in Indonesia knows that the only good communist is a dead one.

Chapter Forty-Two: Borobudur: The Big Rock Candy Mountain

"The Big Rock Candy Mountain": Burl Ives

Borobudur now, in the present day

When you first see this "mountain" planted in rice fields, you feel like it is a gigantic spaceship that is waiting for the Buddhist monks to ascend to heaven. I remember the medieval fairy tale the "Pied Piper of Hamlin" in West Germany, leading the children, as Neil Young would later sing, "to a new home in the Sun". Borobudur is like a large layer cake, getting smaller as you ascend, topped with small stupas and hundreds of Buddhist statuses. When awe-struck Hindus first saw this building, they called it Mount Meru, the legendary abode of the Gods. Borobudur was built in the eighth and ninth centuries A. D. and is the largest Buddhist temple in the world.

How Borobudur looked when Raffles "rediscovered" it in the 1820s

Borobudur is a textbook in stone of Buddhist life in the ninth century A.D. Its carved stone panels show every aspect of Buddha's life, and then there are high relief stone carvings that depict life at the time, from clothing to work, to dancing and to war; this gives us an intimate portrait of what life was back then. The structure itself is a literal symbol of Buddhist belief. The five-story mountain starts with a base terrace that shows a man in a debased state. The next level shows men committing good and evil deeds and how karma works to reward or punish based on your behavior. The third level shows man gradually shedding his desires but still earthbound. The fourth and fifth levels have carved reliefs that reflect man's struggle to overcome the world of the senses. By the time he reaches the square terraces right below the rooftop, he has controlled his emotions and eliminated all desires. Once he reaches the top, he sees the stone stupa, which is a symbol of Heaven (Nirvana).

In its heyday, Borobudur would have had huge Thanka banners draped over the sides, chanting monks in saffron robes and the all-pervading smell of pungent incense (truly a sweetly smelling Big Rock Candy Mountain).

Then suddenly, at the beginning of the 14th century AD, Borobudur was abandoned. There are many causes for this abandonment: one was a severe earthquake and volcanic eruption at the end of the 13th century, which damaged and covered it with volcanic ash. Secondly, starting at the end of the 13th century and the beginning of the 14th-century Muslim kingdoms defeated the Hindu rulers and made central Java a bastion of Islam. Buddhists were no longer welcome, and the surviving Hindus founded their own Kingdom in Bali. Borobudur remained hidden, covered with trees and tropical growth for over 400 years. There were more volcanic eruptions, more volcanic ash, and jungle vegetation that took over and buried the entire bottom layer of Borobudur as well as covering the highest levels of the monument. However, what preserved Borobudur was the Javanese superstitions that this site was emblematic of evil spirits and bad luck, and the locals stayed away.

The British adventurer and founder of Singapore, Stamford Raffles, rediscovered it in the early nineteenth century and partially cleaned and removed the vegetation of this grand monument. This was the great age of the discovery of lost civilizations. Just ten years later, a New York diplomat, John Lloyd Stevens, rediscovered the Mayan civilization in the jungles of Honduras. Here was a huge city covered in vegetation that was completely unknown. Stephens was accompanied by an architect and engraver, Frederick Catherwood. Catherwood drew a series of lithographs showing the Mayan ruins covered with vines and strangling trees, yet the awe and majesty of the buildings and statuary were undiminished. This is what makes traveling so exciting that you are standing in the footsteps of these great explorers and scientists that showed us a world that rose and fell a millennium ago.

You are reliving the discovery: walking in the footsteps of Buddhist priests, chanting sutras and climbing the worn stones of Borobudur to reach nirvana.

Frederick Catherwood lithograph of a Mayan stele at Copan

When the Dutch took over, they stabilized and shored up Borobudur from collapsing. The Dutch also rebuilt the large stupa crown at the very top. But they couldn't change the sense of calmness that you feel when you climb this holy place. It is best at sunrise and sunset; the former bathes it in crystal purity, while the latter burnishes it in bronze and gold.

When you climb the Empire State Building, the building disappears, and you feel the energy of the city around and below you. At Borobudur, the energy is directed upward; your thoughts are focused on the stone architectural carvings, the Buddhas and the stupas as you ascend the stone mountain. You excitingly anticipate reaching the top, where symbolically, you will find the peace of Nirvana.

Bali

The artist village of Ubud, Bali 1900

Chapter Forty-Three: Land Of Milk And Honey

"If there be a paradise on earth, this is it; this is it, this is it," seventeenth-century Indian Emperor Jahangir on first sight of the Vale of Kashmir.

"A Taste of Honey": Lenny Welch (Theme song of the excellent 1961 British movie "A Taste of Honey")

After staying up to catch the late-night ferry from Java to Bali, I was tired but avidly looking forward to Bali. I was traveling alone; Bert, my Swiss friend, had stayed on in Jakarta. As the first rays of sunlight appeared, I came upon the green hills of Bali. I disembarked and got on a bus to Denpasar, Bali's capital. On the bus, I befriended a German from Berlin, Loetz, and we decided to room together in Kuta Beach. We drove past beautiful temples, thatched wood cottages, coconut trees, and picturesque hill-climbing rice terraces. We drove through the morning, watching women bathe, men shitting in the creeks, and children running wild everywhere.

We arrived in Denpasar, which is a dirty, dusty, car-congested city, and immediately caught a bus for Kuta Beach in the afternoon. We found a beautiful little loesman (small hotel) where we booked our rooms. My room was very clean and airy: the floor, walls, and ceiling were all constructed of different kinds of wood. The room was crystal bare, as in an Andrew Wyeth painting. After settling in, we changed (I in my cutoff jeans and Loetz in his tight-fitting, bulging front and barely covering his ass swimsuit that Europeans have universally adopted as their standard beach uniform) and headed for the beach. Kuta was once a sleepy fishing village, and you could still see the fishermen pulling in their nets at sunset. The beach is one long arch, soft, fine-grained white sand, crystal blue water, and no rip tides.

There were Freaks everywhere: bearded, long-haired French freaks dressed in white flowing robes; bronze, topless, Australian sunbathers, protectively surrounded by clean-cut Aussie volleyball players; and an English couple trying to fly a dragon kite. As you walk along the surf, you hear a cacophony of languages coming from the tribal enclaves of different nations. The musical Swiss-German from Bern or Zurich, the Cockney slang of Liverpool, and the highbrow Oxford English of London. You overheard the strains of "Mate" and "Sheila" from boisterous Australians, the cultivated and flowery French from Paris, and the mumbled, guttersnipe French of Marseille. Then you had the TV newscaster English of Californians and the nasal Brooklynese in small pockets. You looked out at the ocean and saw dozens of surfers, straight strings on wave crests, as if they were a marching band gliding in lockstep cadence. Freak girls with long, dark hair and colorful batik sarongs walking along the surf and herds of Germans riding bicycles everywhere. This whole beach scene was reminiscent of the 1940s-1950s Coney Island paintings of Reginald Marsh.

Coney Island Beach by Reginald Marsh 1951

Loetz and I spread our beach towels, lit a Sumatra joint, and sat back to watch the best free show in Bali: the incredible sunset; the red sun lay like an enormous egg on the blue sea. The faces of the Freaks were transformed from cream white to ochre yellow to satin vermillion and finally golden bronze by the changing rays of the falling red egg. We were both mesmerized by the show; Loetz was silent in his private world, and I was singing softly "Wish They Were All California Girls" by the Beach Boys. And for that moment, they were.

Chapter Forty-Four: Confessions Of A Mushroom-Eater

(Thomas De Quincey Goes Native)

"I ran into pagodas and was fixed for centuries at the summit or in secret rooms: I was the idol; I was the priest; I was worshipped; I was sacrificed. I fled from the wrath of Brama through all the forests of Asia: Vishnu hated me: Seeva laid wait for me. I came suddenly upon Isis and Osiris: I had done a deed, they said, which the ibis and the crocodile trembled at. I was buried for a thousand years in stone coffins, with mummies and sphinxes, in narrow chambers at the heart of eternal pyramids. I was kissed, with cancerous kisses, by crocodiles; and laid, confounded with all unutterable slimy things, amongst reeds and Nilotic mud."

— **Thomas de Quincey,** <u>Confessions of an English Opium Eater</u>

Clovers: "Love Portion Number Nine"

I felt like I had taken this magical love potion because everyone I met was beautiful.

Indonesian girl 1900

Indonesian girl 1972 (author's photograph)

You don't need mushrooms to see how beautiful Indonesian children are.

Bali is a natural paradise; mushrooms make it a supra-natural paradise. Magic mushrooms are psilocybin, which is a mind-altering drug. Magic mushrooms have been taken for hundreds of years all over the world. Many historians have postulated that people under its influence were burned as witches. The Salem witch hysteria may have been caused by impressionable women gathering and eating these psilocybin mushrooms.

In Bali, the cows shit in the meadows, and small, white mushrooms sprout out of the shit. When you buy a bag full of these mushrooms, there are usually small clumps of cow dung attached to the mushroom stems (there is no label on the bag to "wash before eating", but you would be wise to do so or carry a strong mouthwash).

On my second day in Bali, Loetz and I tried the psilocybin mushrooms for the first time. At first, I felt only stoned, but then I began to see the most brilliant colors. Waves so blue, trees so green, and people like works of art, some ethereal beautiful like Botticelli's "Venus", others were stepping out, cubistically alive, from Picasso's "Les Demoiselles d' Avignon". This was my first experience with a "mind-altering" drug. I didn't see "God" or "angels" (unless you count that beautiful Australian girl on the beach, who looks very angelic {sans wings}). I talked to everyone I met, saying, "You're beautiful," their faces were all aglow, suffused by the red glow of the setting sun. We walked on the beach like *homo erectus* men who just came down from the trees and saw the incomprehensible ocean for the first time.

We started skipping along, doing semi-cartwheels in the water, laughing, praising the beauty of nature and how insignificant we are next to it. Yet you want to acknowledge it, somehow to glorify Nature or God: to build a new Stonehenge or carve new Aku Aku, Great Stone Head Gods, which greet the Sun on Easter Island. I felt resentment towards anything artificial (electric lights, cars, etc.) I wanted to reintegrate into Nature, just the sea, trees, sand, and my friends. It was great being with Loetz because we were both feeling incredible, fantastic joy.

We felt like Saints who would give all our possessions away freely; if only we could bottle this joy, "Happiness from Bali", and send it to all of the World Leaders. There would be no war, just peace, and harmony with everyone. I'd love to send a bag of mushrooms to President Nixon with the instructions: "Keep eating until you realize what a jerk you are and then change." With mushrooms, you must be honest, speak what you feel, and recognize beauty and ugliness for what they are. If someone calls you ugly, it shouldn't hurt you (however, if it does bother you being called ugly, you could always resort to my favorite reply, adjustable to any situation: "Really! That's not what your mother/girlfriend/wife/grandmother/boyfriend(?) said last night when I was with her {him/them} because everyone is ugly (Dana Wynter may be the one exception), next to the majesty of nature." I realized that beauty, creativity, and harmony coexist in every man. You just need to look to your inner self to discover this truth.

Now that we had solved world peace, we felt we needed a little R&R to celebrate this great revelation. We lay back on the beach and watched the warming red egg lay sunny side up and slowly liquefy into the skillet of the sea. The mushroom high had dissipated, but the pantheistic beauty of nature swirled all around us, enveloping us serenely.

Chapter Forty-Five: Balinese Art

WHERE ART COMES ALIVE

"Mona Lisa": Nat King Cole

Balinese Painting by I Lunga 1995

Ubud is the artistic center of Bali. Here hundreds of artists paint and carve everything from chachkas (crude stick-lie Balinese women) to frightful Garudas to intricately carved Balinese Gods that seem to pulsate alive from their wooden stands.

Traditional Balinese sculpture is all religious in the same way that medieval artisans only produced religious and devotional works: to praise, honor, and worship their God. Balinese temples are not architecture in the true western sense but elaborate hand-carved sculptures. A typical Balinese temple is carved from stone with sculptures completely filling out the exterior and interior of the temple; like the medieval artists in Europe, the Balinese sculptors remain anonymous. While I was walking around the marketplace in Ubud, I found a small sculptural tableau, which the merchant said was a scene from the Ramayana, the ancient Hindu epic poem. The Ramayana is a great adventure tale, but it is also a religious tale, which is dramatized in the barong dramas, traditional dance, sculpture, and the paintings of Bali. In this sculpture that I purchased, every inch of the wood is carved. What strikes you is the fecund depiction of nature: the exuberant tree leaves, the dangling vines, the dripping fruit, lush flowers, and the mythical religious animals: this is the primeval garden of the gods, and man is secondary to the majesty of pantheistic creation.

Balinese sculpture that the author bought in Ubud

Every inch of the wood panel (14 inches tall x 7 inches wide) is carved and gouged out, and in the background is a delicate Balinese temple.

Balinese painting Is sculpture transposed to canvas: myriad Balinese people, monkeys, barongs (dragons), and everywhere dripping and drooping flora, fruit-laden trees, lush green mountains, rice fields, and curlicue streams. When you view a Balinese painting, you are instantly transported to a surreal spiritual reality. Mythological themes and characters of the Ramayana coexist and mirror the struggles of ordinary Balinese, all set in the verdant greens of the Balinese landscape. You become lost in this magical dreamscape but subconsciously absorb the ultimate conflict of good vs. evil. I would call Balinese painting "Magic Realism", but that would be applying a western art style to a distinctly Balinese expression of the Spirit World that is embodied in their lives and art.

However, the paintings on sale in the markets of Ubud are the results of the fusion of western art techniques and native Balinese artistic traditions. Ubud, in the early twentieth century, was a small village specializing in producing herbal medicine (the name "Ubud" means medicine in the Indonesian language). In the 1930s, a German artist, Walter Spies, arrived (unlike Gaugin in Tahiti, who came solely to paint a primitive paradise and get laid), and he established a school that taught the Balinese Western art techniques. He gathered artists from all over Bali and not only encouraged their native tradition but actively proselytized it. He invited such celebrities as Charlie Chaplin, Noel Coward, and H. G. Wells to see and sell them this 'fusion" art. This, in turn, spread its influence in the western art world, both as a new art and a highly valuable one. Within a decade, Ubud became an artistic center; other painters came. The Dutch artist Hans Snell in the 1940s, developed a unique synthesis of Western and native Balinese painting, which greatly influenced the "next generation" budding artists of Ubud. In the 1950s, another Dutch artist Arie Smit started the Young Artists movement, which greatly revived anew the original Balinese artistic vision. Here the figures have no faces, and many are painted by children, which portray a dreamlike fantasy world of spirits.

Here's where I enter the story: enter the Freak stage left. Being a stone head Freak, I wanted something useful as well as artistic from the artisans of Ubud. I entered the shop of an old carver in a back street and asked him to make me a working bamboo bong that I could use to smoke grass or hash. I told him it would have to have traditionally carved Balinese Gods, monkeys, and mythological creatures. He laughed but told me to come back in three days. When I returned, I found a unique and beautiful work of art waiting for me. Then I asked him to paint it in bright Balinese colors-the final bong was a masterpiece! When I asked what he wanted for the bong, he told me my shirt! This was an Arrow brand pink-striped dress shirt that I had bought in Korea to wear and look presentable, getting me through tough customs officials' inspections (wearing this shirt projected an image of:" Look, I'm a tourist, not a drug-smoking freak!"). I reluctantly agreed. Luckily, I had an identical shirt; this one had blue pinstripes. He drove a tough bargain, but I got my bong. "Get it on! Get it on! Bong the Gong!" to paraphrase T. Rex.

The Author's Balinese Bong

The vibrant paint has since faded and peeled off, but the carving remains beautiful, and the bong is still in working order (no batteries required).

Chapter Forty-Six: Jan De Troop - Synthesis of Art Nouveau and Javanese Art

Instead of a specific song, I recommend the reader listen to any gamelan recording to lose themselves in the Javanese/Balinese spirit world.

"The Three Brides" Jan de Troop 1893

While serving in Germany, I got a chance to roam all over Europe and discover the architecture and paintings of the Art Nouveau artists (1890-1910).

Entranceway to Hotel (Apartment Building) Beranger, Paris by Hector Guimard
1898

The swirls and whiplash coils of Hector Guimard's Entrance to the Hotel Beranger (see above) seem alive, a nest of snakes ready to strike. (I also visited Barcelona, home of Gaudi and the Spanish Moderna Movement, but since I was with my German girlfriend, I mostly experienced beaches and hotel ceilings).

I bought artists' books on Art Nouveau paintings and particularly enjoyed the posters of Alphonse Mucha. Here you have beautiful women with long swirling coils of hair which dominate the entire painting or poster. This is a decorative surface art, and it's perfect for selling cigarettes, beer, and bicycles.

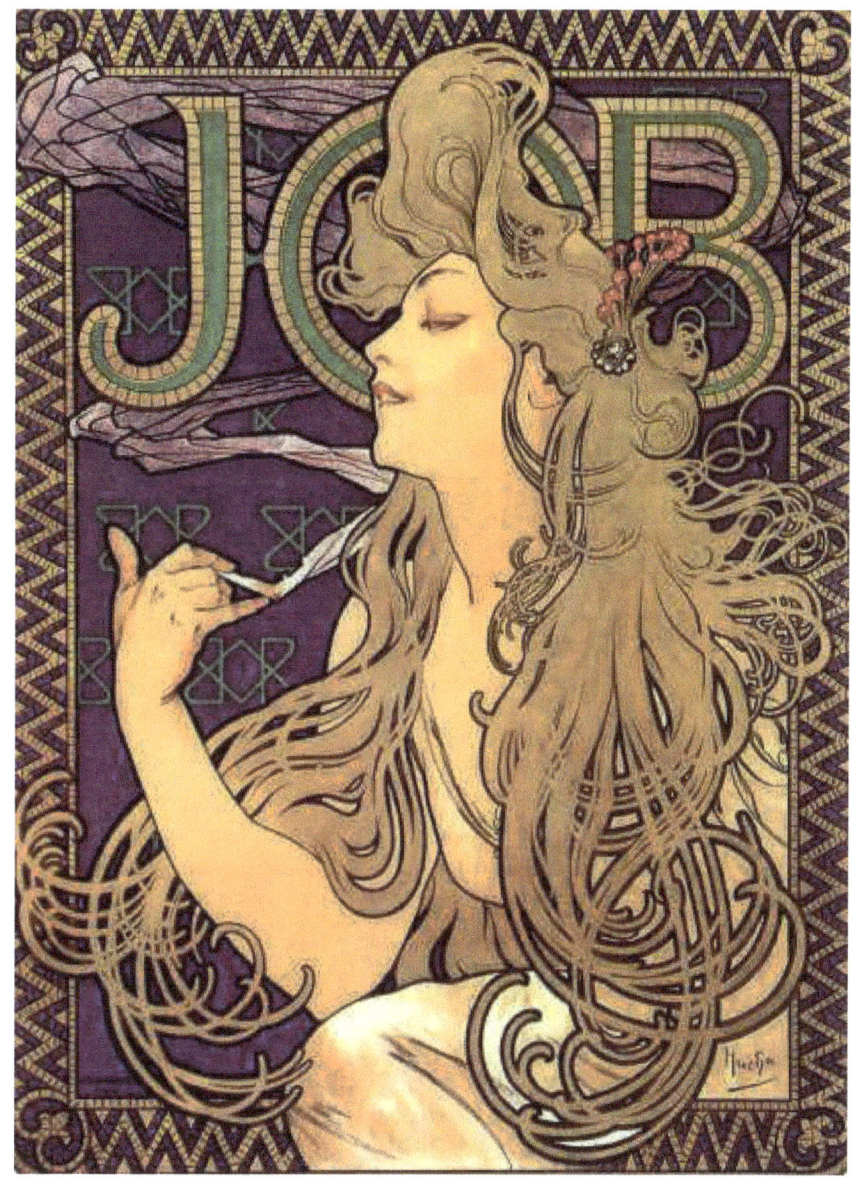

Alphonse Mucha: JOB Cigarette Poster

"You can "Light my Fire" anytime, Darling"

At the same time, in England, there was the Pre-Raphaelite art movement with artists like Dante Gabriel Rossini and Edward Burne-Jones. What strikes you immediately is the extraordinarily luminous beauty of the women in various medieval and Grecian dresses. Here the women become the visionary embodiment of some obsessive religious or mythological fantasy: the virtuous Lady guarding the

Holy Grail, the shimmering Lady of the Lake or even the mesmerizing temptress La Bella Dame Sans Merci (Please don't get me started raving again about the ethereal beauty of the bewitching Sans Merci POD woman Dana Wynter). However, these are the 19th-century versions of Vogue models; instead of a Versace gown, you are illustrating a particular myth in period dress.

JAN DE TROOP IN AMSTERDAM 1892

Here's where Jan de Troop enters the picture. Jan de Troop was born in Sumatra to a Dutch Civil Service family. Although he left the Dutch East Indies at age 11, Javanese art and Indonesian Shadow Puppets made a lasting impression on the young budding artist. Troop's Art Nouveau women were tall, wavy, wayang puppets, curved dramatically in whiplash or noodle configurations. These stereotypical identical Javanese faces and lithe bodies flow all over the canvas, taking every inch of space like Balinese paintings of the period. In his best pieces, you see the Javanese spirits embodied in a struggle between good and evil, just like the Shadow Puppet performances.

I interpret de Troop's "Three Brides" (shown above) not as three separate women but as the different stages in a woman's life: the one on the left is the naive woman in love. Here the spirits fill her with goodness and expectation. The middle bride in a light veil is a woman entering maturity, questioning, confused, facing responsibility for the first time, and realizing that life is not all wine and roses. Here the spirits are fighting for her soul. The bride on the right is the "femme fatale", the mature woman that knows what she wants out of life and is determined to get it. Here the evil spirits give her counsel, and it seems she is plotting evilly on how to fulfill her darkest desires. This otherworldly art isn't a fairy tale or historical representation but phantasmagorical images from a nightmare where the Javanese spirits are fighting for the very soul of the artist.

Troop, like Mucha and Toulouse-Lautrec, was famous for his posters. One poster advertising a cooking oil became so popular, with its noodle curves and slinking Javanese maidens, that all Dutch Art Nouveau art has been dubbed "salad oil" style (I'll have my salad a la carte with room service).

Jan de Troop's Delft Salad Oil Poster (1893)

Chapter Forty-Seven: A New Etymology of a Familiar Four-Letter Word

"All paths are the same: they lead nowhere. However, a path with heart makes for a joyful journey; as long as a man follows it, he is one with it."

Carlos Castaneda: "The Teachings of Don Juan."

Tibetan God Chakrasamvara statue in Yab-Jum union with his consort Vajravarahi

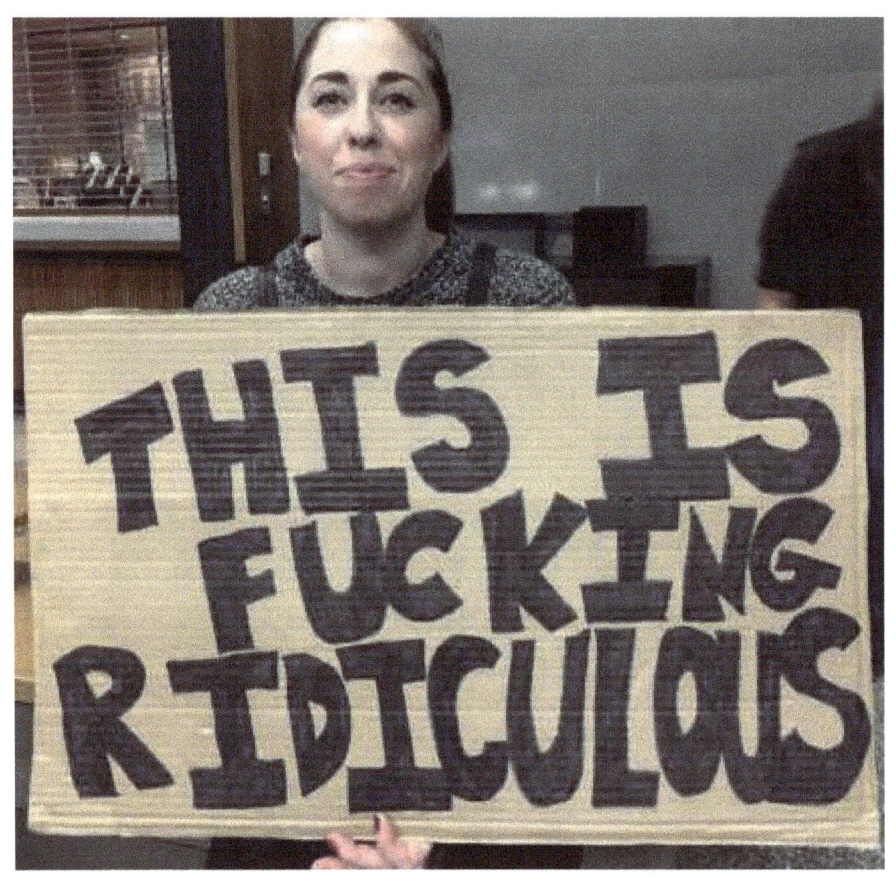

Protestor against President Trump's Border Wall, San Francisco Airport 2017

Here we have two different etymologies for the same word; you'll find a third meaning if you keep reading.

Loetz and I went to a nearby village to see our first barong: the eternal Ying and Yang battle between Barong, the good dragon hero and the evil witch, Rangda. The audience, eagerly anticipating the dance drama, the eerily hypnotic gamelan music and the colorfully costumed actors, all put us into a sustained trance. The elemental battle between good and evil is brought to life by the contorted, spellbound faces of the performers. They are purging evil from their island, not for the tourists, but for their own salvation. We, too, had been cleansed of evil spirits.

It was now after midnight when we got back to Kuta beach, I brought out a bag of mushrooms, and we decided to pull an all-nighter. We took the mushrooms and were still talking about the barong when the mushrooms kicked in: incredible joy in the beauty that surrounded us. We were walking on the beach, wading in the incoming tide; the water was warm, and the starlight reflected in the tidal pools. I felt complete, at one with nature.

I was living like God would have wanted me in this Garden of Eden. I thought of Adam and Eve in the Garden and realized that what they had was innocence: no shame, no guilt, no passion. It was just the natural order of joining to form a whole. I thought of the word "Fuck." What does it really mean? A joining of two separate halves to create one entity. It isn't just the sexual act, in the heat of passion or a choice curse word or as the protestor above feels the word "Fuck" describes an absurd situation, but a means to express love (in a Tantric Buddhist sense of God; a chance to reestablish the cosmic order of Ying and Yang, just like in the barong drama we had just witnessed).

The sexual act in Tibetan Tantric Buddhism is a means to access your inner self, to master your consciousness to achieve nirvana. Viewing the word in this light, "Fuck" is Love. "Fuck" is Truth. "Fuck" is Beauty. "Fuck" is Joy, and "Fuck" is Sorrow. "Fuck" is the creation of the world, and "Fuck" is the destruction of the world. And most important to me, "Fuck" is wholeness, oneness in a Taoist sense with the Cosmic Order of Nature.

Loetz was in a state of rapture, looking at the moonlight illuminating the shimmering water in a tidal pool: "Look at the swirling water pattern. I'm sure this is how the Balinese conceived of batik, so in harmony with nature: the frothing foam makes the most unusual batik pattern."

"Yes, Loetz, I see what you're saying." In a reverie, I saw thousands of water fingers, molding sand and water, creating a huge tapestry of batik, the design surreally changing with each new wave.

Robert Smithson's Spiral Jetty 2005 (Photograph by Soren Harward)
CREATIVE COMMONS ATTRIBUTION-SHARE ALIKE 3.0

I thought of Robert Smithson's "Spiral Jetty", a haunting earthwork that captured the rhythm of Nature: the man-made interplay of stone, sand and water that formed a naturally curved spiral that encapsulated the natural rhythm and, at the same time, idealized the force and transience of nature. This "artwork" eventually just washed away and was gone forever. "All true art imitates nature from the earliest cave painting of ritualistic bison to Picasso's cubist imitation of African sculpture." Loetz agreed, saying, "the grotesque demons that the Balinese carve and paint are their way of exorcising the evil spirit and restoring the natural balance of the universe."

"Yes, isn't it strange that we westerners need mushrooms to make us see the infinity of beauty found in nature? However, once you have trained your eyes to accept the beauty that surrounds you, everywhere you go is a 'Garden of Earthly (and Ethereal) Delight'."

"Yes," Loetz said, "but you need someone close to share this joy; otherwise, your heart will burst."

"This is the way that Jesus the man, not the God, felt: to give his love freely and without bounds to all of mankind. I feel very close to you, Loetz, and I want you to say anything you feel to me."

Loetz countered, "Yes, I can be completely open with you because I trust you." I was lost in ecstatic reverie, "your heart is too full to keep the joy bottled up. You must shout it out. You become obsessed with it. I now know what it means to be insane. You feel incredible joy, screaming to the world, laughing and crying uncontrollably, needing to share, to give this great joy you feel for others. Hosannah! Love of man and God. This feeling makes you truly free!"

We had walked all night and fell exhausted in our beds just as the sun was coming up.

Chapter Forty-Eight: The Balinese Religion

The one thing that stays in your mind about Bali is how religion dominates and pervades everything the Balinese do. There are about twenty thousand temples on this small island, and every day you can see processions of women bearing fruit and flowers for their gods. I was also curious to understand how Bali stays Hindu while the rest of Indonesia (98%) is Muslim.

Elaborate gateway entrance to a Balinese temple (author's photograph)

The Majapahit Empire, a Hindu kingdom in Java, conquered Bali and made Hinduism the state religion. When the Muslims conquered this kingdom in the fifteenth century A. D., all of the Hindu priests fled Java for Bali. The Balinese accepted Hinduism outwardly, but their real religion was animism, which was practiced in Bali for thousands of years.

Evil spirits are all around them, and the offerings you see headed for a local temple are all a means to appease these spirits. Their symbolic dances, like the barong, show how good gods can defeat evil ones. We laugh at fate when a black cat crosses our path, but to the Balinese, this is an evil portent and must be exorcised. Everything the Balinese do reflects this dualism in their outlook. For example, wood carvings depict grotesque ghosts and goblins in the true meaning of Halloween, and every house has clay figures of gods who will dispel evil from entering. This animism reflects the Balinese belief in opposites: heaven and earth, man and woman, and god and demon. Like ying and yang, when the opposing forces are in harmony, then the world and personal destiny are orderly and fortunate.

The Balinese are, on the surface, very polite and friendly but beneath their smiling facade is a mind that sees only opposites of good and evil. In 1965 during the Communist uprising, these gentle people hacked to death 50,000 of their countrymen. It wasn't because of the Communist ideology that they hated Communists in the political sense; it was because the Communists were literally the evil devil, and it was the duty of the good Balinese to kill evil and restore the natural balance between good and evil.

The Balinese form of Hinduism doesn't worship two of the three main deities of Indian Hinduism: Brahma and Vishnu, but they worship the "shrine of three forces", which combines totemic gods of earth, animal, and sun and certain Hindu gods (Shiva and his consort Paravati are a popular god pair). There is a nominal caste system, but people intermarry between castes on a normal basis, and there are no Untouchables in Bali.

But getting back to why Hinduism survived: the main reason why no Muslim kingdom conquered them is that Bali had no spices or ivory. Muslim traders and armies followed the money. The rest of Indonesia had ivory and spices that the Muslims craved. Bali, for us westerners, is <u>the</u> paradise on earth with its lush countryside, inviting beaches, and magic mushrooms which transform this tropical island into the mythical Lotus Land of "The Odyssey", but it had neither elephants nor vast groves of spices, and the Muslims left it alone.

When the Muslims finally thought of attacking Bali in the seventeenth century A.D., they stopped the attack because a new enemy threatened their kingdom and spice livelihood: the Dutch. The Dutch conquered all of Indonesia, but they, too, left Bali alone; again, they saw there were no spices or ivory to exploit, so why bother? The Dutch kept everything status quo, and local Hindu rule and religion remained unchanged; furthermore, a war between Muslims and Hindus would be bad for business. Finally, in 1906 the Dutch found a trumped-up reason to conquer the island (the Balinese plundered a derelict Dutch cargo wreck) and invaded the island. The response from the King of Bali and his Court was a mass suicidal attack on the Dutch Army, which wiped out the entire ruling dynasty. Even today, Java administers the island's government.

Wrapping the body of the dead Balinese King while mounted Dutch soldiers keep order (1906)

Chapter Forty-Nine: The Balinese Ritual Of Death

The Nagen Ceremony

"We all live, and we all die, but we dress for them all." Anonymous joke

The Balinese ritual of death consists of three parts: Funeral, Cremation, and Purification (Think of it as Crazy glue; you mix the three separate parts together for a perfect bond with God). The first: the funeral is a simple affair. The body is temporarily buried in a cemetery where the mourners offer food and flowers to the deceased.

The second: cremation is a very elaborate and expensive ceremony. A special coffin made from a single tree trunk is carved in the shape of a bull (symbolizing Shiva) for men and a sacred cow for women. These specially made coffins are all brightly painted and brought to the cemetery for the cremation. Prior to the arrival of these coffins, the deceased is dug up, ritually washed, wrapped in white cloth, and transferred to a "waddhu" (tower).

A Balinese Waddhu (author's photographer)

This tower is made of wood, papier mâché and bamboo, painted and decorated in garish colors. The waddhu represents the Balinese universe. The bottom of the cremation structure has a turtle and a dragon, which symbolizes the Underworld. The middle of the waddhu is the World of Man with tree branches and paintings of Nature (i.e., volcanos, rice fields, etc.). The top is a pagoda-like structure representing Mt. Meru, the legendary abode of the Hindu Gods. This tower stands ten to twenty meters high (The richer the deceased, the higher and more elaborate the waddhu.).

The ritually washed body of the deceased is then carried up the tower and placed in the pagoda. The pallbearers then proceed to carry the tower to the cemetery on bamboo poles. This is a joyous time, and people follow the tower, shouting and making merry. The bearers keep turning the tower around and around to keep the Spirit of the deceased in his body and prevent his Spirit from wandering through the village, causing misfortune. There's usually a gamelan band accompanying the tower, and the whole procession is similar to funerals in New Orleans, where there is a brass band playing jazz tunes, following the coffin to the cemetery, attracting hundreds of spectators. Once the waddhu reaches the cemetery, the deceased is removed from the tower, placed in the special coffin, and cremated along with the huge waddhu in a ritual ceremony. (This is a very expensive funeral, and many times poor families ask the wealthy if they can cremate a loved one along with the rich deceased's body, which is usually acceptable to the wealthy family). Now the mourners are happy, remembering their loved ones fondly.

After the cremation, there is the third part: purification. This ritual is performed by the Hindu Priest, who blesses the ashes, which are then thrown into the sea. The Purification or release of the Soul to Heaven to start anew the reincarnation cycle lasts twelve days. The mourning family create effigies of the dead person and burn them again, throwing the ashes into the sea. If you're not near the ocean, the local river will suffice for the burial of the ashes. Finally, on the twelfth day, the Soul is fully purified, and the ceremony is complete. This ritual ensures that the deceased's Soul is in Heaven and not wandering the earth, causing mischief because it has no resting place.

We in America, however, love to depict the living dead wandering around with no resting place, causing mayhem for the living people around them. This is where the deceased zombie rises from the grave and walks around in a trance-like daze, eating the flesh of live humans if they can catch them. The best one of these movies was filmed in a shopping mall, where the dead were slowly, aimlessly trudging through the stores, undecided on that last-minute necessity purchase for the afterlife.

Chapter Fifty: The Incredible Lightness and Darkness of Being

The morning sun rose vividly red, breaking through the morning haze; I was lying in my bed observing the way the tropical light penetrated through the open window. The loseman was surrounded by tropical growth: huge coconut trees, flowering bougainvillea and leafy tree palms. This filtered the tropical glare, baptizing the room with crystal pureness. Each object: the small table and chair, the wooden wardrobe, and the rope bed, all stood out like platonic ideals of their original forms. I imagined I was in an early Netherlandish Primitive painting where everything was minutely detailed. What stood out was the essential bareness of the room; there was nothing extraneous to distract from this pastoral beatitude. I thought of taking a photograph of the room but realized it wouldn't capture that peculiar lightness of being. A color photograph would have captured the distinct colors but not the luminous Aurea; a black-and-white photo would only have reduced the objects to a dull abstract of light and dark.

"Magdalen Reading" by Roger van der Weyden (1437)

There is nothing superfluous in this painting, only the ointment jar and cabinet.

I remembered Casper David Friedrich's rooms of frozen poetry, where the light delineates every detail of a starkly bare interior; this clarity of suffused illumination is what I felt in my loesman room. I contrasted this with the paintings of Edward Hopper, who also painted minimalist light-saturated rooms. However, his vision depicted the loneliness of the American experience: the mundane tawdry life of a woman at a makeup table, the solitary lost usher at a seemingly empty theater and the couple staring furtively at the tall sedge grasses from the front of a neglected peeling paint house.

I returned to my room in the late afternoon, having been burnt clean by the sun and beach, my skin encrusted with salt and sand, and the light now was phosphorus gold, radiating a feeling of peace, languor and timelessness. Here I was extraneous, a small insignificant figure in a luminist New England seacoast painting of Fitz Henry Lane or Martin Johnson Heade. This light was glowingly pantheistic, bringing to life the inanimate objects in a Taoist sense of oneness with nature.

"Shrewsbury River New Jersey" John Frederick Kensett 1859

The extraordinary light fuses water and sky into a pantheistic glow where time and motion stop. Then God commanded, "Let there be light"—and light appeared. And God was pleased with what he saw. Genesis (King James Bible)

I had just come home from a Barong drama in a local village. I had taken magic mushrooms before their performance and became as one with the performers: the elemental battle between good and evil Barong versus Rangda. Barong had defeated Rangda, and all was well in the universe: the Ying and Yang were restored to their rightful equilibrium. I fell into a deep sleep only to be overwhelmed by garish surreal images of intense color: villages being burned, women being luridly raped, and a row of white-clad Balinese, each kneeling and being beheaded because they were communists and evil; splashes of crimson red staining pristine white smocks. I woke with a start: I was in the Valley of the Shadow of Death, and I did fear evil. In the blackness, the furniture assumed grotesque menacing shapes, malevolent and animate. I had come here as a "Stranger in Paradise": the lush countryside, inviting beaches and friendly people. Again, I saw myself as a modern-day naive Hans Castorp, living a hedonistic life in this "Zauber Insel", yet I could not escape the evil and the cruelty that was all around me. Rangda had defeated Barong: communism, western imperialism, and tribalism were all guilty of tearing this paradise apart. This was "The Nightmare" of Henry Fuseli breaking through my subconscious and haunting my reality.

"The Nightmare" by Henry Fuseli 1781

Chapter Fifty-One: The Garden of Earthly Delights

"The sense of space and time were both powerfully affected…landscapes were exhibited in proportions so vast as the bodily eye isn't fit to conceive. Space swells to unutterable Infinity. This did not disturb me as much as the vast expansion of time…of duration far beyond the limits of any human experience."

Thomas de Quincy's "Confessions of an Opium-Eater".

Fiona Joyce's "This Eden".

This song captures the mystical beauty of nature in its wholeness and wonder.

Hieronymus Bosch "The Garden of Earthly Delights" Museo del Prado

I took my third trip on mushrooms again with Loetz because we get on the same wavelength. He has the most original insights, and we feed off each other's thoughts and observations. This time we ate our lunch "mushrooms a la carte" because we both wanted to see those supra-saturated colors in the daylight.

I remember, as a young boy seeing my first dayglow poster under a black light: I was blown away; it was like a religious experience. "For now we see through a glass, darkly; but then face to face: now I know in part; but then shall I know even as also I am known." (First Corinthians, Chapter 13, King James Bible) God and Light were One. This was not the pastel prettiness of a San Francisco Victorian but the raw starkness of living color. Magic Mushrooms thrusts you into the majestic pantheistic aliveness of the cosmos.

We were walking on Kuta Beach when the mushrooms kicked in. I stared at the deep blue ocean, and far out, I saw a straight string of surfers similar to my first day on the beach when they looked like a marching band in lockstep, but now they were cresting the high, diamond-glistening surf, and I felt I was witnessing the ecstatic transformation that Joni Mitchell hauntingly sang of bombers turning into butterflies ("Woodstock" Joni Mitchell).

The saturated colors of glistening gold dust beaches, the copper-bronze faces of the freaks, the fecund malachite forests, and the enveloping steel blueness of the ocean were like the last trip: a chemical light switch that brought this dayglow world instantly to fruition. But suddenly, there was a breakthrough: you were Saul, a Roman legionnaire, hunting and persecuting Christians when a shaft of luminous light transformed you into Paul, God's messenger to spread Christ's love throughout the Roman world.

Here is the vision of Hieronymus Bosch's "Garden of Earthly Delights", a phantasmagorical setting of strange machines, mismatched paired animals, Christ and Adam and Eve. Yet this was not the Biblical nor the Islamic Garden of Eden, but a strange, surreal version.

Art critics have spent years trying to decipher the meaning of the "Garden of Earthly Delights" (and medieval theologians spent years speculating on how many angels can dance on the head of a pin?). Now there seems to be a consensus among art critics that these fantastic machines in the painting are alchemy vials, boilers, and artifacts. Alchemy is the pseudoscience that attempted to turn the "Philosopher's Stone" into gold ("Richer Living through Chemistry"). Besides turning stone into gold, another important concept of alchemy was the "Philosopher's Egg". This magical egg could grant immortality in the Faustian sense and symbolically signified a "rebirth "or cleansing of the soul. Alchemy, like mind-altering drugs, offered an "Instant get into heaven (green) card" without believing in the eternal life offered by accepting Christ into your heart. So, looking at the painting in this light, it becomes a morality tale of the foolishness and arrogance of man. The last panel then shows mankind suffering the fires of hell in highly bizarre fashions. For example, a witch offers false hope to a group of gullible sinners partaking in a "Last Supper". Instead of the body and blood of Christ giving eternal life, you are feasting on the yoke of the cracked open "Philosopher's Egg" with the head turned Devil smiling at <u>You</u>, the viewer of this folly.

There were people of all shapes and sizes, running, riding bicycles, kissing, and smoking chillums, all in a fantastic landscape of rainbow-colored umbrellas and volleyball nets that stretched to infinity. I saw all of this as a living tableau of pulsating sexuality and human eroticism. Here was a tribe of Westerners that had left conventional morality, attitudes and lifestyles behind to discover a Brave New World, a world of drugs, sex and hedonism. Their behavior mirrored the carefree lovers in the center panel of the "Garden": a medieval version of "Plato's Retreat"; these lovers are too self-absorbed in lust and debauchery to worry about salvation.

However, we are in Bali, and this hedonistic behavior becomes a living barong drama: the eternal battle of good versus evil, Barong the good dragon and Rangda the evil witch. In my super-heightened mushroom consciousness, I saw the freaks in the throes of sensual abandonment. But I was not a dispassionate observer. I was a willing participant in this frenzied funhouse. I was the lecherous fondler of the naked young girl in the spinning glass ball in the painting's center panel. I envisioned my fate in the burning fires of hell as depicted in the third panel of Bosch's triptych masterpiece. Was this a prophetic vision of what would become of me? Bosch's Hell suddenly transformed into Stephen Dedalus's burning Catholic Hell with phantasmagorical sinners screaming in flaming agony. I turned my face to the sun to burn this hallucinogenic nightmare away. I focused on the horizon: Robin's egg blue of the sky melded with the darker Dresden blue of the ocean into a hermaphrodite oneness, and the carefree laughter of playing Balinese children brought me slowly back to a sense of the equanimity of the natural world.

As I walked on the shallow waters, I saw an Edvard Munch painting come alive, a beautiful woman standing at the sea, immersed in awe of nature. As I walked closer, she changed to a golden bronze hue, but it was her bright white sarong with the lamest prayer, repeated over and over in reddish-purple lettering, that fixated me. I had been speaking German with Loetz and approached her, "Das es ein schones kleid, hast du im Katmandu gegangen?" (That's a beautiful sarong. Have you been to Katmandu?) Surprisingly, she answered in German, but it was Schweitzer Deutsch (German Swiss). "No, I bought it here. I hope to get the prayer translated one day."

"So, you're Swiss! I love the way you speak German, so musical, your intonation up and down, like you're climbing mountains back home." She laughed, and I said goodbye and walked faster to catch up with Loetz.

"The Voice, Summer Night" Edvard Munch 1896

Chapter Fifty-Two: And Now Meet the Real Bali

I am but a rider

A rider of days

The sun and the clouds

How they dance, and they sway

"Rider of Days": Patty Griffin

Loetz and I decided that we would climb Mount Batar, the tallest mountain in Bali. To do that we had to get a guide and we met our guide in the late afternoon. His name was Gude; he was wearing an Australian bush hat and khaki pants, roaring in on a Honda motorbike like Marlon Brando in "The Wild Ones". We planned to meet early in the morning and then went to our hotel. After a freezing night, we got up at 5:30 to see the sunrise: a great ball of red fire rising out of the side of the mountain. The mountain was covered with clouds, and below were vast stretches of green; the Balinese were setting up their market, a scene straight out of Andean South America.

We got some supplies (no Twinkies, but Marie's Biscuits and Bintang beer) at the market; the mountain looming above and the lake below. We met Gude, along with two other Irish travelers and got into old dugout canoes, paddling across the lake to a small village, where we were beginning the ascent. I was really well-prepared, wearing only flip-flops. The terrain here is remarkably like New Mexico – wildflowers, ravines, bulging rock formations and cacti everywhere. The Irish lads were in the front, boisterous and confident; we were in the back, taking in the breathtaking scenery. After a struggling hour and a half, we reached the top. This was like a mountain on the moon: no vegetation, smoke rising and many places warm from the volcanic activity. Below us, half of the valley was black, the remains of lava from the last eruption in 1964. We walked along the top of the crater and saw the new cone crater below; this was also highly active and had erupted, killing three people in 1968. The downward descent took its toll on my feet, but I came through it with few physical injuries. No Whining! We reached the valley floor and paddled back across the lake to the town, where we rented ponies to go to Penelokan, quite a distance from where we first started.

The lush beauty of Bali countryside (author's photograph)

From Peneloken, we walked and visited a fantastic temple: beautiful stone carvings, large gates and apparently abandoned. Then we came upon a small village where Loetz and I were outplayed shamefully in soccer by the local Balinese teens ("Silly Rabbit, TRIX are for Kids"). We then hiked to the oldest, holiest temple,

Purapesikah and then walked back to our starting point, where we stayed the night. Loetz, sleeping on two chairs stacked together and I, sleeping on a low table. In the morning, we walked around the town and came upon a small family shrine that had been carved in stone and painted. We spoke to the creator-artist, who explained a bit about the Balinese religion and the expense of keeping up their temples and shrines. After some subtle pressure by Loetz, we were asked to stay for dinner: rice, peanuts, spiced vegetables and chicken gizzards, a simple but delicious meal. After dinner, we talked about the Communist massacre of 1965. Fifty thousand people were killed in Bali alone, and a half million people throughout Indonesia. The artist's wife was a communist who had been spared because she was a woman. All of the male communists were killed in a ritualized ceremony (dressed in white and beheaded) to purify the island of evil. This couple was typical of most Indonesians in that they liked Sukarno because "he was an international figure" that brought attention to Indonesia. They asked me why the US did not like him. I skirted the question, saying that the United States was very anti-communist, and that satisfied them. However, I thought to myself, flamboyant figures, especially Sukarno, however bad or good they are, die very slowly in the imagination of their followers.

We no sooner got back to our losemen than we planned a two-day bicycle trip around the east end of the island. We took a bus to Klyngkund with our bicycles strapped on top. From there, we pedaled along a beautifully winding road filled with stately banyan trees, white-washed temples and fields of sugarcane and rice. We finally reached Tinganran, the village of Bali Aga, a pre-Hindu Balinese people. Here they make fantastic tightly knit weavings called geringsing, using pure vegetable dyes. Simple-looking scarves take months to weave and sell for only fifteen dollars. A farmer, who lived outside of the village, told us that only people who have not married outside of the Bali Aga can live in the actual village. He explained some of the customs and the origins of the Bali Aga. He described how the people of the village long ago were given a large tract of land by an ancient King of Bali. One day the king's favorite horse went missing; this made the king very anxious, and it was finally reported dead by the villagers of the Bali Aga. The king was very grateful for the courage shown by the villagers in reporting the unfortunate death of his horse, and he wanted to reward the people of the village, saying he would give the people all of the lands with the smell of his dead horse. So, one very bright villager cut up a part of the horse and concealed it in his sarong. The Bali Aga people got an excessively big piece of land because this man walked around with the boundary-makers with the odorous horse piece in his pocket. (This adds a whole new meaning to Richard III's line: "my kingdom for a horse".)

The village has very curious swings: three-tiered, where three sets of children careen through the air without colliding. The village holds less than four hundred people, and we spoke to the head priest's son, who managed the temple. This temple is set off apart from the village, about a mile away. It is set in a shady grove, sheltered by a huge banyan tree. We walked there and sat down, contemplating the temple and drinking coconut milk straight from the trees.

We left the village and headed for Tritoganna, passing hillsides terraced with rice, sandwiched between the sea and the mountains. We passed small villages, and as the sun was about to set, my bicycle broke down. I makeshift fixed it, and we stopped for dinner in a small village restaurant under an immense banyan tree. We had fish, tea and tapioca gruel, surrounded by at least fifty kids and elders gawking at us while we ate. We finally broke away and pedaled into rice fields and, in the pitch darkness, found the beach. It wasn't like Kuta Beach; it had black sand and reefs of stone and coral. We camped on the beach, and both of us huddled under my blanket. At about 3 am, it started to rain and then I developed chronic diarrhea, having to get up every 15 minutes to crap. At 4:30 am, I was on this dark dirt road leading to the village when I was passed by a nonchalant fisherman, who didn't seem particularly surprised to see me. I was met by other fishermen coming out toward me, their outlines silhouetted in black by the grey dawn. It had stopped raining and was getting light; fishing boats were visible on the horizon, and suddenly, a huge red ball started popping out of the sea. We arrived at the village, and I was thoroughly exhausted, draining one tea after another just to get warm.

Old King of Bali Fountain (author's photograph)

We took off on our bicycles and headed for Triliganna. After a hellish climb, we came to this beautiful gurgling fountain tower, centered in a large water tank pool, pouring into the crystal-clear pool surrounded by gargoyle-like animals. All around us were light and dark green rice paddies and small brooks, where children were swimming, and women were washing their clothes. The rice harvest was in full swing as we watched the men and their water buffalos working in the fields. We stripped naked and hopped into the water tank, swimming in the old King of Bali's fantastic water pool. The water was cold, but it hit the spot. After about a refreshing half hour, we lay in the lush grass to dry off. We left the pool and started to pedal back to our original destination. The sun was beating down on us, and after about two hours, we stopped along a roadside brook, stripped again and cooled ourselves from the overbearing heat.

Woman bringing offerings for the local village temple (author's photograph)

Bicycling back was a real torture, mostly uphill, but the scenery was magnificent: small villages holding cock fights, tiny temples plopped in the middle of verdant emerald rice fields, serviced by a procession of flower and fruit-bearing women and children everywhere screaming "Hello, where are you going?" We were so exhausted that we stopped for a swim in the ocean by a fishing village two miles out of Klyngkund. Here the sand was black volcanic ash, and the water was the deepest blue I have ever seen. The waves were very strong but didn't crash down; you could swim in the darkly azure water, yet the riptide was strong and the water deep, almost immediately from the shore. When you swam in, it almost knocked you down. Reaching Klyngkund in the late afternoon, I collapsed in the tea house, again having one chai after another. In the morning, we found the bus back to Kuta Beach, again storing our bicycles on top. When we arrived, we collapsed in our loseman and slept the whole day.

Chapter Fifty-Three: Durian

"Ooooh, That Smell": Lynyrd Skynyrd

Durian botanical print by Hoola Van Nooten (Dutch, active 1863-1885)

Indonesia is a cornucopia of delightful exotic fruits. Every day stoned or sober, I would bargain in the local markets for fresh mangoes, rambutans, mangosteens, and lychees.

When I got to Java, I experienced a new high: the durian. This is a brownish yellow, heavily spiked fruit about a foot high and half a foot wide and weighing about three to five pounds. You cut it into sections and cut out the cream-colored pods (I can't seem to escape from PODS!) and eat the moist fruit around the black seed. Durian emits a powerful stinking odor: the Limburger cheese of fruit.

What does it taste like? Alfred Russel Wallace, the American naturalist who gave Darwin a run for his evolutionist theories, said first it tasted like a custard flavored with almonds. On a second taste, he said it tasted like cream cheese flavored with onion sauce. Still, others were more imaginative, calling it: stale vomit and another skunk spray. The best description I heard was from the American travel and food author Richard Sterling in his book, "The Adventure of Food: True Stories of Eating Everything": "Pig shit mixed with turpentine and onion garnished with sweaty gym socks."

The Indonesians love this fruit. Many a poor laborer will spend half of a day's wages on a durian for his family. They also consider the durian an aphrodisiac. The Indonesians have a saying: "When the durian falls, the sarong rises."

I found it creamy: the consistency of flan and a taste of garlic-flavored vanilla. Taste description is like interpreting Japanese Zen Gardens: there is no right or wrong taste sensation. However, I can say with some certainty the durian does <u>not</u> taste like chicken. It is an acquired taste, but after two durians, you're hooked. One stoned fantasy I had while eating a durian: we might never have had a theory of gravity if Newton had sat under a durian tree instead of an apple tree. The fall of a spiked durian would have left him brain-dead!

When I returned to New York, I was able to find durian in Chinatown. However, like kimchi, if you don't eat it together with your partner, you may be looking for a new girl or boyfriend. Also, if you leave an open durian on your kitchen table, there is a good chance your neighbors will call 911 to report a week-old dead body in your apartment.

Sign Poster at the entrance to Singapore Mass Transit

Chapter Fifty-Four: Loetz's Going Away Party

1 I'm just a poor wayfaring stranger,

I'm trav'ling through this world below;

There is no sickness, toil, nor danger,

In that bright world to which I go.

I'm going there to see my father,

I'm going there no more to roam;

I'm just a going over Jordan,

I'm just a going over home.

2 I know dark clouds will gather o'er me,

I know my pathway's rough and steep;

But golden fields lie out before me,

Where weary eyes no more shall weep.

I'm going there to see my mother,

She said she'd meet me when I come;

I'm just a going over Jordan,

I'm just a going over home.

3 I want to sing salvations story,

In concert with the blood-washed band;

I want to wear a crown of glory,

When I get home to that good land.

I'm going there to see my brothers,

They passed before me one by one;

I'm just a going over Jordan,

I'm just a going over home.

4 I'll soon be free from every trial,

This form will rest beneath the sod;

I'll drop the cross of self-denial,

And enter in my home with God.

I'm going there to see my Saviour,

Who shed for me His precious blood;

I'm just a going over Jordan,

I'm just a going over home.

"Wayfaring Stranger: American Folk Hymn 1780 (public domain)

The best free show in Bali (author's photograph)

Loetz was leaving Bali the next day, and together we decided to celebrate his departure, not with a big dinner and drinks, but a farewell mushroom party. I scored a bag of mushrooms; Loetz and I ate them about sundown. The technicolor high took effect just as the sun was dissolving into the horizon and the fishermen were pulling in their nets for the day. I had a full pack of kretek cigarettes, and we started walking down the beach. The dusk turned dark. The Milky Way was bright and close, giving the beach an ethereal luminosity: a white floor of heaven that went on forever. Every few moments, a shooting star cascaded down the umbrella of stars and disappeared into the ocean. The stars were alive, like millions of fireflies that had orchestrated their slow-motion strobe light show just for us. We were two pilgrims lost in this paradisiacal wilderness.

I felt very close to Loetz, united in a spiritual quest to find out who we are, what is really important, and whether we can sustain this youthful idealism we both felt.

We spoke of our families: how Loetz's mother, pregnant with him, had to flee Czechoslovakia after the war ended. The Czechs were killing the Sudetenland (the former ethnic German province of Czechoslovakia) Germans, and she barely made it out alive. His father was a U-boat officer who survived, but the family had nothing at the end of the war. Loetz spoke of the struggles his father had to support his mother and himself. His father worked as a carpenter, tram operator and taxi driver just to put bread on the table. I told him of my father and mother: a taciturn Swiss who worked two jobs to support us and a loving immigrant mother who was verbally abused by her husband and sacrificed her own ambition, living only for her son. We were the new generation: would we find the answers that eluded our parents as to what the good life is?

We spoke of Marxism, of Communism working towards a common goal to improve all lives. India, beautiful and ugly, all intertwined in the yin and yang of the cosmic order. We were on the Tao; nature, in all its rawness, was flowing all around us. We were swimming in its current, sinking in the consciousness that unites us with the universe.

We both asked ourselves if we would still believe that we could make a difference when we got back to our respective countries. I thought teaching would be the best way to keep the American dream alive for all the disenfranchised and poor. Lutz was always good with his hands, and his goal was to make beautiful furniture. He had a degree, so he could support himself by teaching carpentry and furniture-making skills in vocational schools in Germany.

I envisioned living in New York City, while Loetz saw Berlin, with its free "luft" (air), would be his home. We both asked ourselves if we could sustain this vision of life that mushrooms had opened for us or would we be like our parents were: bogged down, as in Harry Chapin's song "Cats Cradle", with bills to pay, a hassle job, and never making the time to keep the family together.

We both saw drugs as a false God, but as far as the true God, we both had many questions. I still believe in Christ's sacrifice so all men could receive everlasting life, but the pantheistic TAO and the Eightfold Path to the Nirvana of Buddhism made more sense to me than the Christian theology I was taught in my church. And there was always India ahead, promising some new spiritual rejuvenation to give my life meaning.

I told Loetz what Christine from Thailand had told me, that she was afraid she would never find the "thing" that was missing in her life. I thought about her and the other women in my life and asked myself, would I find salvation in the arms of a woman, get married, have kids, and become as Carly Simon so prophetically crooned, "That's the Way I Always Heard It Should Be".

We walked until dawn, talking, smoking a whole pack of kreteks and revealing ourselves, something I had never done with a man before. This is what true friendship is all about: to know the inner person, not to be afraid to be naked emotionally and to listen with an empathy that makes no judgment.

The white way dissolved in the morning sun. We had walked miles from our loseman, but I had found the brother I never had.

Loetz's dream is to live on a small island in the Finnish-Baltic archipelago, leading a simple life with a woman who shares his "Welt Anschauung" (world view). I hope he keeps this dream alive and finds his soulmate to share it with him.

I know that I will miss him, not in the homoerotic sense, but in the emotional and spiritual "Geist" that unites us: two wayfaring strangers, just going over Jordan.

Chapter Fifty-Five: Sandra

Black is the Color

Black is the color of my true love's hair,

Her lips are something rosy fair.

The prettiest face and the daintiest hands,

I love the grass whereon she stands.

I love my love, and well she knows,

I love the grass whereon she goes.

If she on earth no more I see,

My life will quickly heed ye.

I'll go to troublesome to mourn, to weep,

But satisfied, I ne'er shall sleep.

I'll write her a note in a few little lines,

And suffer death ten thousand times.

Black is the color of my true love's hair,

Her lips are something rosy fair.

The prettiest face and the daintiest hands,

I love the grass whereon she stands.

Traditional Anglo-American Folk Song 18th century (Public Domain)

Medea by Frederick Sandys

I first saw her walking alone on Kuta beach, a big girl about 5'9" and solidly built. She wore a tight-fitting sarong and had long, frizzled black hair. I thought she was a Midwest girl, her first time off the farm. I approached her, starting a slightly incoherent babble about how beautiful the beach and surf were. The minute she answered in her nasal Brooklyn accent, I knew I had found a kindred spirit.

We talked non-stop, and it was frightening to find someone like myself who looked at life with such a critical, perhaps caustic attitude. Sandra had the same stereotyping reflex, knowing everything and commenting on any issue with that peculiar New York sense of sardonic humor. Each of us is trying to out due the other in life's experiences. Both being loud and going overboard in our opinions, we were "superior" to anyone else, we were "New Yorkers", and the rest of the world could "eat cake", as Marie Antoinette cluelessly spouted.

I was half stoned, coming down from a mushroom high, but I felt she was the real New Yorker, not F. Scott Fitzgerald's glamorous golden girl in her summer dress; she was his shop girl, working late on Christmas Eve selling fancy dresses she could never afford for herself. She was a working-class daughter of a sweatshop father and a raw-boned practical mother who pinched pennies to give her a better life thru education. Now she was a PhD candidate in Psychology, taking the summer off to see the world before finishing her studies. She is the embodiment of the American Dream, achieving success through hard work. Yet she seemed vulnerable in her romantic expectation of finding that one person who would accept her on her own terms. I saw myself in her, feeling somehow outside, living a lie. I, too, was raised in a working-class family in New Jersey, reading vociferously, and role-playing the "intellectual" New Yorker on weekends. The forever tourist who dutifully walks across the Brooklyn Bridge carrying his copy of Hart Crane's "The Bridge" poem, stands for hours in line to hear the latest protest folk singer in the smoke-filled dives of Greenwich Village or frustratingly tries to score a Bernard girl at Thalia's French film festival.

The first time we made love was in a verdant pasture, where the Balinese farmers leave their water buffaloes for the night. Amid the cattle mooing and piles of dung, we laid down a beach towel. I kissed her and started to undress her, burying my head in her fulsome breasts and caressing her with slow even strokes. I moved down, kissing her vagina, lost in the tangle of black hair and warm wetness. I moved away, and she took my penis in her lips, french toughing my crown. We were both at a fever pitch; I turned her to face me as I eased my penis into her. We were heaving up and down; I foundling her breasts, and she gripping my behind like a girl on a motorcycle clutching the driver to keep from falling off. We both climaxed; I didn't stop, still moving in her until I went soft. We held each other, silent and staring upward at the Milky Wave until we fell asleep. I awoke in the early morning to see a huge water buffalo eying us with a coveted stare while munching grass less than two feet away, a Balinese alarm clock that you don't have to set.

We spent the next two days lying on the beach, talking books, philosophy, ambitions and NYC. One night we went to a Balinese comedy/drama in a local village. This was not for the tourists but for the Balinese. There was a live Gamelan band and the most incredible kris (Balinese sword) fight. The audience was spellbound, little kids awe-struck and quiet, and their parents knew the story by heart. This was an elemental depiction of good versus evil, and when it ended at 3 AM in the morning, everyone, performers, villagers and ourselves were cleansed of evil spirits.

The next evening, we watched an Indian film in Hindu with Indonesian subtitles. The film "Hara Krishna, Hara Ram" was easy to understand, although we had to put up with terrible acting and broad-stroke stereotypes of Indians and hippies. The story was about evil hippies (Westerners with long hair playing guitars) who kidnap a lovely pure Indian maiden. She is then saved by her handsome brother (but not before we had to endure endless song and dance scenes). The main hippie villain was like the cartoon character Snidely Whiplash from "Rocky and Friends". In the end, we all laughingly cheered for the good Indians. The evil hippies were defeated, and we all went home happy. This was the second-night evil was banished from the land, but this was the "Bollywood happy ending" (in three-part harmony and dance), not the visceral catharsis of the live exorcism.

I once asked her if she thought travelling like we were doing would change us: we both said no, but I hope it will, at the least, make me more sensitive and more attuned to people and the natural beauty of nature.

I took her to the bus in Den Pasar; she was off to Hong Kong. I felt like Bogie at the end of Casablanca. (Why do we always trivialize our emotions by identifying ourselves with some Hollywood tearjerker? Sandra is a real person who is leaving my life, not some wet dream celluloid fantasy farewell).

Chapter Fifty-Six: Bali: Farewell to Paradise

"Urge For Going": Joni Mitchell

This song is interesting because the first half tells of the man's going, and the second half deals with the woman going. A song of Paradise Lost, a golden land which becomes barren and cold once the lover leaves.

"I told you, Eve, that we couldn't afford that luxurious beachfront bungalow at Kuta Beach."

Michelangelo's "Expulsion from Paradise" Sistine Chapel, The Vatican

I spent my last day in Bali on Kuta Beach, bodysurfing. The beach is gorgeous, with huge waves that glide you effortlessly to the shore. I focused my eyes on the horizon, triggering the supra-real colors that the mushrooms had given me, the natural "high" without the drug "high". This is truly Paradise, so why do I want to leave? Perhaps it is my Protestant upbringing that instilled in me a sense of responsibility to do something important with my life ("Would you like to double-size that order, Sir?) Or was it the thought that I would disappoint my parents, that had struggled so hard to get me a college education (I'll get a job tomorrow, I promise you, Mom)? Or is it that Bali is the "maya" (illusion) that Buddha preached we must abandon to achieve Nirvana? Or does it come down to simply heeding (and paraphrasing) Dean Wormer's advice to Flounder in "Animal House": "Fat, drugged and stupid is no way to go through life, son".

My close friend Loetz was gone, and I had done my "Casablanca" farewell with Sandra. I remembered the Bryds' song "Turn, Turn, Turn" whose lyrics were taken verbatim from the first eight verses of the third chapter of the Old Testament Book of Ecclesiastes:

"To everything- Turn, Turn, Turn

There is a season- Turn, Turn, Turn

And a time to every purpose under heaven

A time you may embrace

A time to refrain from embracing"

I woke up and realized that I had to make a clean break; I was not here in Asia to be a beach bum forever. India was waiting for a true spiritual awakening, not a drug-induced euphoria.

I cringed at the rough times ahead: riding third class over-crowded trains, sweltering on dusty roads, sleeping in mosquito-infested shoebox rooms and eating filthy stall food. Yet this is what traveling is all about, and I accepted this. There was something out there, and like the Byrds' song, "Chestnut Mare", I will find that horse and possess it.

Chestnut Mare Running Free: Sarah Olive 2019 UNSPLASH

Indonesia II

Canals in Jakarta 1900

Chapter Fifty-Seven: Duo in Solo

"Danke Schoen": Wayne Newton

"Portrait of a Young Woman" by Albrecht Durer

I was spending the day roaming the Solo Karta (westerners call the city "Solo") market for batik bargains when I spotted a blond-haired woman in a sea of black-haired shoppers. I went up to her; she was haggling with a shopkeeper over a batik fabric.

She was about 5'5", short cropped blond hair, hallowed cheekbones, a pronounced aquiline nose, dark circles under her ashen gray eyes, and deep lines around her frowning mouth. She looked to be in her mid-30s. She was not good-looking; she had that Germanic "staring" seriousness that Albrecht Durer unflatteringly captured in his portraits of stolid burgers' daughters.

"Are you getting a good price on that?"

She turned around, gave me the once over, and said with a sigh, "I hope so, I've been here for fifteen minutes, and he still will not give it to me at my price."

"Well, look at the bright side: you'd pay three times the price at home, so you're getting a bargain."

She started to walk away, and the shop owner called her back. She got this beautiful batik sarong at her price. I congratulated her and introduced myself; she said her name was Uwa. I offered to buy her a chai or beer, and she accepted the latter.

She was from a small town outside of Mannheim and was here in Indonesia for a two-week holiday. She had come from Bali and was headed back to Djakarta to fly home. "How did you like Bali?"

"The beach was beautiful, and the Balinese I met were very friendly. I stayed in a luxury hotel on Sanur beach and didn't meet anyone except stodgy European businessmen and vacationing families with screaming kids." She told me she had visited the woodcarvers' center in Ubud and bought some exquisitely carved statues of a Balinese god and a colorful garuda bird. She had also attended a barong dance that the hotel had staged for its guests. She really liked the haunting gamelan music that had accompanied the colorful dance. We had a lot to talk about, and I asked her to dinner. I will pick her up at 7 PM at her hotel.

I had met quite a few conventional tourists; many were lonely, single women in their 30s, hoping to find romance and adventure in foreign lands, things that were missing back home. They booked four-star hotels, ate at the best restaurants, and had a planned vacation for two weeks. They did not dare to leave their silk cocoon, did not explore the back alleys and muddy streets, meet the locals or experience the dust, sweat, bad-smelling toilets, crowded trains, and bureaucratic insolence. They checked the boxes: Taj Mahal, Bali, the Tiger Balm Garden, wait, not even conventional tourists should have to check this box, but they never found Prince Charming or even an exciting adventure that they could brag about to their friends back home. Well, Uwa, let's see if you're ready to live a little and take a "Magic Carpet Ride" with a total stranger.

I arrived at her hotel, and it was definitely first-class, with a fancy doorman and a marbled floor lobby, complete with potted palms and leather club chairs. I was dressed in my best freak outfit: Chinese fisher pants, open linen shirt, and sandals. She wore a brightly printed summer dress and full makeup, and her hair was done up in a permanent. "You look ravishing. If I had known you'd be dressed to the nines, I wouldn't have sent my tux to the cleaners." She laughed, and we went to a small restaurant in my low-rent district. We ordered skewed chicken sate in peanut sauce, accompanied by 16 oz bottles of Bintang beer to wash it down. After dinner, I asked her if she smoked hash. She said she tried it once back home but didn't get high and never did it again. We walked around the market, buying exotic fruit and more bottles of Bintang. After about an hour, I suggested we go to my room and get high. She was a little taken aback, but I assured her, "I am with the IRS, the tax office - you can trust me. I am only here to help you." We walked to my hotel, telling her the doorman was off for the night, but I provided personalized room service. "Welcome to my humble abode, a deluxe single bed, petite mahogany table, and my personal form of air conditioning, the ceiling fan."

We smoked a large blunt of Sumatra #1 (guaranteed high or your money back). She coughed a little but soon got the knack and was able to keep it in, getting a nice buzz out of it. Soon we were both sky-high, gorging on rambutans, swilling beer from the bottle, and laughing at everything we said. We were sitting on the bed, and I leaned over and kissed her. She laughed and kissed me back, pressing her hand on my crotch. Still laughing, she stood up and asked me to unzip the back of her dress. Soon we were both naked, lying in my bed, kissing and touching each other. My hash high focused on her breasts, kissing the nipples until they were rigid hard. I sat up and brought her face to my penis. She tongued it lightly and then began moving slowly, fully enveloping it in a rhythmic motion. When I was rock hard, I moved her head up and asked if I should get a rubber. She was wearing a diaphragm and said it wasn't necessary. I lay back and pulled her on top of me. I found her sweet spot, eased my penis in, and she sat up, her hands on my shoulders as she slowly gyrated up and down. I fondled her breasts as she increased her motions. Her face was aglow with expectation; she was thrusting up and down with a frenzied urgency. I came, and she a little later, but we kept up the dance until I fell limp. She eased off, and we lay back silently, lost in our private reveries.

She was staying one more day, so we got up early and canvased the market, buying gifts for her family and friends back home. That night we ate Chinese food and wondered around the town.

Uva and I were walking around the old city, stopping for fruit and beer, when we came upon a Shadow Puppet Show. It was on a wooden stage that had been erected in the market that afternoon. There was a huge white sheet, lit from behind by electric lights and an array of puppets. On the side of the stage was a small orchestra playing old Javanese folk music, as in a motion picture soundtrack.

Wayang performer shown manipulating puppets behind a white lighted sheet, accompanied by gamelan musicians

Wayang (shadow) Anyang (puppet)

Wayang Anyang dates to before Buddhism came to Indonesia (8th Century BC). The puppets were dead ancestors who came back to speak with their descendants. They came back to curry the favor of the gods and exorcise evil spirits that were plaguing the living family members. The first puppeteer was probably a shamanistic priest that mediated between the living and the dead souls, represented by the puppets.

After Indonesia became Hindu, the two Indian epics, the Mahabharata and the Ramayana were incorporated into the Wayang as a means to propagate the Hindu religion. These stories are still wildly popular today, with their demons, brave heroes, monkey kings, and giants.

When the Muslims converted Indonesia, they incorporated their own legendary and literary figures into the stories. The puppets, both good and evil characters, were made ugly and grotesque and given outrageous costumes and colorations because of the Muslim ban on the reproduction of the human form. They became symbols rather than figural characters.

The puppet theater has also kept up with the times: they have stories about troubled marriages, contemporary political issues, and action dramas, where puppets utilize kung fu and stylized sword fights.

Wayang Anyang is performed almost everywhere, from makeshift stages, like we were watching, to Broadway-style theaters, where hundreds view expert puppeteers and "live" puppets that smoke kretek cigarettes, puffing out smoke and "bleed blood" when stabbed with a kris.

Shadow puppets have survived in the age of movies because the puppets aren't just good and evil. They have all of the virtues and faults of the common man: honesty and courage, as well as weakness of character and jealousy. Good trumps over evil, but we are sympathetic to "evil" characters because they have all of our own human traits, both good and bad (like Milton's Devil in "Paradise Lost").

Afterward, we returned to my room for another night of getting high and lovemaking. Our bodies were now attuned to each other, and the hash-high intensified our pleasures.

She took off the next morning via an air-conditioned bus. Auf Wiedersehn, Uwa!

Chapter Fifty-Eight: The Kris

"God is on our Side" Joan Baez

Kris with golden scabbard from Java

There is a fifteenth-century Hindu shrine Chandi Sukah in Central Java where Bhima (a Balinese Hindu God) works the blacksmith's fire. Ganesh elephant-headed son of Siva supplies the iron for the blade. Arjuna, the avatar of Vishnu, operates the firing billows. All the Gods working together to create a (Soulful) kris. The typical kris is an asymmetrical wavy blade dagger that has a separate Spirit or Soul. Krises possess a unique personality. (i. e. some krises are known for good luck; some krises are known for bad luck {If you are in a dangerous situation and you happen to have a "bad luck" sword, all you can do is "kris" your ass goodbye!}).

Chandi Sukah Temple Stone Relief: The Hindu gods forging a "soulful" Kris

The kris is made up of five elements: water, wind, fire, earth (meaning wood and stone), and spirit. Its origins go back over a millennium, with bas-relief carvings at Borobudur showing a Prince striking his foe with a kris in battle. Today the kris is a sanctified heirloom, a ceremonial dress accessory, an indicator of social status, and, of course, a deadly weapon used in battle for hundreds of years (this is like the old American saying: "you can have your cake and eat it too").

The finest made krises come from Java, and the creative process is similar to the making of a Samurai sword in Japan. Layer upon thin layer of fine steel is forged together to create a flexible and strong weapon. Kris can have either a wavy or straight blade. A handle with plain wood, or an intricately carved mythological head or bedecked with precious jewels. The scabbard can either be finely wrought gold or elaborately carved wood. The royal kris had supernatural powers, and the prince wielding it could vanquish his foes with this magical "Soul" weapon. In every war, every nation likes to repeat the mantra that God is on our side. Here God is in your hand!

Kris maker Java 1854

Chapter Fifty-Nine: Down and Out In Jakarta

"Tom Thumb's Blues": Bob Dylan

I arrived at the Jaxa Street Youth Hostel around 10:30 at night, after seventeen grueling hours on a train from Surabaya to Jakarta. Physically exhausted, I was told there was no room at the inn, not even a straw manger. I went to a neighboring loesman, woke up the owner at 11:30, and had him set up a cot for me. After a shower, I went to bed, and then the nightmare started; I had no mosquito net and was continually attacked by these bloodthirsty critters all night. Finally, I couldn't take it anymore and cleared out at 5:30 in the morning. I found a one-eyed rickshaw driver and asked him to find me a loesman. It took about an hour and then finally we found the loseman, that he had recommended.

This loesman was in the heart of a lower-class Indonesian neighborhood (If I'd been in New York City, this would be called the barrio). It was next to one of the largest outdoor markets in the city, and my fellow lodgers were small-time hustlers, sailors, and whores-a rather likable crew.

The room was spacious, but the bed sagged badly, the table was worn and marred badly with cigarette burns, and the large, grimy window looked out into a garbage-filled alley. The saving grace was that the ceiling fan worked.

In all of my previous travels, I had stayed with fellow freaks or conventional tourists; here, I would be alone, "a Stranger in a Strange Land". If I made friends with the locals, it would be on my own and not with the "crutch" of fellow travelers.

The meeting place for the loesman was the cafe next door. In the States, the icebreaker is to have a beer and talk sports; here, the lingua franca was dope. I was befriended by Tenah, who claimed to be a former gangster, banished from

Singapore, and Abyasa, a Javanese sailor who made the Jakarta-Singapore Ocean run, once a month. We smoked Sumatra grass with black Javanese tobacco, a heady joint that gets you stoned in only five or six tokes.

A Javanese Cock Fight Jakarta (author's photo)

Together, they showed me the underbelly of Jakarta. The first afternoon we went to an abandoned factory, where I saw my first cock fight. Here people were frantically betting, shouting at favorites, and crying in disgust when their bets were lost. The old Javanese trainers/owners lovingly handled their prized fighters, extolling the attributes to increase the betting odds.

The fights were bloody; there must have been ten fights-to-the-death contests. This cruel "sport" is immensely popular in Java and Bali.

Tenah apparently knew the favorites and made some good money that day. We celebrated his good fortune with an elaborate dinner at a Chinese restaurant; then, they took me to a local dance club. This was a pale imitation of the Bangkok scene: the "girls" were closing on middle age, and the emphasis was on pushing drinks and paying to dance. I paid for a "dance", and the woman held me tight, trying in broken

English, to get me to "come upstairs, honey". My companions were having a great time, joking, drinking and fondling the hostesses.

Jakarta Canal (author's photo)

The next day, I spent walking around Jakarta's Chinatown: old crumbling Dutch architecture, white-faced Chinese, good stall food, and endless traffic, both foot and car. I walked back to the hotel along Jakarta's canals; they are really filthy. I took a photograph from an overpass: at one end of the canal, children are playing in the water; a little further on, women are doing their wash in the brown water; and still, further on, people are squatting and shitting in the canal. Yet no one seems to mind; I heard that they even use canal water to make ice.

Walking around Jakarta, I passed one smelly canal after another, all lined with sheet metal, scrap wood, and cardboard hovels. It seemed that half of Jakarta lived lives that were "nasty, brutish and short". However, despite all this, I really loved Jakarta: the girls in their colorful sarongs, drinking coffee in the early morning with rickshaw drivers, who pour it into their saucers and slurp it, and the amusing entrapments of older, streetwalking whores, who make furtive attempts to sell themselves. Jakarta is a different city at night: multi-colored strings of light around market stalls, people everywhere, shoving, laughing, smoking, eating: this city is sensuously alive.

Back in the loseman, I met yet another tenant. I was alone, smoking Sumatra grass and working on my journal when someone knocked at my door. I opened it, and in steps Mahali, one of our resident ladies of the night. I had spoken with her before in the café, so I knew her in passing. She speaks broken English and asks if I'm lonely tonight. She is in her late thirties and looks to be half-Chinese and half-Javanese. She still has a decent body but a face bitter with years, a mask of its former beauty. She seemed desperate, or maybe she just saw me as a foreigner, an easy mark. "You want special; good price!" We finally agreed on the "special ". She undressed and lay on my bed. I got undressed and lay down beside her. She knelt over and started working on my penis, caressing it with her tongue until it was erect and throbbing. She lay back, and I found her sweet spot and eased my penis in. She moaned and murmured, "Oh, you are so big, so good." We started moving together, I kissing her face and breasts. I soon came and she whispered, "You the best." We got up and she asked expectantly, "I come again tomorrow?" I nodded and she left. I laid back on the bed, feeling sorry for her; she flattered me just to entice me so that she could come back again. I thought about her situation. She would have a few more good years, and then what? Clean houses, cook, take in the wash: no family, no savings, no skills. It is an awfully hard life, just like the girls I had known in Korea.

Jakarta celebrated its 445th anniversary, and there were over a million people in the main square: pushing, laughing, blowing horns, and dancing in the street - Times Square on New Year's Eve has nothing on Jakarta. All the pretty girls in their finest summer dresses, the boys ogling and touching them; Javanese are very sensual people. There were all kinds of wood platforms set up in the Square, showcasing a wide variety of music, from Indonesian Pop Rock, whining Chinese erhus and old Javanese folk music. Floats paraded by, with high school girls doing a sexy boogaloo on top; others had shadow puppet performances, accompanied by lively gamelan ensembles and endless places to eat, drink, or just sit, enjoying the spectacle. Everyone was friendly, even if a little boisterous. I was escorted to the festivities by a wild bunch of young Javanese, who thought I was made of money: everyone from America is rich. I finally lost them, and then I was "saved" by two high school students, intent on practicing their English on me. We wandered around together for over an hour, and they bought me an iced cola drink, which did me in (they were right about canal water ice!) We were trying to get around the crowd when out of nowhere, Miss Jakarta rode in on a chariot float, driven by a young would-be Roman in a toga and pulled by huge white plaster horses. It was so incredulous and hallucinogenic that I felt that I was experiencing a surrealistic vision of James Ensor's "Christ's Entry into Brussels."

"Christ's Entry into Brussels" by James Ensor

However, I was in no real mood for observation because of diarrhea that was about to explode. There I was, stuck in the middle of a million swirling, dancing, and singing people, and I had to escape. I finally made it to the first fetid canal, dropped my drawers, and let it go: "Bombs Away!!" I really embarrassed my student friends, but I really did "give a shit"!

The next day, I recovered and went to the Boger Botanical Gardens. I was escorted around by a young, mustached Javanese man of about twenty. I told him I wanted to visit the gardens, so he took me a short distance from the main entrance, and we entered the gardens through a hole in the fence. He showed me around for hours, just wanting to practice his English, and didn't ask me for any money.

He told me his name was Atjep, and he was studying English so that he could work in the tourist industry or be hired by one of the large hotels that catered to Westerners. He still lived at home with his parents and six siblings, three younger brothers and three unmarried sisters. The family did not have money to send him to university, so, in his mind, the best way to get a good job was to learn English. Atjep had a fundamental grasp of English, and we spent hours talking while exploring the gardens. In the end, I thanked him and gave him a small tip, which he profusely thanked me for. Like the other students I met, there were so many bright young men that had so few opportunities under the grandiose schemes of Sukarno. Hopefully, President Suharto will stabilize the country and address these needs.

All of the exotic fruit that I had been eating in the markets were hanging in fecund wonderment in the Gardens. High trees, dripping durian, papayas, mangos, and dozens more exotic varieties. If I had to visualize the mythic Garden of Eden, it would be here (sans the serpent and, alas, no naked Eve either).

I returned to my loseman in the late afternoon. Jakarta has a surreal, almost ominous sunset: the sun usually stays a pale-yellow orb but doesn't set; it just hangs in the air and fades slowly away, and you never see it fall onto the horizon. This is probably due to smog, but the effect is eerie and dreamlike. It was at that moment that I had the strangest vision. I was in the alley, near the café, when I heard a rumbling behind me. I turned and saw a young Javanese riding a WW II-era antique Harley-Davidson. He rode right past me and seemed to disappear into the fading yellow orb of the sun. On the surface, there was nothing strange about this: a man on a motorcycle passed me on the street. But I saw it as a prophetic warning, I must leave Jakarta and continue my journey. That was the symbolic me on that Harley, showing me there's so much more to experience and people to meet; I must ride into that sunset. Early next morning, I booked a passage for Singapore: India was beckoning me.

An Eerie Motorcyclist: Yasser Abu-Ghraib UNSPLASH

Singapore II

Wife of a rich Chinese Businessman 1900

Chapter Sixty: Singapore Redux

"THE PLEA"

"Let Me In": The Sensations

Singapore Dock in 1890

We landed in Singapore harbor from Palembang, Sumatra. Remembering my first entrance to Singapore, I cleaned up my act: no dope, and I was wearing my cleanest shirt, had combed my hair, and had trimmed my beard. However, the Indian Customs official still thought I was a drug addict and wanted to send me back on the boat. I tried appealing to his sense of civic pride: "Whatever happened to: "give me your tired, your poor yearning masses, wanting to be free; this is a democracy, isn't it?" Well, that didn't fly. Then I tried indignation: "Moi, how could you think that I use drugs? The only reason I look a little scruffy is because my tux is in the dry cleaners." That didn't go over, either. Next, I tried begging: "My mother is sick; please let me in so I can get a plane to see her." When he still shook his head, I knew it was going to be a hard sell. Thoughts raced through my mind: bribery, "Oh look, there's a shiny $20 dollar bill at my feet. It's not mine; it must be yours". Converting to Hinduism: "If you let me in, I promise to shave my head, wear saffron robes, and chant 'Hara Krishna, Hara Rama' all day long." Providing sexual favors: "It's not who you know, it's who you blow." Promising him my firstborn: "Don't worry honey, I'm just taking the baby for a little trip; he does have his shots, doesn't he? I'll call when I get there."

Finally, after threatening him that I would make an official complaint with the US Embassy ("427, is that your badge number and is that an "a" in your last name?"), he relented and gave me a 24-hour visa, which was enough time to get out of Dodge to Malaysia.

I went to the youth hostel and saw so many people that I had known before when I was here four months ago. There were these two Swiss guys I'd met, Franco and Joseph, who had come all the way from Zurich overland in a psychedelic painted Volkswagen bus. Here they finally ran out of money, shipped the van home, and were flying out to London the next day. Franco told me, "Well, we missed Bali, but Goa was a real trip." Their story follows.

The next morning, I got on a bus leaving Singapore for Malaysia. Riding out of the city, I saw all of Singapore unfold before me: green lawns with Indians playing cricket, old stooped-over Chinese in front of their stores, and young Malay kids with slicked-back hair, mod clothes, and motorbikes. Singapore is beautiful. There are people everywhere: shopping, walking, eating, smoking; this is a city on the move.

Chapter Sixty-One: Two Swiss and a VW Bus

"On the Road Again": Willie Nelson

A Psychedelic Painted Hippie Van: Photo by Vasilios Muselimis (vasiliosmuselimis@vasilios.com) (UNSPLASH)

My friend Joseph and I decided one day that we would quit our jobs, buy a Volkswagen bus and drive it to India. Joseph was very good at fixing automobiles, but as the Beetles would sing, "We got a driver but no car." So, we bought a five-year-old VW bus and modified it for the trip. We took out the back seats fitted in two beds that pop up to the sides when not in use. We bought essential spares like fuel pumps, spark plugs, hoses, four extra tires, and a good mechanic's tool kit. Now the bus was ready, but what did we need? We bought a kerosene two-plate cooker, a fully stocked first aid kit, essential supplies like bags of rice, beans, soups, coffee, ten cartons of cigarettes, and about twenty cassette tapes of our favorite music.

We would be leaving Zurich in March, so we needed winter as well as summer clothing. We got maps of all of the countries we planned to see and checked with embassies for what visas we needed to get before starting.

We knew that we wouldn't have any problems until we hit Istanbul, and we didn't. Driving through Italy and Yugoslavia was a breeze; Bulgarian customs were thorough, but we weren't carrying any dope, so that wasn't really a problem either. We had about four thousand U. S. dollars, mostly in traveler's cheques, and between us, we spoke German, French, and English.

In Istanbul, we got up-to-date information about which route was safest, where there were traveler hotels, and most importantly, those essentials we might need that we had forgotten. Lastly and probably most important, we got haircuts, and Joseph shaved his beard. We had heard too many stories about travelers getting in trouble because they looked like druggies and hippies at the border crossings.

As luck would have it, we were sitting in the Pudding Shop in Istanbul, and we met two Germans who also had a VW bus, and they, too, were headed to India. We decided to team up and head out together. They fit the part of hippies with their dress and manners, and we found out later that they were really "stoners" and not really prepared. Well, we can't all be Swiss, Yahh!

We figured the trip to the Indian border would take about three and a half weeks, depending on weather, road conditions, and how well our van held up. The first few days were fine. The weather was dry, and the Turkish scenery was all desert. We were on our way and driving ten hours a day. At night we would find a shady spot, hopefully near some water source. We were a little leery of leaving our vans in the Turkish towns for fear of losing our tires or having the van broken into. Our German friends didn't seem to mind going into towns and getting some hash and whatever supplies they needed for the trip.

Joseph and I had smoked hash occasionally back in Zurich, but we promised ourselves that we would stay clean until we got to India. Our friends smoked every night, but we still got along, and everything was fine.

When we were close to the Iranian border, I told our German friends that they should dump their remaining hash or face stiff jail time. They agreed, smoking it all. Boy, did we a going over at the border. We had to unload all of our gear, and they searched our van thoroughly. After about five hours, they finally let us go.

Iran was different. There were still endless deserts, but in the towns, there were beautiful mosques and madrasas (schools) decorated with blue tiles and lattice stone carvings. Here we met friendly people, many of whom spoke English. There were good roads, and everything was great until our friends' bus blew out their gas tank, and we had to stop for three days while it was getting fixed.

We made the best of it by eating local foods and seeing the sights. Our friends also enjoyed themselves getting stoned day and night. We finally got started again, and we pushed on to the Afghan border. Afghanistan is one of the most beautiful places in the world. They people were extremely friendly, the cities were colorful and exotic, and this was a drug paradise. Hash and opium were available everywhere and were dirt cheap. We kept driving through the most gorgeous mountains dotted with small villages. Coming from Switzerland, I know mountains, and these truly surpassed the Alps. We hit Kabul and went to Siggi's restaurant. Here we met dozens of travelers, ate delicious western food (Siggi was an expat German who had lived in Kabul for the last ten years), and got the latest updates on what to expect until we hit India. We also lost our German friends. They decided to stay in Kabul due to the cheap drugs and great food they were having here. We crossed into Pakistan border via the Khyber Pass, the path of conquerors, explorers, and two hippies like us. It was breathtaking and heart stopping: the Pakistani truck drivers nearly drove us off the road and blindsided us on every dangerous curve with their reckless speeding. In Pakistan, we stopped at Peshawar, which is one of my favorite places, and it felt like we were already in India. The bazaar was like a fairy tale full of exotic foods, handicrafts, and dope; the "Street of Storytellers" was rife with tribes' people carrying their weapons openly in the streets. We stayed here for three days and enjoyed every moment, from the food to the people to the exotic atmosphere. We finally moved on, and four days later, we crossed over the Indian border near Amritsar. We had made it in one piece, and we celebrated by buying some hash from a fellow traveler and having our first smoke in India. But as they say in the fairy tales, "For every ending, there is a new beginning." Goa, here we come!

Chapter Sixty-Two: A Liberated Woman, Berliner "Luft" And Lady Jane

"Yes, and I ain't saying you ain't pretty. All I'm saying is I'm not ready for any person, place, or thing to try and pull the reins in on me."

"A Different Drum": The Stone Poneys (featuring Linda Ronstadt)

Louise-Marie

In my travels, most of the people I met were male and ranged from ex-GIs to philosophy seekers, martial arts students, university students, and regular tourists. In north Asia, there were no freaks and even fewer women outside of the bar girls. Once I arrived in Southeast Asia, the situation changed: there were lots of women, but they were mostly tourists, students on a university break, and dedicated career women like Margaret. Many were English and Australian that came to Southeast Asia for the gorgeous beaches and to soak up a little culture or escape from meaningless jobs or unfaithful boyfriends. You also had lonely tourists like Uve, looking for romance and excitement, who came to Asia on vacation to pluck the gold ring on the merry-go-round of life. Most of these women did not smoke hash, and we're definitely not "freaks". The closest woman to the freak worldview was Christine in Thailand. She, however, could not throw it all away (i.e., job. loving parents, self-respect, and responsibility) on an extended self-indulgent quest of self-discovery. I felt she would always regret that she had not found that which, she honestly told me, would have given meaning and purpose to her life.

What is a "freak"? To me, a freak is a mental attitude; dope is usually part of that attitude, not the drooling in your chai heroin kind, but the hash and grass high. You see yourself as rebelling against the puritanical society back home, but that is not the defining answer. A freak, above all else, is a seeker: trying to understand himself, his goals, and what is important in life, whether it be a religion, a philosophy, or a relationship. You are also in Asia to see the wondrous glory of past empires, ruined cities, totally different lifestyles, and the gorgeousness of unspoiled nature. You proudly exhibit your "Red Badge of Courage" by regaling other freaks with horror tales about third-class rail crowdedness, sleeping in bedbug-infested hostels, enduring the bureaucratic hassle of getting visas, and using the incredible smelly and filthy toilets. You are the freak Columbus, discoverer of paradisaical secret islands. You look with scorn at the tourist buses that zoom past you on the road while you're hitchhiking. Those poor souls, they only know what their tour guide tells them to see.

If I had to use one word to describe a freak, I would say it is a sponge. A freak absorbs all experiences, the good, the bad, and the ugly. Only by experiencing everything can your mind make choices of what is really important and what is only ephemeral. Then there is that indefinable quality of "air" as Loetz spoke of about his hometown, "Berliner Luft". You can be anyone, do anything, and share that liberation with like-minded individuals because you are all experiencing that liberating air. You are totally free from society's morality and constrictions; you can totally remake yourself and start anew; you are in the frontier of your mind. For me, traveling in Southeast Asia's luft is like being baptized in the water of life; you are born again.

Enter stage left, the first woman freak, Louise-Marie from the French-speaking part of Switzerland. She was about 5 foot 6 inches tall, with long chestnut brown hair, sapphire sparkling blue eyes, and a hauntingly refined face that spoke of hidden sorrows: a fragile beauty that could shatter into a thousand infinitesimal pieces if she let go of her emotions. What I missed in my once-over, cursory look, was her wellspring of confidence, her animated (and sexy) French-inflected English, and her calmly assured self-possessiveness. Here was a delicate petite woman that knew what she wanted and, through sheer willpower, achieved it. We met at a cafe on the beach in Batu Firangi in Malaysia. "I came from a strict Catholic household where we attended church two or three times a week. I had a normal childhood, but when I grew up, I found I was stuck in a boring job and with an even more boring boyfriend. I saw myself becoming my mother: a respectable, dutiful wife that goes through the motions without really experiencing life. My only joy was reading about exotic places: Casablanca, Bombay, and Bangkok. I dreamed I would go there one day and live a totally different life, but I said to myself, 'girls like you don't do these crazy things; they get married, have children, and live a normal hausfrau life'. However, after a particularly climatic week, where I saw my best girlfriend get married to a pathetic conformist bore, and my boyfriend was nudging me toward the same fate. So, I just quit work, kissed my family and boyfriend goodbye, and bought a one-way ticket to Bangkok, taking all of my meager life savings with me. When I got off the plane, I knew I had made the right decision: for the first time in my life, I felt truly alive and free. This is where I want to live for the rest of my life."

I admired her adventuresome spirit and even envied her a little for her resoluteness in doing whatever it took to remain in Paradise. While we were talking, her "freak of the week", a big brawny Aussie, jealously ushered her away from me. He had taken her in and paid for everything in return for her "knowing him" in the biblical sense. "I depend on the kindness of strangers," as Blanche in "A Streetcar

Named Desire" so delicately phrased it. Whether she loved or just used these freaks, I will never know. The end result, however, was that she could live rent-free and continue her wanderlust. She was the first person I knew who used drugs not so much for pleasure but as a controlling tool in her survival shop kit ("Get 'em high, and they'll give you anything you want").

I left her on the beach with her stud in tow and continued on my travels to Borneo and Indonesia and did not see her again for four months when I bumped into her in the traveler's hotel on my return to Singapore. In the interim, she had gone "native" and introduced me to Salim, her latest arm candy, who was a handsome young Malay stud that she met in the port. I found out through another freak that she had left the Freak Farm League for the big city Major League, striking it rich by screwing wealthy Chinese businessmen to give her the freedom and resources to indulge in the local talent.

When I looked at her lifestyle, I thought of those adventuresome 19th-century English noble ladies that I had read about, like Lady Hester Stanhope, who left stodgy England to find romance and adventure in the clean air of the Arabian Desert. Lady Hester was a strong-willed, cultivated English woman that just happened to be born a woman while her instincts, behavior, and courage were more like the adventuresome Englishmen that went to Asia to make their fortune. Lady Hester found her Arab Prince, and she became known as "Queen of the Arabs", a role she relished because she could not have the power nor the fame as a woman in Victorian England. However, a better analogy would be Lady Jane Digby, who lived her life for love and flaunted conventional Victorian morality.

Lady Jane was born into a distinguished noble family, a naive, beautiful girl whose dance card was always filled. She married young, at 19, to a man twice her age of noble heritage, but unfortunately, he was politically ambitious and neglected her. Soon this bored but spunky girl started secret liaisons with half the nobility of Europe. She divorced, married, divorced again, had numerous children which she left behind in England, and even had an affair with King Ludwig of Bavaria of Disneyland castle fame ("Fairy tales can come true, it can happen to you if you meet the right, rich, randy girl.") Yet all of her relationships were founded on love, not for material gain. She was England's first flower child, 100 years before Tiny Tim stole her crown.

She slept her way through Europe, and at age 46, she arrived in Damascus. A bewitched, visiting Englishman, Edmond Abbott, wrote of her beauty, which was remarkably like Louise-Marie, who is only in her mid-20s. "She is tall and svelte without being thin… she has large blue eyes, deep blue like the depths of the sea, and beautiful chestnut hair, lit with warmer golden tints. Her well-preserved skin has the milky whiteness which belongs so essentially to England and which blooms best under thick English fogs." (This could also be a glowing description of Dana Wynter, except you would have to mention that she sprang fully formed from a giant snow pea pod).

It was the desert air that reinvigorated her ("Have another hit…of fresh air": Quicksilver Messenger Service). Here in a landscape of endless spaces, phantasmagorical mirages, scorching winds, and fiercely individualistic tribespeople, she met her Chief Charming, a cultivated Bedouin, who whisked her away from her current lover, a clueless Scotsman and set her up as his queen in a tent, surrounded by a tribe of robbers, camel herders, and skilled horsemen. Lady Jane herself was an expert horsewoman, and the two would ride off for days alone to enjoy the splendors of solitude and that liberating air. Lady Jane adapted to the harsh life of the Bedouins with a naïve sense of love overcoming all obstacles. I can imagine when she first came to the desert and her proud Prince Charming, trying to impress her, throwing back the tent flaps and revealing the majesty of the wide-open desert as far as the eye could see: "Stay with me and all this will be yours" and Lady Jane in true Monty Python fashion says "What, the tent flaps?" She lived a long and happy life with her desert sheik, never to return to the staid society of England. I hope Louise-Marie finds that same love because, like Lady Jane, she could never go back to that rigid morality and stifling lifestyle of her former heimat (home). Here in Southeast Asia, the air is fecund and dripping with overgrown life, a Garden of Eden that regenerates new beginnings and animal vitality. This air offers life in all its many splendors, a refuge for "A Stranger in a Strange Land".

Lady Jane Digby by Joesph Karl Stieler 1831

Malaysia II

Woman lighting Joss candles (Author's photo)

Chapter Sixty-Three: Outcasts of the Islands

"Song for No One" Victoria Bigelow

Urban loneliness is no different from being lost on the Road

I stopped in Johore Bahru looking for my friends at the Youth Hostel in town. As I sat in a cafe drinking chai, I thought of Terry and all of the people I had met in this dusty town.

Asia is a cruel mistress; it casts a spell and never lets you go.

I first ran into Terry Ben Ali in Hong Kong. He was a native Malay that had been adopted by a British couple and taken back to England with them. He had everything going for him: loving parents, university, and a place in society. Then he discovered drugs and became heavily addicted, abandoned his schooling, and just left England for the road. He was now 31, and he said he would be traveling for the rest of his life.

Terry was very soft-spoken, quietly relating his travels while cooking vegetables in coconut oil and smoking hash in the small Hong Kong hostel. He had a twitch and suffered from gallstones, but that didn't stop him from being on the road. When I left him in Hong Kong, he only had ten US dollars. Then I met him again here. He had worked as a deckhand on a freighter that took him to Singapore from Hong Kong. The drug-free, puritanical Singapore did not suit him, so he crossed over to Malaysia and joined the freak circus at Johore. I saw Terry as a modern-day Ibn Battuta; however, he was not on a religious pilgrimage but on a dope quest. The strange new worlds took a back seat to the places where the dope was plentiful and cheap.

At the hostel were the same drug-addicted freaks that I had met four months before on my way to Indonesia. Dope was cheap, the surf was inviting, and there were fellow freaks to share this "Maya" existence. One of these resident freaks (in a rare coherent conversation) told me that he remembered Terry and told me he had left on a freighter from Singapore, headed for Pakistan and Afghanistan. It's amazing how far a proper Oxford English accent will get you!

Joseph was a Belgian ex-painter in his early forties. He had worked on cargo ships for fifteen years. "What's money? Throw it away!" And he did, on booze and women, but he told me, "I had to leave, or I would become just like those old homosexual sailors that have no life apart from the sea."

He was now an itinerant handyman living in fleabag hotels and heading for an island off of Australia where he had been promised a job. "Maybe I'll settle there and get back to painting." It had been three years since he last held a paintbrush (unless you count the various stores and houses that he painted as a handyman).

Saul

It was about 1:00 o'clock on a hot steamy day in Bangkok, and I was eager to talk to some travelers about their experiences and maybe find new destinations to explore. I overheard an older mid to late 30s male traveler speaking to the waiter in English. What struck me was the accent: the nasal Brooklynese, which immediately identified him as a New Yorker. Uh hah, a fellow compatriot that would give me an update on what's happening in the City, which I had left close to three years ago. I introduced myself and asked if I could join him. He told me his name was Saul and that he was from Sheepshead Bay.

He was of medium height, stocky, with receding black curly hair. He had a broad open face and limpid watery eyes. But what stood out was his nervousness: he was constantly moving his hands and face, chain-smoking one cigarette after another. I could tell right away that he was a junkie: not the drooling in your Chai stereotype, but the manic talkative type that seemed to be impatiently "Waitin' for the Man", who had the magic Excelsior. He was a typical New Yorker, the kind that will tell their life story to a complete stranger just because they are lonely, and that's just the way New Yorkers are.

"I was raised in Brownsville to poor but loving parents who made sure that I studied hard, and it paid off: I got my degree in Economics at City University. I was a rising star at an export-import firm, got married to a beautiful woman, and had two kids and a comfortable house in Sheepshead Bay. I was living the American dream. On my weekends, I took the kids to see the Yankees, and I even helped to coach the Little League baseball team that one of my sons was playing in. Then at one after-hours office party, a coworker offered me some heroin to snort. It was like a different world; everything made sense. I thought I had found answers to what I had been missing in my life. But I knew I had to be careful; I wasn't going to be a helpless junkie like the blacks in Harlem. I kept my habit under control and occasionally snorted on the weekends, but soon I wanted more. I started snorting in the bathroom at work, and that affected everything I did. I failed to return calls, missed appointments, and my boss called me in to say shape up or ship out. I tried keeping off the stuff, but it was too powerful. Some nights I even stayed in the city in a fleabag hotel, just getting high. I neglected my wife and kids, blew through my weekly paycheck, and started eating away at my savings. I still needed more money for my habit, so I second mortgaged my house and started blowing through that money too. When I got my pink slip at work, my wife realized that something was radically wrong.

She tried to get me help to go into counseling and rehab. I lasted a week in one rehab center, and then I split for the city and my heroin connection. I didn't care about baseball, the kids, or anything. It was only dope that mattered. When my wife saw that I wouldn't get any treatment, she took the kids to her mother and, after a month, filed for divorce. She got the house, and the kids, a huge alimony, and I got my habit. Now I had started shooting up, and I met this junkie who told me about Thailand: the cheap drugs, the beautiful women, and the easy lifestyle. I had nothing going for me here, and I knew I had to get away. I bought a one-way ticket to Bangkok, and that was close to two years ago. At first, I was the kid in the candy store: I used to get Ten Miles High every day and didn't leave my hotel room for days at a time. Then I looked at myself in the mirror and said you've got to change; otherwise, you'll wind up dead like those French junkies that were found in their room after three days, stinking with a needle in their arms.

I started controlling my habit: I still needed to get high, but I only shot up once a day and was able to function and figure out what I wanted to do with my life. My money was running low, and then I thought I could get into the smuggling business. I approached my dealer and gave him a proposition. I had worked in export-import, so I knew how to set up exports with all the forms and declarations. I had visited foreign markets as part of my job duties and knew how to get a container through customs. If the supplier had connections in New York, we could distribute the smuggled goods, and we'd all make some money. The dealer talked to his low-level boss, and he was interested. I laid it all out for him. I told him I would accompany the shipment when it went through customs at Port Elizabeth. I still had some connections with port and customs officials and the trucking companies; if he had a means of distribution, we could make a pretty good business of it. I'm not talking about putting the cartels out of business, I'm talking about small packets of pure heroin that we could ship to Chinatown in burlap bags of rice, maybe 100 kilos in a full container of rice to his connections there. He could cut it down, and the street value would be close to half a million, not a bad day's work. I told him that I would shepherd the shipment to the final destination and take all the risks. If it worked out, we'd go into business together and could increase the flow depending on the market. I'm supposed to meet the top boss and sell him my pitch later this week. If it works out, I'll be moving out of this dump and getting myself a nice apartment with an indoor swimming pool and maid service. I've even been seeing a Thai girl, and we'll move in together if this deal comes through. I'll never go back to the States, at least not for good. I have everything that I want here."

He suddenly stopped, got up, said goodbye, and walked out the door. I guessed he saw his connection and wanted to get that fix before he went into withdrawal. That was the last I saw of him, so I'll never know if that scheme ever worked out.

These men did not have a "Lord Jim" sin to expiate, nor were they disreputable, immoral scoundrels, like the scheming Peter Wilhelm in the original Conrad's "Outcast of the Islands" (although I imagined Saul in a sequel, the continuing saga of the "Confidence Man" Peter Wilhelms). Nor were they pining for some lost romance and traveled to Asia to forget:

Tell me not (Sweet) I am unkind,

That from the nunnery

Of thy chaste breast and quiet mind

To war and arms, I fly…

I could not love thee (Dear) so much,

Lov'd I not Honour more.

"To Lucasta, Going Off to the Wars" Richard Lovelace

They were just addicted to booze or drugs and saw no future other than aimlessly wandering from one steamy Asian port or country to the next, never finding inner peace or a place that they could call home.

Chapter Sixty-Four: An Ocean Too Far

"Into the Mystic": Van Morrison

A Zheng He "Treasure Ship" 1405-1433 A.D.

While visiting the Stadys Museum in Malacca, I came across an exhibit dedicated to a Chinese naval explorer and adventurer who landed in Malacca in the early fifteenth century. This was a full century before the Portuguese conquered the city. This extraordinary man was a heavy-set Muslim eunuch in the service of the Ming Emperor of China, Zheng He. From 1405-1433 A.D., Admiral Zheng led seven naval expeditions, visiting all of Southeast Asia, the Horn and East Coast of Africa, and Arabia covering a distance of over 200,000 nautical miles.

His mission was threefold: display a dynamic show of Chinese force, extend the Chinese Empire Tributary system, and seek out opportunities for trade and conquest.

His "treasure ships" were the largest wooden sailing ships ever built: four hundred and thirteen feet long, seventy-one feet wide, nine-masted with four decks carrying soldiers, sailors, diplomats, and scholar-scientists. The typical wooden warship of the British Navy in the 18th century was only about one hundred and sixty-five feet long and thirty feet wide.

Zeng He brought gifts of gold, silver, porcelain, and silk and, in return, received tributary gifts of ivory, ostriches, apes, and even a giraffe. He suppressed the Chinese pirates preying on Chinese coastal vessels, conquered the Kingdom of Ceylon, and on his fourth voyage, brought back forty envoys of the lands he had visited, bringing with them "tribute" from these "vassal" states.

His significance is one of the greatest "what if" stories of Chinese history. Zheng was a leader of the Eunuch faction, which vied with the Confucian scholar bureaucrats for the attention of the Emperor. At stake was the vision of what China should be: an Expansionist "Superpower," controlling all of Asia as the eunuchs wanted, or an "Isolationist" country, having no need of Asian conquest and expanded trade opportunities. China, in the scholar's vision, was the greatest and richest country on Earth, and they need not bother with the barbarians of the world.

The eunuchs lost out, and the voyages ended; Zheng died at sea on the seventh and last voyages. China shut itself off from the new technologies and ideas developed in the west and slowly declined. It chose to rebuild the Great Wall to stop the Northern Mongol incursions instead of funding ocean voyages for trade expansion and territorial conquests, and five hundred years later was easy prey for the technologically superior western powers.

What is fascinating is that there was a similar naval expedition in U.S. history, which also determined the vision of what our country would be.

The U. S. Naval Expedition exploring Antarctica 1840

The U. S. Exploring Expedition of 1838-1842 had a scientific as well as a trade/expansionistic mission. President John Quincy Adams wanted a scientific, mapping, and trade expansion expedition, but this wasn't approved until President Martin van Buren obtained funding from Congress in 1837. There were three main exploration vessels under the command of a Naval Officer, Lieutenant John Wilkes. The expedition roamed the Pacific Ocean, mapping and collecting biological and anthropological specimens. The expedition carried the leading scientists, cartographers, botanists, philologists, taxidermists, and artists to collect, record, and sketch the flora/ fauna and peoples of the two hundred and eighty islands they visited. They brought back 60,000 bird and plant specimens, 4000 Native artifacts like Fiji war clubs, intricately woven baskets, and colorfully feathered Pacific Islander ceremonial dresses. These specimens and artifacts became the nucleus and first collections of our "National Museum," the Smithsonian. The expedition also performed extensive mapping of the Oregon coast (then under the control of the

British Hudson Bay Company) and California (under Mexican control) for military and trade purposes.

What would America become: a country dedicated to acquiring an overseas empire like Great Britain, or would we concentrate on developing our own country, inventing new technologies to make a garden out of a vast desert? This was the vast unexplored country that we acquired with the Louisiana Purchase in 1803. Inventions like the Fulton Steamship, the Cotton Gin, and the Bessemer Steel Furnace served to unify the country.

At play was the seafaring New England states with their whaling and China Trade vessels vs. the New York City financial and industrial interests. In 1820 the Erie Canal opened up the Midwest farm products to the East Coast and made New York the most powerful and richest city in the country. It was not only the credo of "Money talks": it was the incredible wealth and unification power of railroads, steel for new cities to be built in the wilderness, and endless waves of amber fields to make America the breadbasket of the world. Just as important was the indelible image of the West as a symbol of the self-made man. New York City won out, and New England declined into an economic backwater.

At the same time as Lt. Wilkes was leading the U. S. Naval Expedition, the U. S. Topographical Office in Washington D. C. commissioned an Army officer in 1840, Charles Fremont, to map out a northernly route to Oregon to aid the scores of pioneers traveling there. In 1842, he headed a second expedition to map a southernly approach to California.

Whereas Wilkes wrote of his naval expedition in the dry language of a scientist, Fremont chronicled his journey with the skill of a romantic novelist. This was thanks to his imaginative, literary wife, who "ghost-wrote" the narrative. She recounted tales of adventuresome "Mountain Men," struggling pioneers in their Conestoga wagons, and life-and-death skirmishes between Indians and dashing U. S. Army calvary men.

John Charles Fremont 1856

Fremont became an overnight hero, nicknamed "the Pathfinder", and his account of the expedition inspired hundreds of thousands to "Go west, young man." Along with the promise of fertile new farmland in Oregon, there came the California Gold Rush of 1849 (There's gold in them thar hills!). The frontier offered the opportunity to remake yourself and amass great power and wealth, just as India did for the ambitious but poor young Englishmen.

It's ironic that after the historian William Jackson Turner declared the American "frontier" closed in 1890, it was only eight years later that America started its own overseas empire, taking the Philippines, Puerto Rico, and Guam as spoils of the Spanish American War.

Chapter Sixty-Five: "The Searchers" Meet "Waiting For Godot"

Ethan: Injun will chase a thing till he thinks he's chased it enough. Then he quits. Same way when he runs. Seems like he never learns there's such a thing as a critter that'll just keep comin' on. So we'll find 'em in the end, I promise you. We'll find 'em. Just as sure as the turnin' of the earth.

"The Searchers", 1956 John Ford Western

VLADIMIR: "Tomorrow, when I wake or think I do, what shall I say of today? That with Estragon, my friend, at this place, until the fall of night, I waited for Godot?"

"Waiting For Godot": 1953 play by Samuel Beckett

"Missing" Everything but the Girl

A lover disappears, and the sorrow overwhelms you.

Dave, my English friend, split from me in Johor. He wanted to stay on the beach; I wanted to photograph the old city of Malacca. I found a small traveler's hotel in the historic district, smoked a Sumatra blunt, and headed out to get dinner.

She was sitting alone at a table with an untouched plate of fried rice, just gazing into space. Aha, a stoned freak! But how would I approach her: sarcastically: "Ground control to Major Tom. Can you hear me, Major Tom?" The good Samaritan approach: "Hi, weren't you with a group of travelers, looking for a cheap hotel? I got one that is perfect". The worldly, complementary approach: "What's a good-looking dame like you doing in a gin joint like this?" or the sincere boyish approach: "Hi, I just got into town and don't know anybody. May I join you?" I decided on the sincere wimpish boy approach, which would probably work unless she was paranoid and saw me as a soft-spoken serial killer. All my efforts were for naught: I delivered my well-rehearsed line, and she barely looked up, half nodded and fell back into her trance. If, at first, you don't succeed, try something else." You look so familiar. Are you sure we haven't met in some Greenwich Village coffee house? Oh, by the way, I'm Gordon. How are you?" (as I took a chair opposite her). She roused herself to look at me and mumbled, "I'm Lisa". "It speaks; the monster lives", now if I only had a crowbar, I could pry open her mouth and get a few more words out of her. However, she slowly revived herself and apologized, saying she must have smoked some heroin-laced hash and got really spaced out.

Lisa

She was from Portland and bummed around Southeast Asia for a few weeks. She had befriended a group of travelers, and they had smoked this strong shit. Somehow, she had wandered off and found herself in this restaurant. She was medium height, about 5' 6", and very thin, with her blond hair in a tight bun. Her face had a slightly pinched look owing to her high cheekbones, small mouth, straight, longish nose, and wire-rimmed glasses, accented by her lack of makeup. After we had talked for about half an hour, she confessed that she had come to Southeast Asia to find her boyfriend, Josh. He had gone to Singapore as a master's candidate in government. He was there to study Lee Kwan Yew's form of state-guided democracy. Then he had gone to Malaysia for a vacation break, and she had not heard from him in over a month. He had not returned to his lodging in Singapore, and calls to the American Embassy in Singapore got her nowhere. In desperation, she flew out to Singapore to find him. After inquiring about him at his Singapore hotel, she tracked him to Malacca.

After a week of searching, she found him strung out in a fleabag hotel. They both had smoked grass in university but never did the hard stuff. Now she found him addicted to heroin, hanging with some hardcore freak addicts. He seemed happy to see her but couldn't stop his addiction, begging her for money. He told her that he had gone to a Chinese opium den just out of curiosity, and it felt so good that he went back for five days in a row and became hooked. The next step was shooting heroin, which was cheaper and less hassle than opium because the police regulated the opium den. He was shooting up with these stoner freaks, selling his camera, and watch, and blowing through all his money. She cleaned him up, got him food, and they moved to a good hotel together. The very first night there, while she was sleeping, he stole all her money and traveler's checks and disappeared.

She spent days looking for him to no avail. Then she met these freaks who knew him but not where he was now. They offered her a joint that was laced with heroin, and after smoking it, she disgustedly ran out and ended up in a trance-like stupor in the restaurant where I met her.

"What are you going to do now?"

"I dunno, I guess keep looking until I find him again and try to get him back home for treatment." I had seen these drooling-in-their-chai junkies and avoided them like the plague. They usually stole from other freaks when strung out and sat zombie stone-faced when high. I thought of Joan Baez's "There but for Fortune go you or I".

"Can I help you?" She looked at me incredulously, saying, "Oh God, yes, thank you." I got Lisa a pedicab to her hotel and told her I would pick her up at 9:00 AM to start the search. In the morning, we checked his old hotel, no luck, but found out from some freaks where the opium den was located.

Chinese smoking in an opium den in San Francisco in 1890

We went down a garbage-strewn back alley and came to a rusted steel door with no signs and knocked to get admitted. We entered a dimly lit, low-ceiling dormitory-like setting with about a dozen wood table beds where emaciated old Chinese men were laying and smoking opium through long wooden tubes. There were also roughhewn wood bunk beds on the side walls, with more old men just gazing into space. The air was stuffy, thick with the mingled smells of sickly-sweet burned opium and sweat. It was early afternoon, but at least half of the beds were occupied. Other Chinese men were kneading and rolling the opium into small balls to stick at the end of the long wooden pipes. The old men lay with their heads on curved wooden saddles, inhaling the fired opium balls. Each ball gave the smoker four hits.

The scene was like one of the rings of Dante's "Inferno"; there were no cries or screams, but the fires of lighted opium, the overpowering smell, and the calm resignation of the rail-thin smokers gave a horrifying picture of Hell.

We asked one of the opium makers if there were any frequent foreign users, and Lisa showed him a photograph of Josh, a handsome guy, smiling without a care in the world. "No, he no come here." We left these lost souls and headed for the hotel where she had smoked with the freaks last night. The "New Paradise" hotel was a real dump. There was no lobby: the owner sat behind a grimy plexiglass shield atop the front counter, which sealed him in; the only decoration was a marked-up Chinese calendar. We asked him if he had seen the man in the photograph. He shook his head "No". Just then a shabby, long-haired freak came down the stairs. I approached him and quietly asked where I could score some heroin. "You gotta go to the harbor, ask for Sun Lee. But be careful, it's a rough area, and they rolled a couple of freaks there." I thanked him and showed him the photograph, but he didn't know Josh.

Malacca River Port 1907

The harbor was a bustling place, with not many big ships but lots of fishing boats and covered barges. After about a half hour of fruitlessly asking for Mr. Lee, we found a foreman who pointed us to the right place. It was a huge old brick warehouse, a remnant of Malacca's colonial past, with an ornate Georgian front and stately peeling Corinthian columns supporting the open plan main bay. Everywhere there were loaded pallets of rice, tea, canned goods, and consumer electronics from Japan. Dozens of Chinese laborers were moving goods in and out of the dusty cavernous space. We spotted a small office in the rear of the building. We were stopped by a Chinese "slicky boy" who took us to his boss when we told him what we wanted. The boy ushered us into a dirty office; behind a large worn, cigarette burned wood desk sat a rounded, smiling, middle-aged Chinese man, surrounded by half a dozen smoking and laughing "slicky boys".

"What you want?"

"I look for brother, he buy from you, you know?" I showed him the photograph.

He looked at it, frowning, "He no come here. You buy now?"

"Maybe your boys see?"

He showed the photograph around, but they all shook their heads. "You no buy, you leave!"

We took back the photograph and left. Outside the warehouse was another group of rough-looking Chinese boys, smoking and lounging on their Honda motorbikes, giving Lisa covetous looks. We walked quickly and hurriedly found a pedicab to get the hell out of Dodge.

An old warehouse building in Malacca port (author's photo)

We were back to ground zero and didn't know what to do next. Lisa was close to tears, and I took her for chai. I told we would try tonight, going to the outdoor freak hangouts. I asked her if she wanted a smoke to calm her. She agreed despondently, and we went to my hotel room. She just sat on the chair, her mind lost in thought. I rolled a joint, and we shared it. The grass made her sleepy; she said that she had not gotten much sleep last night. I told her to lie down on my bed; she fell asleep almost immediately.

After about three hours, she awoke, and I took her to a restaurant for some food. Afterward, we resumed our search. We returned to "New Paradise", but we still couldn't find the freaks. We showed the photograph to all the freaks who came in or went out, but no one knew him. After about an hour, we split for the old fort, which was a popular freak hangout, but no Josh. We tried all the main squares and freak restaurants, but nobody knew or saw him.

It was now after 10:00 PM, and I offered to take her back to her hotel. We got a pedicab there, and I was about to say good night and that we could try again tomorrow. She stared into my face and said quietly that she didn't want to be alone now. We got to her room, and she slumped down on the bed, tears streaming down her cheeks. I sat beside her, holding her silently. She wiped her tears with her hand, looked at me intently, and kissed me. "No…Are you sure you want this?" She kissed me again, and I kissed her hard, holding her face in my hands. We were now in a frenzied dance to undress each other; we fell naked on the bed, kissing each other furiously. I came on top of her and entered her. We thrust together, hard rhythmic punches. I soon excitedly climaxed, but she kept thrusting her whole body at me. Finally, she was exhausted and stopped. Her body went completely limp, and I held her until her breathing became normal; she fell into a deep sleep. I looked at her, her breasts heaved slowly, and for the first time, her face looked calmly relaxed and at peace. I, too, fell asleep and awoke to see her dressing.

"How are you feeling?" "For the first time in weeks, I feel like an incredible weight has been lifted off me. I feel free. I see now that I've been chasing an impossible dream. I'm going back home to try to pick up the pieces of my life. Thank you for last night and all the help you gave me; I won't forget what you did for me."

I never saw her again, and I hoped she would move on with her life; she deserved it.

"Waiting For Godot, Avignon, France 1987

Chapter Sixty-Six: The Freak Becomes a Landlord

"Our House": Crosby, Stills, Nash & Young

This is the way I felt about the bungalow I rented.

I left Jahore Baru by bus, arrived in Penang, and decided to spend some time on the local beach, Batu Firangi.

For the first time in all my travels, I finally rented a full house. This was an old, all-wood, palm-thatched cottage set back from the road. It had fine lattice balcony windows and a beautiful veranda overlooking palm trees. The house had one bed, a few mats, and the water well and outhouse were off to the side, outside of the building. It was a pretty chaotic atmosphere; at one time, we had five people staying, other times, three. People came and went, and no one kept count. Nobody paid any rent, which was unfortunate for me, but we all had a good time, smoking hash and enjoying the incredible sunsets from the veranda.

The days turned into weeks; images float into your mind that captured the essence of Batu Firangi. A cowherd moving down the beach driven by a wizened old Malay, who was sweet talking and scolding them; the fishermen sleeping out in the grassy area of the beach, next to their boats. Two strong Malay boys out casting their nets and walking two abreast with a fish-laden net, bringing in their catch. The colorful painted boats, the bright-eyed Indian kids, playing in the soft dusty afterglow of the Penang sunset. The palm trees standing out, silhouetting the three-humped mountains and the orangey smoked and streaked horizon, dissolving slowly into the blackness of night. On Sundays, I went to Georgetown, the historic district of Penang, sitting in the park of St. George's Church, watching the old men sleep on the monuments and gravestones and the young Chinese kids playing with a dragon kite. Walking around the old city, seeing the old Chinese women with their granny glasses, sitting on doorsteps, or watching their sons work in their shop. At night watching the young Malays in the latest Western leisure suits and mini-skirts, bumping and grinding away to the pleasures of western pop-beat music. Leisurely sampling the exotic fruits of the market and sitting in Parisian-style cafes, drinking endless cups of chai as I watched the spectacle unfold before me (Pass the popcorn, please).

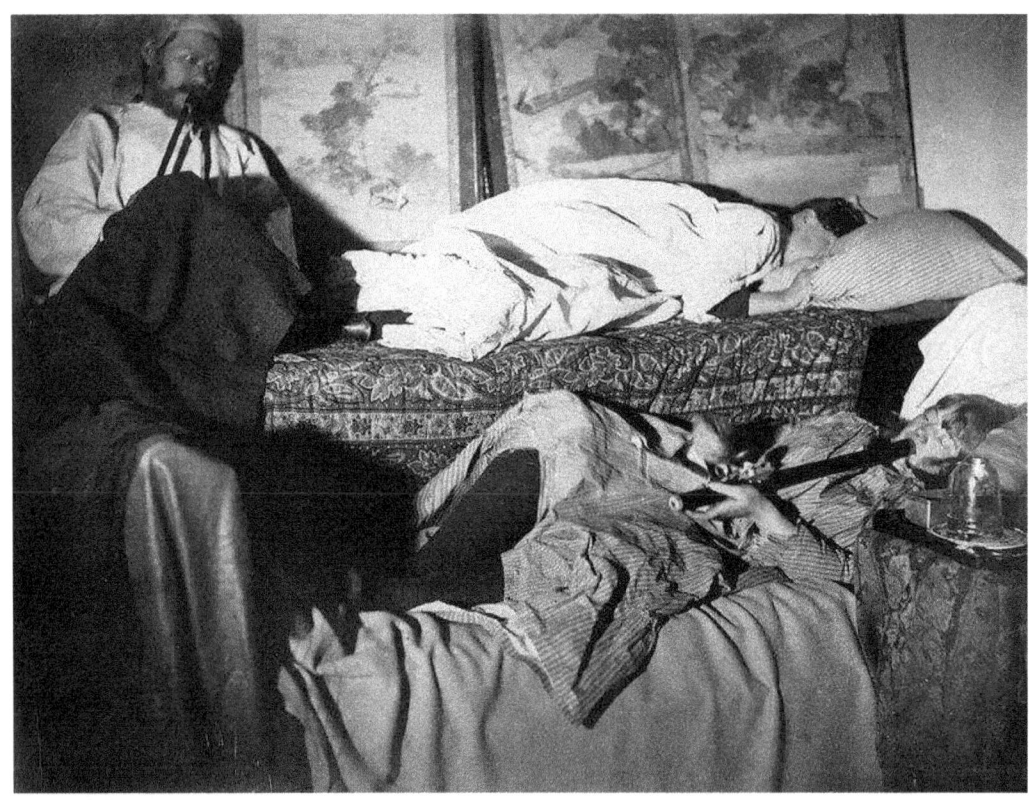

Opium smokers in Chinatown San Francisco opium den 1890

In my wanderings around Georgetown, I stumbled upon an opium den frequented by old Chinese men. Being young and stupid and disregarding my sordid adventure in the seedy opium den with Lisa in Malacca, I thought I'd check the box: smoking opium, so I could say with a swagger, "been there, done that". The entrance was a non-discrete metal door with no signage. I knocked, and the door was opened by a rotund middle-aged Chinese man who asked me what I wanted; I told him and paid him what he asked. He then led me into a small, dimly lit subterranean room. One emaciated Chinese man was sleeping above in a bunkbed, two others slowly motioned me to come over and lay down on a wooden bed, resting my head on a curved wooden saddle. They mixed the opium pipes; you smoke four to six pipes. Afterward, I felt very spacey and calm. I was completely relaxed, but I did not feel high. Two friends who also tried opium got sick, but I just felt a calming stillness that made everything around me seem surreal-everything seemed normal, but the buildings seemed to dissolve when I walked by them, and it was as if I was invisible because there were people all around me, but they did not seem to see me.

I felt like Major Tom from the Elton John song. I walked out of the mirage of the city into the darkening countryside. I was happily adrift, moving fearlessly in a vast dark space, guided on my way home by an incredible Milky Way starlight showcase, illuminating a silvery path. I entered a palm canopy where it was pitch black and when I emerged, the stars were embedded sparkling diamonds on a horizonless black felt jewelry display tray. It brought back a memory when I was a child, and I entered a black night room, which was suddenly set ablaze by the brightly illumined multi-bulbed Christmas tree, a reassuring beacon that banished the darkness.

I tried to make some sense of my experience by reading "Naked Lunch" by William Burrows, but he was very paranoid in his trip and hallucinogenic in the language he used to describe his addiction. I thought he exaggerated his addiction, and the meaningless stream-of-consciousness passages were incomprehensible; I couldn't finish this overindulgent bore of a book.

Years later, I was still trying to understand how opium affected me. Then I watched a Grade B French thriller about a failed bank heist, "Killing Zoe". I won't go into the plot, but what fascinated me was the reaction of the hero. He had just smoked opium and was taken to an underground jazz nightclub in Paris. As he listens to the black saxophonist playing a sonorous riff, he becomes one with the music. He is mesmerized into a Tao harmony where the notes become tangible: he sees each individual musical note floating by in space coming out of the saxophone horn. I realized then that each star stood out in crystal clearness, assuming a life of its own, a microcosm of the whole universe and I was an integral part of this vast canvas. Somehow, I walked back to my beach house, but I didn't remember how I got there.

The next day at the beach house, I felt very warm and realized I had a fever. I took a bicycle cab to Penang hospital. There were no lines, just mobs of people moving en masse from one area to another. The first doctor I saw told me I was fine, but since I was still running a fever and felt very tired, I felt it might be hepatitis. I wanted a second opinion. The second doctor thought I might have hepatitis but really didn't have a cure for me. The hospital was filthy, it looked like the nurses were using the same hypodermic needle on everyone, just wiping it with alcohol to disinfect it. If I didn't have any serious disease, I surely would have contracted one if I remained in that hospital, so I quickly left. I decided to try my own homeopathic cure. I bought several types of prescription-type antibiotic drugs (no doctor's authorization was required to buy these drugs in the local Malaysian drugstores), Chinese herbal medicine, and Malaysian vitamins to combat the sickness.

I stayed out of the sun, drank lots of beer, and slept. The house scene was changing for the worse. I now had two heroin addicts shooting up on the veranda. I had this feverish, delusional dream that transposed Rick's Café Americano in "Casablanca "to this tropical beach. The junkies since they sat immobile most of the day, I would place them one on each end of the veranda, dress them in red Beefeater overcoats, and give them each a large Sikh turban. Then I would drape a large banner overhanging the veranda railing: WELCOME TO GORDON'S AMERICAN FREAKLAND. I would hire a Malay rock band, and we would have a freak discotheque on the ground floor, complete with a bar that would stock every type of booze, drug, and hallucinogen. I would be in a dark tux with an Uncle Sam stove pipe top hat, welcoming the freaks. There would be shady French dope smugglers, drunk Aussies, straight English university girls, ex-GIs with vacant, hallowed stares, and dewy-eyed, flower child, California hippie girls. Between band breaks, I would have a Chinese torch singer doing the sultry Lee Wiley chanson, "As Time Goes By" while I stare out onto the beach, waiting hopelessly for Christine from Chiang Mai to saunter into my gin joint, "Play it again, Saeed."

After a week, I got better but still felt weak. The house scene went from bad to worse: now I had four junkies here, each shooting up and sitting stone-faced, and the only life I saw was the drool coming from their open mouths. There was no one I could even have a simple conversation with, and someone had stolen my pet rock, so I was out of luck there too. I decided it was time to move on. I gave up the beach house and took an eight-hour bus trip to Phuket, Thailand. At the hotel on the beach at Phuket, I met my friend, Dave, the Englishman that I had traveled with four months before.

Chapter Sixty-Seven: On Traveling

Friendship or "Friends with Benefits" on the road

Guy freaks

When you're traveling, it's usually easy to find male companions, but most are ephemeral and depend on your circumstances and mindset.

There is a whole network of freak hostels and small hotels throughout Asia where you are always bumping into people you have traveled with before. Then there are the freak "convention centers" like Goa or Katmandu, where everyone knows everyone, and you have your "31 Flavors" to choose from for a traveling companion.

My French friend Marc was great if you do not want to have a long conversation (or <u>any</u> conversation, for that matter). He was constantly stoned and said nothing for hours, which is fine if you're in the same condition. The few times he was cognizant, he was barely tolerable unless we talked about or ate food in the local market. Then there are the fellow freaks who are trying to sell you something. This could be a philosophic or religious idea. They have studied a particular subject, and if it works for them, it should work for you ("Taoism is like a Hoover vacuum cleaner, it sweeps up everything in its path"). They are spreading the "good news" gospel. I learned a great deal about important issues this way. I think my time with Don walking all night in Taipei (because they closed our hotel) was one of the richest experiences I have ever had on the road. But it wasn't friendship; it was a teacher/student lecture/discussion.

One of my best friends on the road was the English guy, Dave. We spent about a month together in Malaysia, and we could talk about anything, stoned or not. He had a great sardonic sense of humor, "India is the only place in the world where shit grows on houses." (In reference to the Indian villages where cow dung is made into paddies and stuck on house walls to dry and later be used as cooking fuel.) We shared the same goals (or lack thereof, since we got stoned together quite a bit) and were always there for each other.

He was slowly making his way to Australia for a new life but took the time to "smell the roses" (in his case, it was "inhale the dope"). He was open to new experiences but shy about what he really wanted out of life. We never "unburdened our souls" to each other, perhaps because that wasn't the "manly" thing to do. "Life is hard; you take the punches it gives you and then move on. Don't get all mushy about it."

Why is it that I will tell a strange girl whom I've known for two days my innermost desires and fears and not share them with a guy that I have known on a daily basis for over a month?

Ego and an aversion to appearing weak in another's eyes or even finding the right words to express secret fears or vulnerabilities created a silent barrier we never tried to breach. So, we took the easy way out and got stoned.

Traveling with chicks, straight or freak.

"Just you and me, kid against the world": A perfect HALLMARK moment

(Photo by Louise Burton on UNSPLASH)

Traveling with chicks is a whole other ball game (not like baseball, but more like throwing the "unspun stone"). There is always that unspoken tension of "will I sleep with this one?" And that affects "pure" friendship. Even if you're not attracted to your female companion, the sweaty closeness, the sensitivity of observations, and the give-and-take of frustrating daily travel all affect your attitude toward her. Being stoned only amplifies all of the above. "She chose you to travel with; what are you waiting for, boy?" If you don't have sex, you become critical of her faults and idiosyncrasies. You say to yourself, "Why am I putting up with this shit? I'm better off alone." So. you end up going your separate ways after a time.

If you do have sex, you are now a "couple" with all of the petty domestic grievances that come with it. The upside is that now you have a "shared vision", and hopefully, you become less selfish and more concerned about each other's wellbeing. Isn't sharing your experiences why you're traveling in the first place? She gives you different viewpoints, and thought-provoking insights, and you can articulate your innermost feelings without any sense of nervousness or subterfuge with someone you care about.

On the downside, you now "possess" her; you become jealous if she leaves you out of any interaction with other travelers. You wall yourself off from others, suffocating your openness: "This is our world to discover; everyone else, get out!" Sex becomes a refuge, not a joy.

This leads to the premarital trap: either you or she have found your "soulmate". You, for your part, want to bring her back to the States. She's the "Image of a girl you've always missed", the one you were always searching for. You want to introduce her to your mother ("I just know you two will get along, you have the same hobby, collecting Bakelite radios"). "You'll love Gary, Indiana, once you get used to the factory smells, black dust, and crime. I'll show you my favorite bowling alley, and we'll eat in the best Diner outside of New Jersey."

She, for her part, sees you as serious, adventuresome, and cultivated, "You had the balls to come to Asia alone to rescue me from that horrible French junkie". You are not like the party drunks and stuck-up jocks going nowhere that she slept with in the "Animal House" university she went to. She thinks to herself, "He may be a little wild, but I can tame that. I know he will look great in a wedding tux; once we cut his hair and shave his beard. My dad will get him a job in his factory, {"Helium, my boy, is an "expanding" industry and a real "gas" to be around"} I'll be the envy of all my girlfriends. I do hope I don't get another lousy fondue set for a wedding gift. I can't wait to buy that house of my dreams (Oh daddy dear, you promised me!) in Shaker Heights and start having our 2.5 kids".

Chapter Sixty-Eight: Dinner and A Movie

"Movies": Weyes Blood

This song satirizes our love of movies. We have no real individual feelings that can compare to feelings we see and vicariously experience on the "big screen".

Malaysia is a collection of small colorful towns and beautiful tropical beaches. Most towns have a movie theatre, and after a succulent dinner of fried rice with pork (Chinese), sizzling shish kebob in coconut sauce (Malay), or fiery lamb vindaloo (Tamil Indian), you could either get stoned and lay out on a beach, watching the stars and surf or get stoned and see a movie. My friend Dave from Manchester, whom I traveled with, enjoyed movies, so it's on to the big show (We have a "really big shew" tonight, folks).

We tried Malay soap operas and comedies, but most didn't have subtitles, so we had to make up the dialog. This was great fun for us. I taught Dave the comedic skit "John and Marsha". Dave played John, and I was Marsha. For a dramatic scene, where the woman confronts her husband over a suspected infidelity: "John!!" "Marsha?"

And for the tender love scene: "Oh…John" "Oh…Marsha".

However, the Malay theatergoers didn't quite see the humor in this (too droll, I suppose) and constantly "Shh…ed" us until we shut up. We endured the rest of this potboiler in bored silence, "Johnn…" "Marshaa…" (zzzzzzzz).

We then tried Indian films, mostly romantic song and dance comedies. Boy falls for girl; the girl is forbidden to see the boy by parents because the boy is poor. The boy is given fortune by a rich uncle; the boy gets girl after many boring adventures and song and dance interruptions. These movies were subtitled in English, but the acting, plot, and comic scenes were terrible. Even the song and dance routines couldn't save these turgid, lovestruck melodramas. You needed a double shot of hash just to sit through these insipid love stories (which, of course, had no sex, maybe a brief kiss at the end).

Speaking of sex, I remembered the first pornographic film I ever saw in Europe: a supposedly sex education film from Sweden called "I Am Curious Yellow". It was in Swedish, and the subtitles were in Dutch and French, but you didn't really need dialog to enjoy the film. Watching this blond vixen romping from one sexual position to another was very, very educational; I even took notes. You know I will be tested on this subject matter, and this will go on my permanent record!

Poster for the film "Sword Master" 2016

So, we finally discovered Chinese swordplay movies, and we were instantly hooked. The movies were like old-time American westerns. A typical plot: the town is held by bad guys, who threaten the heroine, and in walks (there are no horses here), the hero. He goes to the local tavern and proceeds to get drunk, observing how the bad guys control the village and threaten to deflower the local damsel in distress. There is usually some comic relief from the bumbling bar owner, but the film gets right down to action, usually a tavern fight that is destroyed in the foray, while the hero dispatches the lackeys of the Big Boss. The Big Boss then brings in all his big guns (swords in this case) for a showdown in the OK town square (remember, there are no cattle or horses in the movie). The hero again defeats the bad guys with amazing, flying-through-the-air sword feats. Finally, there is a climatic showdown where the Big Boss has kidnapped the clueless damsel, and the hero dramatically kills the Big Boss (in three-part harmony) and frees the maiden. He then walks off alone into the sunset, without even kissing the dewy-eyed heroine ("Just doing my job, Mam"). All that was missing was a cute little Chinese boy, at the end of the movie, crying, "Shane Yu, please come back!"

There was one hero in these sword epics that stood out: a tall, good-looking Chinese actor named Wang Yu, and his story follows.

Chapter Sixty-Nine: Wang Yu

"Everybody was kung fu fighting. Those cats were fast as lightning"

"Kung Fu Fighting": Carl Douglas

I was searching through the used VHS tapes at my local thrift store in New York in the 1970s when I came upon a copy of "The One-Armed Swordsman" from 1967 starring Wang Yu. Instantly, I was transported back to Malaysia and those stoned nights when I would be enthralled by the sword and Kung Fu epics of Wang Yu.

"The One-Armed Swordsman" started a whole new action genre for Hong Kong cinema and was the first film to make over $1,000,000 Hong Kong dollars, in no small part to the charismatic acting and handsome persona of Wang Yu and the direction of Chang Cheh. Before this, Hong Kong films in the 1950s and 60s were domestic soap operas and romantic comedies. Wang Yu started a whole new stereotype for an action hero: a man of few words, a Gary Cooper type, who wasn't looking for a fight but don't get him started. The sword scenes were pure poetry in motion (Norse sagas in this instance): acrobatic moves and lots of blood and guts.

Wang Yu went on to make many other films for Hong Kong filmmakers The Shaw Brothers and the director Chang Cheh. In 1970 he started another genre of action films where fists were used instead of swords, based on Shaolin Martial Arts. "The Chinese Boxer" and "The One-Armed Boxer" were smash hits and paved the way for future superstars like Bruce Lee and Jackie Chan.

After the success of "The One-Armed Boxer", Wang Yu broke his contract with the Shaw Brothers and lost the battle in court. He then moved to Taiwan to continue making movies under his own direction. Wang Yu knew how to make lively action films, and he even collaborated with Japanese cinema makers. Here it was Chinese versus Japanese martial artists who fought to the death, with the Chinese beating the crap out of the Japanese, of course.

One of his best movies was "Beach of the War Gods", which was a loosely remade version of "The Seven Samurai". However, it has a spectacular fight scene where Wang Yu and his merry band battles an entire Japanese army and saves the day (and all of China) in a patriotic twist of the original samurai movie.

He also broke the mold of the virtuous hero in Chinese cinema by playing bad guy roles and a vicious criminal in another film. Wang Yu made over 60 films in his career and was the best of these heroic swordsmen and kung fu artists, and I must have seen all of his "epics." He had a great following and a huge fan club and was the most popular hero in Chinese movies until another handsome man, this time a Chinese American named Bruce Lee, blew everyone away with his Kung Fu action movies.

Happy trails to you, Wang Yu!

Wang Yu in 1970

Thailand III

Reclining Buddha Bangkok

Chapter Seventy: Taxi Dancing

"Taxi Dancing": Rick Springfield with Randy Crawford

Movie Lobby Card of the 1927 film "The Taxi Dancer"

Phuket island is an unspoiled postcard beach paradise: smiling fishermen, young children waving and yelling good-natured "Falang" (foreigner), and a "hippie falang" at that. Quiet villages with fine featured women in sarongs, the ever-present water buffalo lounging under huge banyan trees, and the one size fits all school children with their regimented bowl haircut and standard uniform: both boys and girls dressed in white shirts and blue pants or skirts.

Dave and I rented an oceanfront bungalow, the water thirty feet away, and this gave us a constant, cooling breeze that saved us from the heat of the Thai summer. We rented bicycles and visited the beaches: Patong had a bad undertow (not the best when you are stoned), and Haarsurin had very rough waves; the one we liked best was Rawai. This beach had golden sand and gentle surf and looked out on small green islands dotted with sleepy fishing villages and gold-spired, whitewashed wats.

Hitching a ride in Phuket is like a scene from a slapstick movie. I was heading to visit a beautiful waterfall: first, I got a lift from a Thai Road Repair Truck, and next a young Thai picked me up on his bicycle. Lastly, a friendly motorcyclist took me all the way. Every day we had schoolchildren following us, laughing and shouting, "Falang-what is your name- where are you going?" Every night we had the Milky Wave to guide us home, swimming in calm inlets at midnight and waking at noon to hauntingly plaintive Thai music.

Dave and I spent an afternoon in Phuket city, a mainly Chinese city with many joss houses. A joss house is a colonial term for a Chinese temple and refers to the joss (incense) sticks or candles that are burned during religious services. This is another success story, very similar to the Overseas Chinese in Malaysia: poor Chinese came from the mainland to work in the tin mines and rubber plantations. They saved up, and the next generation started small shops and restaurants; they re-invested their monies, and the third generation started banks and small factories. Now they control most of the businesses, real estate, and entertainment venues and built beautiful Taoist and Confucian temples all over Thailand.

While eating dinner in a small Chinese restaurant, we were befriended by a young Thai man, Sarin. He told us he was 36 years old, had two wives, and was a dance instructor. He wanted to talk to us to improve his English and acquire friends to visit if he ever came to the States. He bought us a round of coconut toddy and proposed that we all go to a Thai Dance Hall.

The Dance Hall was the size of an American high school gymnasium, with small tables set around a huge well-lit ballroom. As you entered, you had to buy tickets, five baht each, which you would use to dance with a young Thai girl. The music was blaring out from huge speakers, and the girls sat primly, with numbers on their blouses in bleacher seats. Boys and young men would ask a young girl for a dance, giving her a ticket for each dance. The dancers were very proficient in mambo, rumba, cha cha cha, merengue, and rock and roll. Since our host was a dance instructor, he strutted his stuff, and the girls he chose complimented him perfectly. I picked a girl for a cha cha (the only Latin dance I knew), and she did her best to follow my two left feet. It was great fun, and I really got into it when they played rock and roll. She followed my "jitterbug" flawlessly and didn't even break a sweat while I was drenched in perspiration. Everyone had a great time, fueled by bottles of Singha beer. We stayed for about two hours, and then Sarin took us to a darkly lit nightclub. Here we had live music: a Chinese girls' band that belted out rock and roll, alternating with two Thai singers that sang everything from fast Latin songs to touching "torch" numbers.

The nightclub had beautiful "hostesses" whose main job was to have us buy drinks for them; dancing was secondary. Here we met a rich old Chinese banker. He claimed to own two Mercedes, have 13 children, and is president of a large bank in town. He bought us all drinks and he spoke excellent English. I discussed politics, local economics, and traveling with him. He was lively and witty, even making a cutting jibe at Sarin for having a second (illegal) wife. We were pretty plastered when we said we had to get back; he graciously gave us a lift in one of his Mercedes.

We were sitting and smoking, viewing the incoming tide; I thought about the dance hall and my home city. New York City had over a hundred "Taxi" halls, patronized by 40,000 lonely single men weekly at the height of the Great Depression. They were called "Taxi" halls because they charged 10 cents a dance, the same starting price for a NYC taxicab. Here too, you bought your tickets at the entrance, and the girls all had numbers that you picked for a dance. The girls were usually young; some left broken homes, and others were young divorcees. The "taxi" dancer received half of the ticket price, and if she was pretty and light on her feet, she could make two to three times more than a factory or department shop girl would earn as a daily wage. They lived in apartments with three or four other "taxi" girls and were generally "good" girls, not prostitutes, but girls that wanted excitement and something different out of life. The customers ran the gamut from "green" country boys to out-of-town salesmen to lonely single immigrants. During World War II, NYC was full of soldiers and sailors that sought fun and friendship from the dancers. The management of the halls forbade the dancers from making dates, but many gals and guys ignored this rule.

Hollywood recognized this phenomenon, churning out potboilers like "Ten Cents a Dance" starring Barbara Stanwyck, "The Taxi Dancer" starring Joan Crawford, and a gem of film noir, "Deadline at Dawn" starring Susan Hayward as a "taxi" dancer that helps clear a sailor of murder and finds in him a husband for her troubles.

"Taxi Dancers" in New York City 1938

"Taxi" dancers declined in the 1950s; eligible girls married returning soldiers and sailors, and many halls were closed by indignant politicians, who looked at them as "dens of iniquity". By the early 1960's they were all gone in New York City, the same fate that befell our beloved and unique Automat cafeterias.

Chapter Seventy-One: Paradise Regained

Paradise Regained

By one man's disobedience lost, now sing
Recover'd Paradise to all mankind,
By <u>one man's firm obedience</u> fully tri'd
Through all temptation, and the Tempter foil'd [5]
In all his wiles, defeated and repuls't,
And *Eden* rais'd <u>in the wast</u> Wilderness.

John Milton "Paradise Regained" Book 1

Koh Samui Island

How do you define Paradise? Since the etymology of the word is Persian, we should first see what Islam says: the Muslim depiction of Paradise would be shaded gardens, bubbling fountains, and beautiful women as a reward for the good. Muslims believe that this verdant garden is also the original Garden of Eden. And the quote from John Milton states that Jesus Christ will make a new Eden or Paradise in the "wast Wilderness". We in the modern West see a beautiful golden beach, balmy breeze swaying coconut palms, peaceful animals lying languidly and happy, smiling native peoples, and we say this is Paradise; when in reality, this is just our idea of a perfect vacation destination, this "Peaceable Kingdom" of Hick's painting, a timeshare for two weeks out of our busy schedule.

As a freak traveler, things that are beautiful are magnified with "things go better with Coke" (the drug, not the soft drink). We have the luxury of losing ourselves completely in the beauty that surrounds us. We are Taoists, at one with nature, communing with the cosmos. Yet, we are selfish; we want to all to ourselves, to say we discovered this (Bali without the freak circus and expensive five-star hotels). It is pristine solitude that we seek, not the "Coney Island of the Mind". And we want it on the cheap: look, I only spent 25 cents a night for my room or 35 cents for a complete fresh fish dinner. Paradise is only Paradise if we can get it half off.

We decided to go to Koh Samui Island because it was a New World, to feel the excitement of discovery, like the crew of the "Half Moon" vessel, seeing that first "green spit of Manhattan Island" after months of seeing only endless stretches of steel gray ocean, as Fitzgerald so memorably wrote. And Koh Samui was a postcard paradise when we arrived at 6 AM, after an all-night ferry trip: endless coconut groves, verdant green vegetation, and friendly people.

We walked into the main town as the sun was rising. There was a line of yellow-robed monks with shaved heads, sitting with their tin cups out, begging for their breakfast. I gave one a few baht, and after asking for a hotel, he directed us to a small Chinese hotel in the center of the town. The town consists of mostly wooden buildings and a muddy thoroughfare, which led to the main outdoor market, now open for business. We passed mangy dogs and women carrying huge bundles of produce. We bought rambutans, rice cakes and beer for our first meal, the "breakfast of champions". We explored the village, coconuts piled high next to every dwelling, and visited an old weather-beaten wat. Here we met an old monk that spoke fluent English, and we talked about Buddhism and where to go on the island. We walked to a rocky beach and sat smoking grass, watching the fisherman casting their nets in crystal clear waters, the horizon dotted with coconut-covered green specks of islands.

The second day we started walking around the island, dirt roads, small villages with one-table cafes, coconuts piled everywhere, and fishing boats awash on the sand at low tide. We passed a school, and the children were dumbfounded at seeing falangs (foreigners). Yet they still waved and laughingly called out "hello". There were kids playing a soccer game, and my friend Dave joined in; they weren't afraid, and he had fun keeping up with the swift teens. Back at the hotel, we met the owner's son, who spoke good English. I was smoking an Indonesian kretek cigarette (The cloves in the tobacco crackle like grass seeds), and he thought I was smoking ganja. He wanted to smoke, so I rolled a joint, and he ran out (I was a little paranoid that he might bring the Thai cops. But I continued smoking {can't waste good dope}); zap, he shows up holding a 38-caliber pistol.

"It's all over now, Baby Blue", the headline reads: "Ex-GI Captain gets year in Thai jail for smoking marijuana". But he just wanted to show off his weapon: we all had a good laugh and got stoned together. Time stopped (or I should say it had no relevance, we followed the rhythm of life where there is the all-pervading present, no past or future, only the now) as we swam in crystal blue waters, smoked good dope, and ate exotic fruits. We visited a beautiful waterfall, swimming in the small lake beneath, letting the rushing cold-water cascade over us. Here we met some Thai teens that had killed a large lizard with their slingshots. They showed us around, passing wild fruit trees laden with ripe papayas, rambutans, and hanging durians. I remembered the vacation I had with my family to Florida: my mom always wanted to see wild orange and grapefruit trees growing in the Everglades. So, I arranged an outing, and we walked in the tropical forest until we found a few trees bearing the fruit; I was paranoid that we would stumble onto alligators or poisonous snakes, but she trampled on ahead, unafraid until we found the wild, fruit-laden trees. I was happy for her that she got her "bucket list" adventure accomplished. (When we got back, the real action adventure began: scrambling for the smorgasbord goodies at the 4-star hotel luncheon- women and children off the lifeboat).

The next day we hitched to the other side of the island. We stayed on a white sand beach, swimming near some Thai fishermen who were pulling in their catch.

We ate at a small café and met a funny old fisherman who spoke no English but insisted on treating us to a strong Thai arrack whiskey. We shared our Thai cigarettes and drank arrack; he amused himself looking through the zoom lens of my camera. We had been in Ko Sumi for three weeks and finally had to leave this Lotus Land: Dave had to get back to Bangkok, and I needed to check on my Indian visa. As the ferry departed, I felt like a wrathful God had kicked us out of Eden: however, maybe the next Paradise we encounter will have beautiful maidens at our beck and call.

Chapter Seventy-Two: Koh Siracha: Sheep And A Tall Buddha

Photo by Andrea Lightfoot (UNSPLASH)

Bangkok had the usual desultory drug scene: "Yea, man, did you go somewhere? I don't get out much. This shit is soo good!" And that was a long, meaningful conversation! The other freaks we knew were just nodding off in their private reveries.

Since I had a week before leaving for India, Dave and I decided to visit another paradisical island, Koh Siracha (it was either that or get a new pet rock to talk to).

We took a small ferry to the island and wandered around until we found a wat to stay in. The monks were friendly and gave us a private room with straw mats to sleep on. We ate food with them, and at night, one of the monks brought out a guitar, and we sang American and Thai folk songs.

The monastery is picturesquely set on a small mountain overlooking the surrounding sea: its claim to fame is that it has a sacred footprint of the Buddha.

Buddha must have been a pretty tall guy since his footprint was about fifteen feet in length (Ho, Ho, Ho, said the Jolly Green Giant Buddha).

We wandered around the rocky landscape and encountered dozens of herds of domesticated sheep (with all these sheep and no women, I could now understand why the ancient Greeks were tempted). I was beginning to look at these animals in a whole new way; there was this chunky mottled white and black alpha female that was starting to appeal to me.

We found a still beach, bought a durian from a local stall, and sat on the sand eating durian and smoking Sumatra grass. Time again seemed to stand still; Dave spoke heartfully about Australia- he had worked as an auto mechanic back in England, and he was good with his hands, so he might try some other job. We spoke of the Aussies we met traveling, and they all seemed friendly and outgoing. I tried to reassure him, telling him that he was heading out to new territories and remaking himself into whatever he wanted. Besides, there would always be opportunities for someone like him, who could roll a tightly packed joint in under sixty seconds.

We stumbled up small hills and continued our wandering until we came across this beautiful crumbling teak palace, now deserted, with gardens overgrown with heavy vegetation. The outdoor staircases were overgrown with strangler vines, but we climbed up and looked inside. There was a vast ballroom with rounded wood columns. I imagined this palace in its heyday: banquet tables laden with food, the king sitting on a high throne and delicate Thai women performing a royal dance, accompanied by a full orchestra. We walked around the building and met a solitary monk coming out of a large tree overgrown wat. He didn't speak much English, but made it known to us that this was a summer palace of King Chulalongkorn, who reigned over a hundred years ago. We asked him why the palace was deserted, but he didn't know. He had been the caretaker there for over a decade and never had any royal visitors.

We walked back to our "footprint" monastery and ate with the monks. The next few days, we found other beaches and swam in the still waters. We were befriended by three young fishermen, who turned us on to their local "Buddha grass", smoking from a bong (bamboo pipe), sitting in a little tin sheeted house on the beach, just groovin' with them. I felt "Ten Miles High"; I could now see how Buddha got so tall.

The last day we spent on a beautiful beach. The warm sun, cool breeze, and absolute quietude gave me the sensation that this was before time. The God of "Genesis" had made this pristine world and saw that it was good, and then He rested.

Chapter Seventy-Three: The Continuing Adventures Of Flash Gordon

Ming the Merciless in "Flash Gordon Conquers the Universe"

Ming: What do you mean? You destroyed the wrong planet?

Scientist: Ahh... Yes. Both Earth and Venus look alike, covered in clouds. I destroyed Venus by mistake. I'll do better next time, I promise.

Ming: Guards, take this fool away, execute him and bring me a competent scientist to fulfill my mission!

(The two steel helmeted guards were rejected for the role of the "Tinman" in the "Wizard of Oz", which was shooting at another studio down the street, and this was the only acting job they could get.)

Narrator: Well, boys and girls, we are leaving Flash Gordon at a critical moment. Ming the Merciless has a new and improved Death Ray (this one runs on "Energized Bunny" batteries) now aimed at Earth. Doctor Zarkov has been given a mind-altering drug by a Ming Secret Agent, and all he does is skip around the laboratory and sing "Tiptoe Through the Tulips" over and over. Dale Arden has the "vapors" (a Victorian euphemism for her period) and is indisposed with cramps ("It only hurts when I laugh".) Flash, even though he is now a Pod freak, must pull himself together to battle Ming alone ("Wow! That's far out, man! Do I get to use a ray gun?")

Armed with only a camera and a notebook (plus a bottle of Johnny Walker Red Label to sell on the Black Market), Flash boards a new spacecraft for India, where Ming is raising an army of Goddess Kali assassins. Will Flash defeat the evil Ming and save Earth? Stay tuned; you can find out in Volume III ("From Stoner to Seeker"), coming soon in glorious black and white.

The Continuing Adventures of Flash Gordon…Flash: "Golly, that's so cool! But is there a comic book version?"

I will leave you now, wishing you "Happy Trails" (in three part harmony) and ending with the same quote I used in my first book, "Soldier to Sojourner: The Journal", which has become my personal favorite advice for everyone: never forget the immortal words of the mad scientist, Dr. Emilo Lizardo in "The Adventures of Buckaroo Banzai," "Laugh a while you can, Monkey Boy."

Bibliography

A Quirky, opinionated, and annotated Bibliography

"And now you know the rest of the story," Paul Harvey, American radio political commentator.

For a general introduction to Southeast Asia, I recommend "A Short History of Southeast Asia" by Peter Church (2017, the sixth revision). However, my favorite one volume description of Southeast Asia in the 60s and 70s is the Time-Life "Southeast Asia" by Stanley Karnow, which was written in 1967. This slim volume gives you all the colorful personalities, the varied religions, the traditional way of life and the arts of the individual countries. It has as well beautiful photography showing the pictorial spender of Southeast Asia: the beautiful beaches, majestic mountains, colorful cities and interesting customs. This book is out of print now, but you can usually find a copy on eBay or if you are lucky, in the book bin of your local thrift store.

This bibliography will be different from your standard bibliography in that I try to reference material relevant to the 1970s and 80s; the exception to this would be some of the economic books I recommend which describes the economic miracle and how it developed in the 70s and 80s coming finally to fruition in the early 21st century. This is also true for biographies which start in the 60s and 70s or earlier and end up in the 2000s or beyond.

For current information on a particular country, I am a great believer in travel guides and heartily recommend "The Lonely Planet" guides in each of the countries I traveled to. These are "meat and potatoes" (hold the potatoes) main course books, chock full of historical, political, and social references, as well as describing all the must-see (and the not-so-must-see) attractions, usually with a wry sense of humor. The best cultural guides are the "Blue Guides" series which go into excruciating detail on the monuments and ancient cities, with detailed maps and planned itineraries. The last two series of travel books, "Insight" and "DK" Guides give you a photograph, drawing, or old print of the temple, shrine or city they are describing in words. I will also recommend select guidebooks that capture the particular "Zeitgeist" of a country and its people.

For in-depth history and culture of a country, I have a cherished eleventh edition of the Encyclopedia Britannica (1911) (Frederick Jackson Turner did the part on American history, John Muir on the scenic beauty of the American wilderness, and Bertrand Russell and T. H. Huxley did articles on philosophy). I must also mention my constant, faithful companion that I carried throughout my wanderings (like Alexander the Great with his well-worn copy of the "Iliad"): "Golden Guide to Asia". This little red book was my perennial inspiration (and many times my pillow) on my journey and still has an enduring influence on me and occupies first place on my bookshelf.

As far as the songs I cite at the beginning of many of my chapters; they can all be listened to on "YouTube". I implore you also to listen to a Balinese gamelan recording, traditional Thai, Malay and Indonesian music, and Southeast Asian popular music on this resourceful venue. As for the photographs, drawings, prints, and cultural artifacts that I have embedded in my journal, the majority were found on Wikimedia Commons, which gives legal justification for Creative Commons Share-Alike licenses and public domain for usage and UNSPLASH, which has free photographs to use copyright free if you are a member. For the other images, I have done my best to get "creative common" or fair usage justifications, citing the author or organization that holds the copyright and proper licensing rights. If I missed any attribution, I sincerely apologize to the owner of the image that I used. There is a complete picture index below with all licensing approvals. I have not included any cookbooks or recipes on the food I have described because any exotic dish preparation can be found in easy-to-follow steps on food channels or "YouTube" videos. I have annotated with my two-cent comments on many of the books, magazines, newspapers, and videos that I have read on a particular topic or important issue that merits further investigation. I further divided the bibliography by country, giving general books on individual countries and then in-depth studies on my select issues. Enough of this: all of the above sounds better given by a fast-talking lawyer rapidly going through the disclaimers. "The Really Big Shew Must Go On"

LAOS

An Ordinary Life in Laos

"Before I Became A Refugee Girl" by Samly Matt

This is a story of life in rural Laos before and after the communist takeover in 1975. The book details the experiences of a young girl that grew up in that era and became a refugee from the communist regime.

The Deep CIA State

For the secret war waged by the CIA against the Pathet Lao communists dating back to the late 1950s see "Perilous Missions: Civil Air Transport and CIA Covert Operations in Asia" by W.M. Leary (2006)

An American Hero

Doctor Thomas Dooley wrote two books on Laos, "The Edge of Tomorrow" and "The Night They Burned The Mountain ", concentrating on the Hmong hill people and his struggles to build clinics and hospitals to service these independent tribes' people. These are highly recommended, and they give you a real flavor of the times, which was the middle1960s. I deal with Doctor Dooley more fully in my chapter on him, citing his accomplishments and legacy in this Journal.

Colonial Indochina

To trace Laos's roots in the French colonial period, the best detailed book is "Indochina: An Ambiguous Colonization 1858 to 1954 Volume II" by Pierre Brocheux and Daniel Hemery. This gives an in-depth background to why the French wanted so desperately to hold on to Southeast Asian colonies which resulted in their ignominious defeat at the Dien Bien Phu in 1954.

Southeast Asia Wars

To realize how we Americans did not learn from the mistakes that the French made in Indochina, I highly recommend "Street Without Joy: The French Debacle in Indochina" by Bernard Fall (1961). We fought and lost the Vietnam War the same way the French did a decade earlier.

Off to the Movies

The last reference would be a movie, "Air America" starring Mel Gibson. Here you get the Zeitgeist and the senseless carnage of the CIA American air campaign against the peoples of Laos.

THAILAND

For the general historical background "A Brief History of Thailand" by Richard Ruth will give you all the thumbnail information you need to understand a lot of what I wrote about Thailand in my Journal.

I was especially enamored by the different faces of Buddha based on the historical period in which they were created. An excellent scholarly book about this is "Origins of Thai Art" by Betty Gosling (2004). A similar book with excellent photographs of the different styles of the faces of the Buddha is "Images of the Buddha in Thailand" by Dorothy Fickle (1989). In both of these books you see how the Buddha image in Thailand was influenced by conquerors, traders and Western culture.

Chiang Mai ("I left My Heart in Chiang Mai")

Lonely Planet's "Thailand" has a detailed section on this magical city. You might also want to get a Thai perspective on this city: "Tour Siam/Chiang Mai: The Basic Travel Guide "by Mon Monn. This is only available in Kindle format.

The "Economic Miracle"

As far as the economic growth of Thailand, this is covered along with the other Southeast Asian countries in "Southeast Asia's Economy: Development Policies in the 1970s" by Uttia Mayiat. Thailand is an interesting case study because they have developed a thriving tourist industry as opposed to a heavy industrial (aka, Japan) economy. For example, Bangkok is the number one shopping destination for well-heeled Chinese to purchase electronic and consumer goods. Thailand beaches and resorts are internationally famous, and their farm products are exported all over the world.

Thailand also has an international sex industry which has enriched certain sections of the Thai economy. The sex industry is chronicled by Jonathan Finch in a light and informative way: "Sexy Thai Bar Girls and Me: Sex Adventures in Asia (2016). This is not your usual travelogue to say the least.

MALAYSIA

For general background, "Crossroads: A Popular history of Malaysia and Singapore" by Jim Baker (2022) is a good background book.

Penang and Malacca

I was fascinated by two cities in Malaysia: the first was Georgetown in Penang, which is a British colonial gem that has been lovingly preserved. Penang is an excellent walking city where you can imbibe the cultures of the Chinese, the Malays and Tamil Indians. For this you should pick up "Capturing Penang (A Walkaround Photo Guide)" by James Dugan (2020).

The second city is Malacca and this city is done justice by "The Story of Malacca" by Alein G Moore. This book goes into the history, the interaction of the cultures, the creation of a distinct language spoken by the Chinese settlers, the beautiful Gold Coast mansions of the enterprising Chinese, the colorful port and a fossil Portuguese culture dating back 400 years kept alive by the descendants of the mixed-race Portuguese and local nationals. He also discusses the food and particular ambience of this unique city. I have seen many extraordinary places in my travels, but Malacca has to be one of my favorite places of all time.

The "Economic Miracle"

An excellent book on the economics of how all the countries in Southeast Asia prospered is "How Asia Works" by Joe Studwell (a founder of the "China Economic Review") which was written in 2014. However. it goes back to the 70s and 80s and contrasts the different countries and how they achieved varying degrees of success in the "Economic Miracle" which swept through Southeast Asia in the 1990s and 2000s.

Overseas Chinese

No history of the region would be complete without the story of the Overseas Chinese in Southeast Asia, who were responsible for building the economies of the various nations they settled in. There are two books that I can recommend: "China and the Overseas Chinese and Southeast Asia" by Teresa Chong Carino and "Merchant Princes of the East: Cultural Delusions, Economic Success and the Overseas Chinese in Southeast Asia" by Rupert Hodder. The Overseas Chinese were like the poor Jewish immigrants coming to America; they had almost nothing and they wound up with it all, controlling large industries, banks, small mom and pop stores and on the darker side the opium trade of Asia. Both books make fascinating reading to see how these poor immigrants developed, becoming administers for the British and other European colony overlords and then developing the local industries of the respective countries they were in.

Architecture

A fascinating sidebar to the Overseas Chinese if you are interested in architecture is "Chinese Houses of Southeast Asia: The Eclectic Architecture of Sojourners and Settlers" by Ronald G Knapp and A. Chester Ong. Here you can see the beautiful mansions that the nouveau-rich Chinese built in the late 19th century and early 20th century all over Southeast Asia in beautiful glossy photos- a great coffee table book.

SINGAPORE

If you subscribe to the great man theory of history, then you will see that Singapore is the product of two extraordinary men: the founder: Stamford Raffles and the present ruler of Singapore: Lee Kuan Yew. These two men single-handedly did more than anyone to make Singapore one of the most fascinating and commercially successful cities in the world

The standard history of Singapore, which has gone through three revisions since being published in 1977 is "A History of Modern Singapore 1819- 2005" by Constance Turnball.

I would recommend after this book to read a biography of Stamford Raffles. Raffles was a "renaissance man": an excellent administrator, a respected historian, a collector of Asian artifacts, a botanist and a discoverer and preserver of Indonesia's ancient Buddhist monument of Borobudur. "Sir Stamford Raffles" by Hugh Egerton is a standard biography and out of print but is available FREE on The Guttenberg Project.

After the independence of Malaysia from Great Britain, which included Singapore in 1963, the Overseas Chinese we're persecuted and harassed by the majority Muslim Malay government. They formed their own political party to assert Chinese rights in Malaysia. The Malaysians were afraid of the Chinese influence and mustered enough votes to expel Singapore from Malaysia in 1965. Yew was head of this Chinese party and he single handedly developed a plan to enable Singapore not only to survive, but to thrive and become a world class international city. There is no better history of that exciting times then in Yew's autobiography: "From Third World to First: The Singapore Story: 1965- 2005". Here we see a genius of urban planning, a skilled administrator, an adroit diplomat and premier "snake oil" salesman to bring the world to Singapore, while uplifting the common man of Singapore out of poverty.

BORNEO

White Rajah

Malaysian Borneo or Sarawak is the story of one unique family spanning three generations: The Brooke Family. The book "White Rajah: A Biography of Sir James Brooke" by Nigel Barley (2002) details how James Brooke was able to gain control of a huge part of Borneo and how his family, through good governing and respect for native traditions and lifestyle, kept control of Sarawak for over a century. We as Americans can look back at our sorry history of how we dealt with our native Indian population in contrast with enlightened policies of the Brooke family.

Headhunters

For an early 20th century chronicle of the Dayak people there is a 1927 book called "Borneo Jungles: Among the Dayak Headhunters" by a physician named William Crone. This was written when the Dayak culture was still vibrant and there were headhunters among some of the tribes in Borneo.

Life in a Longhouse

I remember as a college student reading "Life in a Longhouse" by Hedda Morrison (1962) and was enthralled by the descriptions of the self-sustaining simple lifestyle of the Dayak peoples. We were lucky in our time in Borneo to see the Dayaks creating their beautiful weavings. I highly recommend this book for anyone who intends to travel to Borneo. I understand that you can now stay in an air-conditioned longhouse and experience first-hand the disappearing culture of the Dayak people. It would be interesting to see how the Dayaks evolved in the half century since I visited the region.

The Exploitation and Destruction of the Dayak Lifestyle

There is another book that is extremely important in the history of Borneo and that is "The Last Wildman of Borneo" by Carl Hoffman. This was written in 2019; however, it deals with two people in the early 80s: Bruno Manser was self-made ecologist and amateur anthropologist that tried to preserve the ancient way of Dayak life in the Indonesian Kalimantan part of Borneo. Here the Indonesian government has deforested this pristine paradise to plant hundreds of thousands of acres of palm oil trees for export dollars. This is also contrasted with the second main character in the book: Michael Palmaria. This American draft-dodger made his fortune buying original artifacts and art of the Dayak people and selling them to collectors and museums worldwide. The contrast of these two men makes fascinating reading and tells us something about our ambivalent reactions as westerners to an unspoiled primitive culture.

Travel Literature

The last book that I would recommend is by one of my favorite travel writers Eric Hansen, a fellow New Yorker who wrote "Stranger in the Forest" about his walking through all of Borneo and the fascinating tribes and unique cultures that he meets on his journey. Hansen and Bruce Chatwin are, in my opinion, the two best travel writers of the late 20th century and still relevant in the early 21st century.

INDONESIA

Cultural and Historical Background

"A Brief History of Indonesia" by Tim Hannigan is a good introduction, but an even better introduction is the travel book which is a veritable Bible of what Indonesia is and this is as interesting as any personal travelogue: "Indonesian Handbook" (Moon Guide 1989) by Bill Dalton. This is an Indonesia guide by a man that ate, slept, and devoted years of his life to chronicling Indonesia and his love of this country stands out in this excellent travel guide.

Sukarno

No history of Indonesia can be understood without studying the enigmatic first leader of Indonesia: Sukarno. Like all great men he was flawed, but his vision of an independent Indonesia, not beholding to communist Russia nor capitalist America was a dream that was never realized. Whatever his faults, Sukarno kept this thousand island nation together and proud to be Indonesian. There are many biographies of Sukarno; the one that I would recommend is "Sukarno: A Political Biography" by J.D. Legge (1972) written two years after Sukarno's death. This is "the big picture" portrait of the man: his fight for independence, his time in jail for subversion against the Dutch, his collaboration with the Japanese to build up his army, his victorious independence war against the Dutch and his successful effort to unify the country and finally, his ignominious fall after the failed communist uprising of 1965.

Borobudur

If you cannot travel to Indonesia to experience one of the world's greatest monuments: Borobudur, then you should find a good photo book which goes into the history and shows the beauty and monumentality of this great shrine. Borobudur is above all a didactic catechism of Buddha's life. These stone Buddhist "Stations of the Cross" are captured in the book "Borobudur: Golden Tales of the Buddhas" by John Miksic (2017). This book I found remarkably interesting for the history in stone of Buddha's life and the excellent photography of the monument.

Kretek

As a smoker, I particularly enjoyed kretek (clove cigarettes) and the reference book for everything about this cigarette is "Kretek: The Culture and Heritage of Indonesia's Clove Cigarettes" by Mark Hanusz (2004). When I was there in the 1970s, everyone from kids to grandmas smoked kreteks. They are to Indonesians what hamburgers are to Americans and an important industry that supports 10 million people in the making and selling of this product.

Pass the Popcorn

In my travels in Indonesia, I stayed primarily in Java and Bali and to get a real flavor of what Java is like I would recommend watching another Mel Gibson (this "bloody bloke" really gets around) movie: "A Year of Living Dangerously," which deals with an Australian newspaper reporter in Jakarta and the abortive communist uprising in 1965. The director, Peter Weir has captured the majestic beauty, ugly poverty, and haunting mystery of Java.

BALI

BALI is one of the most fascinating places in the world and when I was there it was still relatively unspoiled. However, the natural beauty is so magnificent that I do not see how this could be destroyed, even in the age of mass tourism. Going back to the 1970s, there is a text and photo book called "Entranced: My Travels in Bali in the 1970s" by John Houchin (2020) Here the author combines photos and text like yours truly is also doing. This is an evocative portrait of the pristine island of a time long gone.

Balinese Art

Bali is not only a natural paradise, but an artistic paradise as well and Balinese painting has now become world famous. A comprehensive book on Balinese painting is "Balinese Art: Paintings and Drawings of Bali 1800-2010" by Adrien Wickers (2012). This book is invaluable in showing how modern 20th century Balinese painting was influenced by Western artists in the 1930s–1950s and it is this "fusion" art of East and West that is so popular today.

Balinese Dance and Gamelan Music

To truly understand Balinese dance drama of the eternal struggle of good and evil, you must understand Balinese religion, ritual and the haunting gamelan music. It must be emphasized that this dance drama is not just a cultural artifact or entertainment for the tourists, but an actual struggle between good and evil. This is further explained in lucid detail in the book on Balinese dance drama called "Bali: Sekala & Niskala (the Seen and the Unseen): Essays on Religion, Ritual and Art" by Fred Eiserman, Jr (2009). The author has lived over 30 years in Bali, speaks the Indonesian language and has immersed himself in the culture and religion of the Balinese. I wish I could have had this book when I visited Bali in the 1970s.

MY ALTER EGO

"Flash Gordon" and "Flash Gordon Conquers the Universe" are free to watch on YouTube. Each movie serial has 12 episodes and lasts about three and ½ hours. I remember seeing a few serial episodes at my local theater but was never able to watch an entire movie until I found an old VHS tape of the entire "Flash Gordon" movie in a local thrift store. Flash Gordon is a true "American" hero, not a comic book superhero with supernatural powers. A word of advice: don't buy the German television production of "Flash Gordon" made in the 1960s (Scheisse!) and avoid like the plague the 1970s American movie "Flash Gordon". Stand up for your rights as a red-blooded American: you want the authentic cheesecake acting, the wire-operated spaceships, the paper mache monsters, and the cliff-hanging episodes. I could find no better hero to emulate (well, maybe Groucho Marx), and don't forget the stirring musical theme from Franz Liszt's "Preludes," every time Emperor Ming the Merciless enters the scene.

Illustration Credits

Sojourner to Stoner: The Journal

INTRODUCTION: "AMERICAN GOTHIC" GRANT WOOD: THIS IS A FAITHFUL REPRODUCTION OF A TWO-DIMENSIONAL PUBLIC DOMAIN WORK OF ART. PUBLIC DOMAIN IN COUNTRY OF ORIGIN WHERE THE COPYRIGHT TERM IS AUTHOR'S LIFE PLUS 100 YEARS OR FEWER. THIS IS ALSO IN THE PUBLIC DOMAIN OF U.S. THIS PHOTOGRAPHIC REPRODUCTION IS THEREFORE ALSO CONSIDERED IN THE PUBLIC DOMAIN OF UNITED STATES/SOURCE: U.S. LICENSE: CREATIVE COMMONS CCO

MAP: MAP WAS PROVIDED BY THE CENTRAL INTELLIGENCE AGENCY FROM THEIR "WORLD FACTBOOK" 2020 THIS IS PUBLIC DOMAIN BECAUSE IT IS A PUBLISHED WORK BY A GOVERNMENT EMPLOYEE IN HIS OFFICAL DUTIES AND THEREFORE PUBLIC DOMAIN U.S. LICENSE: CREATIVE COMMONS CCO

CHAPTER 1: "BANGKOK CANALS" PUBLIC DOMAIN FRANK AND FRANCIS CARPENTER COLLECTION LOC-USZ62-5324 (BLACK AND WHITE FILM COPY NEGATIVE) CREATIVE COMMONS CCO

THAILAND I HEADER: BANGKOK "DOUBLE TIER "TEMPLE 1900 PUBLIC DOMAIN. CARPENTER COLLECTION: LIBRARY OF CONGRESS USZ62-5324 (BLACK AND WHITE FILM COPY NEGATIVE) CREATIVE COMMONS CCO

CHAPTER 2: "INVASION OF THE BODY SNATCHERS" MOVIE POSTER: POSTER PUBLISHED BEFORE 1978 (1956) WITH NO COPYRIGHT NOTICE, IT ENTERED PUBLIC DOMAIN UPON PUBLICATION/AUTHOR: ALLIED

ARTISTS PICTURE CORPORATION/SOURCE: SCAN BY HERITAGE AUCTIONS /POSTER IS IN PUBLIC DOMAIN SO THEREFORE PHOTOGRAPHIC REPRODUCTION OF A PUBLIC DOMAIN POSTER IS ALSO CONSIDERED PUBLIC DOMAIN U.S. LICENSE: CREATIVE COMMONS CCO

PHOTOGRAPH OF DONALD SUTHERLAND IN "INVASION OF THE BODY SNATCHERS" 1978 : ALTHOUGH IMAGE IS BELIEVED TO BE COPYWRITE IN U.S., IT QUALIFYS UNDER U. S. FAIR USAGE FOR THE FOLLOWING REASONS: To illustrate the **subject in question**

• Where no free equivalent is available or could be created that would adequately give the same information

• On the English-language Wikipedia, hosted on servers in the United States by the non-profit Wikimedia Foundation,

qualifies as **fair use** under United States copyright law. SOURCE: ttp://archives.thestar.com.my/archives/2012/3/26/lifeliving/f_4jim.jpg

ALL QUOTATIONS, POSTERS AND PHOTOGRAPHS FROM THE "INVASION" MOVIES DISCUSSED ARE EITHER LICENCED AS SHOWN ABOVE OR COVERED BY CREATIVE COMMONS FAIR USAGE BECAUSE THE MOVIES ARE REVIEWED AND COMMENTED UPON, WHICH IS THE SOLE TOPIC IN THIS CHAPTER AND ARE NOT USED APART FROM THIS ANALYSIS.

CHAPTER 3: "REEFER MADNESS" MOVIE POSTER IS PUBLIC DOMAIN BECAUSE IT WAS PUBLISHED BETWEEN 1927 AND 1929 WITHOUT A COPYRIGHT NOTICE AND ENTERED THE PUBLIC DOMAIN UPON PUBLICATION, PHOTOGRAHIC REPRODUCTION OF PUBLIC DOMAIN POSTER IS THEREFORE ALSO CONSIDERED PUBLIC DOMAIN/SOURCE:

POSTERWIRE.COM /AUTHOR: MOTION PICTURE VENTURES/U.S. LICENSE: CREATIVE COMMONS CC0

DANA WYNTER: 1962 STUDIO PUBLICITY PHOTO, PUBLIC DOMAIN: PHOTO PUBLISHED IN U.S. BETWEEN 1927 AND 1977 WITHOUT A COPYRIGHT NOTICE. AUTHOR: ABC, NO U.S. LICENSE REQUIRED

CHAPTER 5: "AMERICAN SOLDIERS IN VIETNAM" PUBLIC DOMAIN THIS FILE IS OF U.S. SOLDIERS WAS TAKEN BY A FEDERAL EMPLOYEE AS PART OF HIS OFFICAL DUTIES. AS A WORK OF THE U. S. FEDERAL GOVERNMENT, IT IS IN THE PUBLIC DOMAIN / 4 APRIL 1968 SOURCE: VA042088, ADMIRAL ZUMWALT COLLECTION, VIETNAM ARCHIVES TEXAS TECH UNIVERSITY / AUTHOR: SP4 DENNIS KURPIUS, 221st SIGNAL CO.

CHAPTER 6: "DRESDEN DESTRUCTION" PHOTOGRAPHER: RICHARD PETER SOURCE/COLLECTION DUETSCHE FOTOTHEK/ DUETSCHE FOTOTHEK OF THE SAXON LIBRARY DRESDEN PROVIDED WIKIMEDIA COMMONS THE PHOTOGRAPH AS PART OF A COOPERATION PROJECT: LICENSED UNDER CREATIVE COMMONS ATTRIBUTION SHARE ALIKE 3.0 GERMANY/ATTRIBUTION: DUETSCHE FOTOTHEK/FREE TO COPY, SHARE, DISTRIBUTE AND TRANSMIT

CHAPTER 8: "BERLIN BLEIBT DUETSCH

- Это
- 1941
- 1945
- 4-я танковая бригада в боях у Мценска
- wot
- Багратион

- [Балатон 1945](#)
- [Белое оружие](#)
- [Белоруссия 1944.](#)
- [Викинги](#)
- [Военнопленные](#)
- [Война на Украине](#)
- [Германия](#)
- [Гражданская война в России](#)
- [Долбодятлы](#)
- [Драчк](#)

Photograph: Soviet Archives

Source: Mihalchuk 1974

PHOTO WAS TAKEN IN 1945 AND COPYRIGHT WAS NOT RENEWED IN THE SOVIET UNION. IT IS THE AUTHOR'S LIFE (ANONYMOUS) PLUS 70 YEARS. THERE WAS NO COPYRIGHT IN U.S. LICENSE: CREATIVE COMMONS ATTRIBUTION-SHARE-ALIKE 3.0 LICENSE.

FRENCH TRAVEL POSTER: PUBLIC DOMAIN IN FRANCE SINCE COPYRIGHT WAS NOT RENEWED FROM 1931; PUBLIC DOMAIN IN U.S. SINCE COPYRIGHT WAS NOT RENEWED AND IT IS PUBLIC DOMAIN BECAUSE OF AUTHOR'S LIFE PLUS 70 YEARS PHOTOGRAHIC REPRODUCTION OF PUBLIC DOMAIN POSTER IS THEREFORE ALSO CONSIDERED PUBLIC DOMAIN. LICENSE IN U.S. CREATIVE COMMONS CCO

CHAPTER 9: "TWO VIETNAMESE GIRLS" 1895 LIBRARY OF CONGRESS PUBLIC DOMAIN LOC: LCUSZ62-98699 (BLACK AND WHITE NEAGATIVE) CREATIVE COMMONS CCO

CHAPTER 10: HYMN: ORIGNAL GERMAN HYMN PUBLIC DOMAIN IN GERMANY, NO COPY RIGHT IN THE U.S./ENGLISH TRANSLATION BY JANE BORTHWICK 1855 NOW PUBLIC DOMAIN, AUTHOR'S DEATH PLUS 70 YEARS U.S. LICENSE CREATIVE COMMONS CCO

DR. DOOLEY PHOTO BY" DUCKS IN THE WATER" JAN 2009 RELEASED IT TO CREATIVE COMMONS ATTRIBUTION-SHARE ALIKE 3.0 IN U.S. THIS PHOTO IS ALSO ON GNU FREE DOCUMENTATION LICENCE,1.2

CHAPTER 11: FRENCH TRAVEL POSTER: PUBLIC DOMAIN IN FRANCE SINCE COPYRIGHT WAS NOT RENEWED FROM 1931; PUBLIC DOMAIN IN U.S. SINCE COPYRIGHT WAS NOT RENEWED AND IT IS PUBLIC DOMAIN BECAUSE OF AUTHOR'S LIFE PLUS 70 YEARS PHOTOGRAHIC REPRODUCTION OF PUBLIC DOMAIN POSTER IS THEREFORE ALSO CONSIDERED PUBLIC DOMAIN. LICENSE IN U.S. CREATIVE COMMONS CCO

CHAPTER 14: DESTRUCTION OF BERLIN SOURCE: GERMAN FEDERAL ARCHIVES ACCENSION NUMBER B145 BILD-PO54320 PHOTO IS PROVIDED TO WIKIMEDIA COMMONS BY THE GERMAN FEDERAL ARCHIVES AS PART OF A COOPERATIVE PROGRAM THIS FILE IS FREE TO TRANSMIT, COPY AND USE FREE OF CHARGE ATTRIBUTION: BUDESARCHIV B 145 BILD PO54320/KARL WEINROTHER (PHOTOGRAPHER)/CC-BY-SA-3.0 PHOTO IS LICENSED IN U.S.: CREATIVE COMMONS ATTRIBUTION SHARE ALIKE 3.0 UNPORTED

CHAPTER 15: THAI DANCER PUBLIC DOMAIN LIBRARY OF CONGRESS CARPENTER COLLECTION LOC USZ62-5324 (BLACK AND WHITE NEGATIVE) CREATIVE COMMONS CCO

"EAST GATE OLD CITY" SOURCE/PHOTOGRAPHER: STEFAN FUSSAN/ AUTHOR RELEASED PHOTOGRAPH TO CREATIVE COMMONS ATTRIBUTION SHARE ALIKE 3,0 UNPORTED WORLDWIDE STATING "PHOTO CAN BE FREELY USED AND DISTRIBUTED FOR BOTH NON AND COMMERCIAL PURPOSES".

CHAPTER 16: "PROSERPINE" THIS IS A FAITHFUL REPRODUCTION OF A TWO-DIMENSIONAL PUBLIC DOMAIN WORK OF ART. PUBLIC DOMAIN IN COUNTRY OF ORIGIN WHERE THE COPYRIGHT TERM IS AUTHOR'S LIFE PLUS 100 YEARS OR FEWER. THIS IS ALSO IN THE PUBLIC DOMAIN OF U.S. BECAUSE COPYRIGHT WAS TAKEN OUT BEFORE 1927 AND NOT RENEWED. THIS PHOTOGRAPHIC REPRODUCTION IS THEREFORE ALSO CONSIDERED IN THE PUBLIC DOMAIN OF UNITED STATES. U.S. LICENSE CREATIVE COMMONS ATTRIBUTION-SHARE ALIKE 3.0

CHAPTER 17: JIM THOMPSON PHOTOGRAPH: ALTHOUGH IMAGE IS BELIEVED TO BE COPYWRITE, IT QUALIFYS UNDER U. S. FAIR USAGE FOR THE FOLLOWING REASONS: To illustrate the **subject in question**

- Where no free equivalent is available or could be created that would adequately give the same information

- On the English-language Wikipedia, hosted on servers in the United States by the non-profit Wikimedia Foundation,

qualifies as **fair use** under United States copyright law. SOURCE: ttp://archives.thestar.com.my/archives/2012/3/26/lifeliving/f_4jim.jpg

CHAPTER 19: NESTORIAN CHRIST

Restoration of a T'ang dynasty Nestorian image which found in Cave 17 at Mo-kao Caves, Tunhwang. The original work dated back to 9th century. According to Dr. Buslig Szonja of Eötvös Loránd University and Prof. Lin Meicun of Peking University, this is an image of Jesus Christ. Source: http://dsr.nii.ac.jp/narratives/discovery/09/index.html.ja (i n Japanese).	
Date	T'ang dynasty
Source	http://www.yuniljung.com/kkansu/pic/009100030120050103R02144096_1.jpg Unknown author
Author	

THIS IS A FAITHFUL REPRODUCTION OF A TWO-DIMENSIONAL PUBLIC DOMAIN WORK OF ART. PUBLIC DOMAIN IN COUNTRY OF ORIGIN WHERE THE COPYRIGHT TERM IS AUTHOR'S LIFE PLUS 100 YEARS OR FEWER. THIS IS ALSO IN THE PUBLIC DOMAIN OF U.S. BECAUSE COPYRIGHT WAS TAKEN OUT BEFORE 1927 AND NOT RENEWED. THIS PHOTOGRAPHIC REPRODUCTION IS THEREFORE ALSO CONSIDERED IN THE PUBLIC DOMAIN OF UNITED STATES. U.S. LICENSE CREATIVE COMMONS ATTRIBUTION-SHARE ALIKE 3.0

KHMER BUDDHA WITH ONE LEG MISSING: SOURCE:MUSEUM GUIMET PARIS/AUTHOR/PHOTOGRAPHER: VASSIL AUTHOR RELEASED IMAGE TO PUBLIC DOMAIN WITH NO RESTRICTIONS LIC IN U.S. CREATIVE COMMONS CCO

EMERALD BUDDHA:

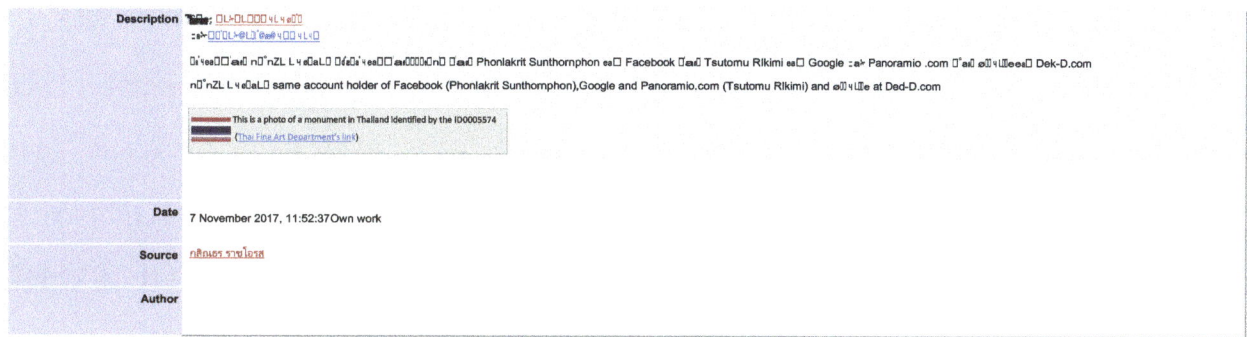

AUTHOR HAS RELEASED THIS IMAGE TO CREATIVE COMMONS ATTRIBUTION SHARE ALIKE 4.0 INTERNATIONAL LICENSE WITH CREDIT ATTRIBUTION OF THE AUTHOR LISTED ABOVE.

WALKING BUDDHA: PHOTOGRAPH FROM THE NATIONAL MUSEUM BANGKOK/SOURCE:068 WALKING BUDDHA SUKHOTHAI STYLE/AUTHOR PHOTO DHARMA FROM SADAO THAILAND, RELEASED UNDER GNU AND THE LICENSE IN U.S. IS CREATIVE COMMONS: ATTRIBUTION- SHARE ALIKE 3.0

CHAPTER 20: BLACK FIGURE ON TRAIN: PEDRO GABRIEL MIZIARA ON UNSPLASH

CHAPTER 21: "THE ROSE LEAF": THIS IS A FAITHFUL REPRODUCTION OF A TWO-DIMENSIONAL PUBLIC DOMAIN WORK OF ART. PUBLIC DOMAIN IN COUNTRY OF ORIGIN WHERE THE COPYRIGHT TERM IS AUTHOR'S LIFE PLUS 100 YEARS OR FEWER. THIS IS ALSO IN THE PUBLIC DOMAIN OF U.S. BECAUSE COPYRIGHT WAS TAKEN OUT BEFORE 1927 AND NOT RENEWED. THIS PHOTOGRAPHIC

REPRODUCTION IS THEREFORE ALSO CONSIDERED IN THE PUBLIC DOMAIN OF UNITED STATES. U.S. LICENSE CREATIVE COMMONS ATTRIBUTION-SHARE ALIKE 3.0

CHAPTER 22 "TWO WOMEN" PUBLIC DOMAIN: THIS IS A FAITHFUL REPRODUCTION OF A TWO-DIMENSIONAL PUBLIC DOMAIN WORK OF ART. PUBLIC DOMAIN IN COUNTRY OF ORIGIN WHERE THE COPYRIGHT TERM IS AUTHOR'S LIFE PLUS 100 YEARS OR FEWER. THIS IS ALSO IN THE PUBLIC DOMAIN OF U.S. BECAUSE COPYRIGHT WAS TAKEN OUT BEFORE 1927 AND NOT RENEWED. THIS PHOTOGRAPHIC REPRODUCTION IS THEREFORE ALSO CONSIDERED IN THE PUBLIC DOMAIN OF UNITED STATES. U.S. LICENSE CREATIVE COMMONS ATTRIBUTION-SHARE ALIKE 3.0

CHAPTER 23: KING PELLES' DAUGHTER BEARING THE HOLY GRAIL: FREDERICK SANDYS 1861: THIS IS A FAITHFUL REPRODUCTION OF A TWO-DIMENSIONAL PUBLIC DOMAIN WORK OF ART. PUBLIC DOMAIN IN COUNTRY OF ORIGIN WHERE THE COPYRIGHT TERM IS AUTHOR'S LIFE PLUS 100 YEARS OR FEWER. THIS IS ALSO IN THE PUBLIC DOMAIN OF U.S. BECAUSE COPYRIGHT WAS TAKEN OUT BEFORE 1927 AND NOT RENEWED. THIS PHOTOGRAPHIC REPRODUCTION IS THEREFORE ALSO CONSIDERED IN THE PUBLIC DOMAIN OF UNITED STATES. U.S. LICENSE CREATIVE COMMONS ATTRIBUTION-SHARE ALIKE 3.0

CHAPTER 24: MALACCA PRINT/FORTESS PRINT: THIS IS A FAITHFUL REPRODUCTION OF A TWO-DIMENSIONAL PUBLIC DOMAIN WORK OF ART. PUBLIC DOMAIN IN COUNTRY OF ORIGIN WHERE THE COPYRIGHT TERM IS AUTHOR'S LIFE PLUS 100 YEARS OR FEWER. THIS IS ALSO IN THE PUBLIC DOMAIN OF U.S. BECAUSE COPYRIGHT WAS

TAKEN OUT BEFORE 1927 AND NOT RENEWED. THIS PHOTOGRAPHIC REPRODUCTION IS THEREFORE ALSO CONSIDERED IN THE PUBLIC DOMAIN OF UNITED STATES. U.S. LICENSE CREATIVE COMMONS CCO, SOURCE/PHOTOGRAPHER: VICTOR COUTO/ AUTHOR HAS RELEASED PHOTOGRAPH TO THE PUBLIC DOMAIN "TO USE FOR ANY PURPOSE".

SULTANATE PALACE: PUBLIC DOMAIN, 2009. PHOTOGRAPHER ADIPUT RELEASED PHOTO TO PUBLIC DOMAIN TO USE THIS PHOTO FOR ANY PURPOSE WITHOUT CONDITIONS

CHAPTER 26: "PORTUGUESE DANCERS"; SOURCE/PHOTOGRAPHER: VICTOR POGADAEV RELEASED PHOTO TO PUBLIC DOMAIN 2016 U.S. LICENSE: CREATIVE COMMONS CCO UNIVERSAL PUBLIC DOMAIN

CHAPTER 28: PRINCESS ARYA AND FLASH GORDON: PUBLIC DOMAIN PHOTOGRAPH IS COPYRIGHT FREE SINCE IT HAS NOT BEEN RENEWED SINCE PUBLICATION (1938) AND 70 YEARS HAVE PASSED NOW IT PUBLIC DOMAIN. U.S. LICENSE: CREATIVE COMMONS 2.0 CCO

CHAPTER 29: SINGAPORE DRAWING/ EARLY PHOTO OF BOROBUDUR: THIS IS A FAITHFUL REPRODUCTION OF A TWO-DIMENSIONAL PUBLIC DOMAIN WORK OF ART. PUBLIC DOMAIN IN COUNTRY OF ORIGIN WHERE THE COPYRIGHT TERM IS AUTHOR'S LIFE PLUS 100 YEARS OR FEWER. THIS IS ALSO IN THE PUBLIC DOMAIN OF U.S. BECAUSE COPYRIGHT WAS TAKEN OUT BEFORE 1927 AND NOT RENEWED. THIS PHOTOGRAPHIC REPRODUCTION IS THEREFORE ALSO CONSIDERED IN THE PUBLIC DOMAIN OF UNITED STATES. U.S. LICENSE CREATIVE COMMONS CCO

CHAPTER 29: TIGER BALM GARDENS SOURCE; ORIGINALLY POSTED TO "FLICKR" AS "TIGER BALM GARDE HK"/ AUTHOR: JANICE WALTZER

/IMAGE UPLOADED TO COMMONS USING FLICKR UPLOAD BOT IN APRIL 2010 BY KT0288. ON THAT DATE IT WAS LICENSED UNDER CREATIVE COMMONS ATTRIBUTION 2.0 GENERIC

CHAPTER 30: STAMFORD RAFFLES: SOURCE: NATIONAL GALLERY LONDON. THIS IS A FAITHFUL REPRODUCTION OF A TWO-DIMENSIONAL PUBLIC DOMAIN WORK OF ART. PUBLIC DOMAIN IN COUNTRY OF ORIGIN WHERE THE COPYRIGHT TERM IS AUTHOR'S LIFE PLUS 100 YEARS OR FEWER. THIS IS ALSO IN THE PUBLIC DOMAIN OF U.S. BECAUSE COPYRIGHT WAS TAKEN OUT BEFORE 1927 AND NOT RENEWED. THIS PHOTOGRAPHIC REPRODUCTION IS THEREFORE ALSO CONSIDERED IN THE PUBLIC DOMAIN OF UNITED STATES. U.S. LICENSE CREATIVE COMMONS CCO

PRINT OF BOROBUDUR DISCOVERY: THIS IS A FAITHFUL REPRODUCTION OF A TWO-DIMENSIONAL PUBLIC DOMAIN WORK OF ART. PUBLIC DOMAIN IN COUNTRY OF ORIGIN WHERE THE COPYRIGHT TERM IS AUTHOR'S LIFE PLUS 100 YEARS OR FEWER. THIS IS ALSO IN THE PUBLIC DOMAIN OF U.S. BECAUSE COPYRIGHT WAS TAKEN OUT BEFORE 1927 AND NOT RENEWED. THIS PHOTOGRAPHIC REPRODUCTION IS THEREFORE ALSO CONSIDERED IN THE PUBLIC DOMAIN OF UNITED STATES. U.S. LICENSE CREATIVE COMMONS CCO

BOROBUDUR OLD PHOTOGRAPH: THIS IS A FAITHFUL REPRODUCTION OF A TWO-DIMENSIONAL PUBLIC DOMAIN WORK OF ART. PUBLIC DOMAIN IN COUNTRY OF ORIGIN WHERE THE COPYRIGHT TERM IS AUTHOR'S LIFE PLUS 100 YEARS OR FEWER. THIS IS ALSO IN THE PUBLIC DOMAIN OF U.S. BECAUSE COPYRIGHT WAS TAKEN OUT BEFORE 1927 AND NOT RENEWED. THIS PHOTOGRAPHIC

REPRODUCTION IS THEREFORE ALSO CONSIDERED IN THE PUBLIC DOMAIN OF UNITED STATES. U.S. LICENSE CREATIVE COMMONS CCO

RAFFLESIA ARNOLDI: SOURCE/PHOTOGRAPHER: MA_SUSKA (MARCH 2007) AUTHOR RELEASED IMAGE TO CREATIVE COMMONS ATTRIBUTION 2.0 GENERIC LICENSE WITH REQUIREMENT OF ATTRIBITON (MA SUSKA).

CHAPTER 31: LEE KWAN YEW: PUBLIC DOMAIN /SOURCE: WHITE HOUSE PHOTOGRAPHIC OFFICE HTTPS.//CATALOG.ARCHIVES.GOV/ ID 7518579 /STATE DINNER8 MAY 1975 PUBLIC DOMAIN THIS FILE IS OF A FOREIGN DIGNITARY TAKEN BY A FEDERAL EMPLOYEE AS PART OF HIS OFFICAL DUTIES. AS A WORK OF THE U. S. FEDERAL GOVERNMENT, IT IS IN THE PUBLIC DOMAIN

ROBERT MOSES: PUBLIC DOMAIN LIBRARY OF CONGRESS HTTP: HDI.LOC GOV/LOC. PNP/CPH3C36079/PHOTOGRAPHER: C.M. STIEGLITZ

CHAPTER 32: SARKIS BROTHERS: PUBLIC DOMAIN IN COUNTRY OF ORIGIN WHERE THE COPYRIGHT TERM IS THE AUTHOR'S LIFE PLUS 100 YEARS OR FEWER. THIS IS ALSO IN THE PUBLIC DOMAIN OF U.S. BECAUSE COPYRIGHT WAS TAKEN OUT BEFORE 1927 AND NOT RENEWED. THIS PHOTOGRAPHIC REPRODUCTION IS THEREFORE ALSO CONSIDERED IN THE PUBLIC DOMAIN OF UNITED STATES. U.S. LICENSE CREATIVE COMMONS CCO

THREE RAJ HOTELS: (1) EASTERN AND ORIENTAL HOTEL, PENANG, MALAYSIA/ SOURCEAND PHOTOGRAPHER: GRYFFINFOR/ PHOTOGRAPHER RELEASED TO GNU FREE DOCUMENTION LICENSE, VERSION 1.2 /IN U.S. FILE IS LICENSED CREATIVE COMMONS, ATTRIBUTION-SHARE ALIKE 3.0

(2) RAFFLES HOTEL SINGAPORE: SOURCE AND PHOTOGRAPHER: ELISA ROLLE / PHOTOGRAPHER RELEASED IT TO GNU FREE DOCUMENTATION WITH AUTHOR ATTRIBUTION: ELISA ROLLE /IN U.S. LICENSE: CREATIVE COMMONS, ATTRIBUTION-SHARE ALIKE 4.O INTERNATIONAL LICENSE WITH ATTRIBUTION (ELISA ROLLE).

(3) STRAND HOTEL RANGOON, BURMA PUBLIC DOMAIN IN BURMA: 50 YEARS HAVE PASSED AND COPYRIGHT WAS NOT RENEWED/ PUBLIC DOMAIN IN U.S. BECAUSE PHOTOGRAPH WAS PUBLISHED PRIOR TO 1927 AND COPYRIGHT WAS NOT RENEWED LICENSE CREATIVE COMMONS CCO/ PHOTOGRAPHER: PHILLIP KLEIR (CIRCA 1900)

CHAPTER 33: BROOKE PORTRAIT: THIS IS A FAITHFUL REPRODUCTION OF A TWO-DIMENSIONAL PUBLIC DOMAIN WORK OF ART. PUBLIC DOMAIN IN COUNTRY OF ORIGIN WHERE THE COPYRIGHT TERM IS AUTHOR'S LIFE PLUS 100 YEARS OR FEWER. THIS IS ALSO IN THE PUBLIC DOMAIN OF U.S. BECAUSE COPYRIGHT WAS TAKEN OUT BEFORE 1927 AND NOT RENEWED. THIS PHOTOGRAPHIC REPRODUCTION IS THEREFORE ALSO CONSIDERED IN THE PUBLIC DOMAIN OF UNITED STATES/CREATIVE COMMONS 2.0 SHARE ALIKE

CHAPTER 34: POSTER OF FRANK BUCK: PUBLIC DOMAIN OF U.S. BECAUSE COPYRIGHT WAS TAKEN OUT BEFORE 1927 AND NOT RENEWED. THIS PHOTOGRAPHIC REPRODUCTION IS THEREFORE ALSO CONSIDERED IN THE PUBLIC DOMAIN OF UNITED STATES/ SOURCE: TRANSFERRED FROM EN. WIKIPEDIA BY SHREEBOT/AUTHOR: SCHMAUSSCHMAUS AT EN, WIKIPEDIA

CHAPTER 35: IKAT FABRIC PUBLIC DOMAIN THIS IS A FAITHFUL REPRODUCTION OF A TWO-DIMENSIONAL PUBLIC DOMAIN WORK OF

ART. PUBLIC DOMAIN IN COUNTRY OF ORIGIN WHERE THE COPYRIGHT TERM IS AUTHOR'S LIFE PLUS 100 YEARS OR FEWER. THIS IS ALSO IN THE PUBLIC DOMAIN OF U.S. BECAUSE COPYRIGHT WAS TAKEN OUT BEFORE 1927 (IF IT WAS EVER COPYRIGHT) AND NOT RENEWED. THIS PHOTOGRAPHIC REPRODUCTION IS THEREFORE ALSO CONSIDERED IN THE PUBLIC DOMAIN OF UNITED STATES SOURCE: HONOLULA MUSEUM OF ART/AUTHOR (CREATOR) ANONYMOUS.

SHRUNKEN HEAD: SOURCE: PITT RIVERS MUSEUM OXFORD GREAT BRITAIN: PHOTOGRAPHER: NARAYAN K28/ RELEASED BY AUTHOR TO CREATIVE COMMONS ,FREE USAGE WUITH ATTRIBUTION OF NARAYAN K28 U.S. LICENSE: CREATIVE COMMONS: ATTRIBUTION SHARE-ALIKE 3.0 UNPORTED.

CHAPTER 36: "NANOOK OF THE NORTH" PHOTO OF NANOOK'S WIFE NYLA 1921 AUTHOR: ROBERT J. FLAHERTY. PUBLIC DOMAIN IN CANADA BECAUSE PHOTO TAKEN BEFORE 1949 AND AUTHOR DIED MORE THAN 50 YEARS AGO. PUBLIC DOMAIN IN U.S. BECAUSE PHOTO WAS TAKEN BEFORE 1927 AND IT IS AUTHOR'S LIFE PLUS 70 YEARS OR FEWER U.S. LICENSE: CREATIVE COMMONS CCO

EVE BY GISLEBERTUS 1130: PUBLIC DOMAIN THIS IS A FAITHFUL REPRODUCTION OF A TWO-DIMENSIONAL PUBLIC DOMAIN WORK OF ART. PUBLIC DOMAIN IN COUNTRY OF ORIGIN WHERE THE COPYRIGHT TERM IS AUTHOR'S LIFE PLUS 100 YEARS OR FEWER. THIS IS ALSO IN THE PUBLIC DOMAIN OF U.S. BECAUSE COPYRIGHT WAS TAKEN OUT BEFORE 1927 (IF IT WAS EVER COPYRIGHT) AND NOT RENEWED. THIS PHOTOGRAPHIC REPRODUCTION IS THEREFORE ALSO CONSIDERED IN THE PUBLIC DOMAIN OF UNITED STATES.

INDONESIAN HEADER: JAVA POSTER PUBLIC DOMAIN IN NETHERLANDS SINCE COPYRIGHT WAS NOT RENEWED FROM 1931; PUBLIC DOMAIN IN U.S. SINCE COPYRIGHT WAS NOT RENEWED AND IT IS PUBLIC DOMAIN BECAUSE OF AUTHOR'S LIFE PLUS 70 YEARS PHOTOGRAHIC REPRODUCTION OF PUBLIC DOMAIN POSTER IS THEREFORE ALSO CONSIDERED PUBLIC DOMAIN. LICENSE IN U.S. CREATIVE COMMONS CCO

CHAPTER 38: OLD BATAVIA: PRINT OWNED BYTROPPENMUSEUM GIVEN TO WIKIMEDIA AS PART OF COOPERATIVE PROJECT/U.S. LICENSE CREATIVE COMMONS ATTRIBUTION-SHARE ALIKE 3.0 WITH THE ATTRIBUTION: TROPPENMUSEUM, PART OF THE NATIONAL MUSEUM OF WORLD CULTURES.

BOOKCASE: SOURCE/PHOTOGRAPHER: BRIAN GIESEN, FLICKR. AUTHOR RELEASED IMAGE TO CREATIVE COMMONS 2.0 GENERIC LICENSE WITH NO RESTRICTIONS/ATTRIBUTION: BRIAN GIESEN, FLICKR

NEW AMSTERDAM PRINT 1664 AUTHOR: JOHANNES VINGBOONS (1616-1670) SOURCE "MEMORY OF THE NETHERLANDS" PUBLIC DOMAIN THIS IS A FAITHFUL REPRODUCTION OF A TWO-DIMENSIONAL PUBLIC DOMAIN WORK OF ART. PUBLIC DOMAIN IN COUNTRY OF ORIGIN WHERE THE COPYRIGHT TERM IS AUTHOR'S LIFE PLUS 100 YEARS OR FEWER. THIS IS ALSO IN THE PUBLIC DOMAIN OF U.S. BECAUSE COPYRIGHT WAS TAKEN OUT BEFORE 1927 (IF IT WAS EVER COPYRIGHT) AND NOT RENEWED. THIS PHOTOGRAPHIC REPRODUCTION IS THEREFORE ALSO CONSIDERED IN THE PUBLIC DOMAIN OF UNITED STATES.

CHAPTER 39: WORDS TO "TAKE ME OUT TO THE BALL GAME" (1908) WAS COPYRIGHT BEFORE 1927 AND THE THIS VERSION IS NOW PUBLIC DOMAIN BECAUSE THIS VERSION OF THE SONG WAS NOT RENEWED.LICENSE: CREATIVE COMMONS CCO

JAKARTA STADIUM: AUTHOR /SOURCE: FLIXII RELEASED PHOTO TO CREATIVE COMMONS-ATTRIBUTION -SHARE-ALIKE 4.0 INTERNATIONAL LICENSE WITH NO RESTRICTIONS WITH ATTRIBUTION OF AUTHOR, FLIX II.

"PELE": PUBLIC DOMAIN IN SWEDEN /AUTHOR: AFP/SCANPIX PUBLIC DOMAIN BECAUSE OF AUTHOR'S DEATH (UNKNOWN AUTHOR) PLUS 70 YEARS OR LESS. COPYRIGHT NOT REGISTERED IN U.S. AND BECAUSE OF AUTHOR'S DEATH (UNKNOWN AUTHOR) PLUS 70 YEARS OR LESS, IMAGE IS NOW PUBLIC DOMAIN IN U.S./U.S. LICENSE: CREATIVE COMMONS CCO

CHAPTER 40: KRETEKS: PHOTOGRAPH OWNED BY TROPPENMUSEUM/ GIVEN TO WIKIMEDIA AS PART OF COOPERATIVE PROJECT/U.S. LICENSE CREATIVE COMMONS ATTRIBUTION-SHARE ALIKE 3.0 WITH THE ATTRIBUTION: TROPPENMUSEUM, PART OF THE NATIONAL MUSEUM OF WORLD CULTURES.

CHAPTER 41: SUKARNO PHOTOGRAPH: OFFICAL PORTRAIT OF THE PRESIDENT OF INDONESIA (1949) THIS PHOTOGRAPH IS IN THE PUBLIC DOMAIN IN INDONESIA BECAUSE THE COPYRIGHT HAS EXPIREED AND WAS NOT RENEWED. THIS IS ALSO PUBLIC DOMAIN IN U.S. WHERE THE PERIOD IS 70 YEARS OR LESS (UNKNOWN AUTHOR) AFTER DEATH OF AUTHOR. LICENSE IN U.S. IS CREATIVE COMMONS CCO.

SUHARTA PHOTOGRAPH: PUBLIC DOMAIN IN INDONESIA, RELEASED TO CREATIVE COMMONS ATTRIBUTION-SHARE ALIKE BY DEPARTMENT OF INFORMATION, INDONESIAN GOVERNMENT SOURCE: PHOTOGRAPH SUPPLIED BY INFORMATION DEPARTMENT GOV. OF INDONESIA TO AUTHOR R.E. ELSON FOR HIS BOOK: "SUHARTA: A POLITICL BIOGRAPHY" CAMBRIDGE UNIV. PRESS 2001/AUTHOR UPLOADED IMAGE TO CREATIVE COMMONS ATTRIBUTION -SHARE ALIKE 3,0 WITH PERMISSION OF INDONESIAN GOVERNMENT WITH NO RESTRICTIONS.

CHAPTER 42: BOROBUDUR (PRESENT DAY) PHOTOGRAPHER: GUNAWAN KARTAPRANTA FROM THE INDONESIAN WIKIPEDIA (2008) AUTHOR HAS RELEASED IMAGE TO GNU FREE DOCUMENTATION LICENSE, VERSION 1.2. IN THE U.S. THE GNU OR CREATIVE COMMONS ATTRIBUTION- SHARE ALIKE 3.0 LICENSE MAY BE USED.

BOROBUDUR (1820'S PRINT): PUBLIC DOMAIN THIS IS A FAITHFUL REPRODUCTION OF A TWO-DIMENSIONAL PUBLIC DOMAIN WORK OF ART. PUBLIC DOMAIN IN COUNTRY OF ORIGIN WHERE THE COPYRIGHT TERM IS AUTHOR'S LIFE PLUS 100 YEARS OR FEWER. THIS IS ALSO IN THE PUBLIC DOMAIN OF U.S. BECAUSE COPYRIGHT WAS TAKEN OUT BEFORE 1927 AND NOT RENEWED. THIS PHOTOGRAPHIC REPRODUCTION IS THEREFORE ALSO CONSIDERED IN THE PUBLIC DOMAIN OF UNITED STATES. U.S. LICENSE: CREATIVE COMMONS ATTRIBUTION-SHARE ALIKE 3.0

MAYAN STELE: PUBLIC DOMAIN THIS IS A FAITHFUL REPRODUCTION OF A TWO-DIMENSIONAL PUBLIC DOMAIN WORK OF ART. PUBLIC DOMAIN IN COUNTRY OF ORIGIN WHERE THE

COPYRIGHT TERM IS AUTHOR'S LIFE PLUS 100 YEARS OR FEWER. THIS IS ALSO IN THE PUBLIC DOMAIN OF U.S. BECAUSE COPYRIGHT WAS TAKEN OUT BEFORE 1927 AND NOT RENEWED. THIS PHOTOGRAPHIC REPRODUCTION IS THEREFORE ALSO CONSIDERED IN THE PUBLIC DOMAIN OF UNITED STATES. U.S. LICENSE: CREATIVE COMMONS ATTRIBUTION-SHARE ALIKE 3.0

BALI HEADER: UBUD VILLAGE: PHOTOGRAPH OWNED BY TROPPENMUSEUM/ GIVEN TO WIKIMEDIA AS PART OF COOPERATIVE PROJECT/U.S. LICENSE CREATIVE COMMONS ATTRIBUTION-SHARE ALIKE 3.0 WITH THE ATTRIBUTION: TROPPENMUSEUM, PART OF THE NATIONAL MUSEUM OF WORLD CULTURES.

CHAPTER 43; CONEY ISLAND BEACH: THIS PAINTING IS OWNED BY THE SMITHSONIAN AND IN 2021 ALL OF THEIR ART AND ARTIFACT PHOTOGRAPHIC REPRESENTATIONS WERE ENTERED INTO THE PUBLIC DOMAIN FOR FREE USAGE U.S. LICENSE: CREATIVE COMMONS-CCO

CHAPTER 44: PRINT OF THOMAS DE QUINCEY

PUBLIC DOMAIN THIS IS A FAITHFUL REPRODUCTION OF A TWO-DIMENSIONAL PUBLIC DOMAIN WORK OF ART. PUBLIC DOMAIN IN COUNTRY OF ORIGIN WHERE THE COPYRIGHT TERM IS AUTHOR'S LIFE PLUS 100 YEARS OR FEWER. THIS IS ALSO IN THE PUBLIC DOMAIN OF U.S. BECAUSE COPYRIGHT WAS TAKEN OUT BEFORE 1927 AND NOT RENEWED. THIS PHOTOGRAPHIC REPRODUCTION IS THEREFORE ALSO CONSIDERED IN THE PUBLIC DOMAIN OF UNITED STATES. U.S. LICENSE: CREATIVE COMMONS ATTRIBUTION-SHARE ALIKE 3.0

CHAPTER 44: INDONESIAN GIRL IN SARONG: LIBRARY OF CONGRESS B&W FILM NEGATIVE/ THE CARPENTER COLLECTION LOC: USZ62-87971. U.S. LICENSE: CREATIVE COMMONS CC0

CHAPTER 45: BALINESE PAINTING OF MAIDENS BATHING: AUTHOR (PAINTER) RELASED PHOTOGRAPHIC IMAGE TO GNU FREE DOCUMENTATION VERSION1.2/ IN U. S. LICENSE IS CREATIVE COMMONS ATTRIBUTION-SHARE ALIKE 3.0

CHAPTER 46: "THREE BRIDES": PUBLIC DOMAIN THIS IS A FAITHFUL REPRODUCTION OF A TWO-DIMENSIONAL PUBLIC DOMAIN WORK OF ART. PUBLIC DOMAIN IN COUNTRY OF ORIGIN WHERE THE COPYRIGHT TERM IS AUTHOR'S LIFE PLUS 100 YEARS OR FEWER. THIS IS ALSO IN THE PUBLIC DOMAIN OF U.S. BECAUSE COPYRIGHT WAS TAKEN OUT BEFORE 1927 AND NOT RENEWED. THIS PHOTOGRAPHIC REPRODUCTION IS THEREFORE ALSO CONSIDERED IN THE PUBLIC DOMAIN OF UNITED STATES. U.S. LICENSE: CREATIVE COMMONS ATTRIBUTION-SHARE ALIKE 3.0

PHOTO OF JAN DE TROOP AMSTERDAM 1892: AUTHOR WILLHERN WITSEN. PHOTO IS PUBLIC DOMAIN IN NETHERLANDS BECAUSE IT IS THE AUTHOR'S LIFE PLUS 70 YEARS. IT IS ALSO PUBLIC DOMAIN IN U.S. BECAUSE IT WAS TAKEN BEFORE 1927 AND NEVER COPYRIGHT AND IT IS ALSO AUTHOR'S LIFE PLUS 70 YEARS. U.S. LICENSE: CREATIVE COMMONS CC0

ART NOUVEAU GATE: AUTHOR: GROUME RELEASED IMAGE FROM FLICKR TO WORLDWIDE SHARING AND U.S. LICENSE: CREATIVE COMMONS ATTRIBUTION-SHARE ALIKE 3.0 WITH ATTRIBUTION OF PHOTOGRAPHER GROUME REQUIRED.

"JOB CIGARETTE POSTER": PUBLIC DOMAIN THIS IS A FAITHFUL REPRODUCTION OF A TWO-DIMENSIONAL PUBLIC DOMAIN WORK OF ART. PUBLIC DOMAIN IN COUNTRY OF ORIGIN WHERE THE COPYRIGHT TERM IS AUTHOR'S LIFE PLUS 100 YEARS OR FEWER. THIS IS ALSO IN THE PUBLIC DOMAIN OF U.S. BECAUSE COPYRIGHT WAS TAKEN OUT BEFORE 1927 AND NOT RENEWED. THIS PHOTOGRAPHIC REPRODUCTION IS THEREFORE ALSO CONSIDERED IN THE PUBLIC DOMAIN OF UNITED STATES. U.S. LICENSE: CREATIVE COMMONS ATTRIBUTION-SHARE ALIKE 3.0

DELFT SALAD OIL POSTER: PUBLIC DOMAIN THIS IS A FAITHFUL REPRODUCTION OF A TWO-DIMENSIONAL PUBLIC DOMAIN WORK OF ART. PUBLIC DOMAIN IN COUNTRY OF ORIGIN WHERE THE COPYRIGHT TERM IS AUTHOR'S LIFE PLUS 100 YEARS OR FEWER. THIS IS ALSO IN THE PUBLIC DOMAIN OF U.S. BECAUSE COPYRIGHT WAS TAKEN OUT BEFORE 1927 AND NOT RENEWED. THIS PHOTOGRAPHIC REPRODUCTION IS THEREFORE ALSO CONSIDERED IN THE PUBLIC DOMAIN OF UNITED STATES. U.S. LICENSE: CREATIVE COMMONS ATTRIBUTION-SHARE ALIKE 3.0

CHAPTER 47: "THIS IS FUCKING RIDICULOUS" AUTHOR: DANIEL ARAUZ RELEASED PHOTO OF PROTESTER AT SAN FRANCISCO AIRPORT 28 JAN 2017 TO CREATIVE COMMONS ATTRIBUTION-SHARE-ALIKE 2.0 LICENSE

TANTRIC BUDDHIST STATUE: SOURCE/AUTHOR JOE MABEL RELEASED IMAGE TO CREATIVE COMMONS ATTRIBUTION-SHARE ALIKE 3.0 WITH THE ATTRIBUTION OF JOE MABEL. ORIGINAL STATUE

IS IN THE COLLECTON OF TRAMELL AND MARGARET CROW COLLECTION OF ASIAN ART, DALLAS, TEXAS.

CHAPTER 48: DEATH OF BALINESE KING: PHOTOGRAPH OWNED BY TROPPENMUSEUM/ GIVEN TO WIKIMEDIA AS PART OF COOPERATIVE PROJECT/U.S. LICENSE CREATIVE COMMONS ATTRIBUTION-SHARE ALIKE 3.0 WITH THE ATTRIBUTION: TROPPENMUSEUM, PART OF THE NATIONAL MUSEUM OF WORLD CULTURES.

CHAPTER 50: NETHERLANDER PAINTING/ SHREWSBURY RIVER/ "THE NIGHTMARE":

A FAITHFUL REPRODUCTION OF A TWO-DIMENSIONAL PUBLIC DOMAIN WORK OF ART. PUBLIC DOMAIN IN COUNTRY OF ORIGIN WHERE THE COPYRIGHT TERM IS AUTHOR'S LIFE PLUS 100 YEARS OR FEWER. THIS IS ALSO IN THE PUBLIC DOMAIN OF U.S. BECAUSE COPYRIGHT WAS TAKEN OUT BEFORE 1927 AND NOT RENEWED. THIS PHOTOGRAPHIC REPRODUCTION IS THEREFORE ALSO CONSIDERED IN THE PUBLIC DOMAIN OF UNITED STATES/ LICENSE: CREATIVE COMMONS ATTRIBUTION -SHARE ALIKE 3.0

CHAPTER 51:" GARDEN OF EARTHLY DELIGHTS" BY BOSCH: THIS IS A FAITHFUL REPRODUCTION OF A TWO-DIMENSIONAL PUBLIC DOMAIN WORK OF ART. PUBLIC DOMAIN IN COUNTRY OF ORIGIN WHERE THE COPYRIGHT TERM IS AUTHOR'S LIFE PLUS 100 YEARS OR FEWER. THIS IS ALSO IN THE PUBLIC DOMAIN OF U.S. BECAUSE COPYRIGHT WAS TAKEN OUT BEFORE 1927 AND NOT RENEWED. THIS PHOTOGRAPHIC REPRODUCTION IS THEREFORE ALSO CONSIDERED IN THE PUBLIC DOMAIN OF UNITED STATES/SOURCE PRADO MUSEUM

MADRID LICENSE: CREATIVE COMMONS ATTRIBUTION -SHARE ALIKE 3.0

MUNCH PAINTING OF GIRL: THIS IS A FAITHFUL REPRODUCTION OF A TWO-DIMENSIONAL PUBLIC DOMAIN WORK OF ART. PUBLIC DOMAIN IN COUNTRY OF ORIGIN WHERE THE COPYRIGHT TERM IS AUTHOR'S LIFE PLUS 100 YEARS OR FEWER. THIS IS ALSO IN THE PUBLIC DOMAIN OF U.S. BECAUSE COPYRIGHT WAS TAKEN OUT BEFORE 1927 AND NOT RENEWED. THIS PHOTOGRAPHIC REPRODUCTION IS THEREFORE ALSO CONSIDERED IN THE PUBLIC DOMAIN OF UNITED STATES SOURCE: MUNCH MUSEUM OSLO CREATIVE COMMONS ATTRIBUTION-SHARE ALIKE 3.0

SOURCE/PHOTOGRAPHER: GOOGLE ART PROJECT IN COOPERATION WITH OSLO MUSEUM

CHAPTER 53: BOTANICAL PRINT OF DURIEN:" PUBLIC DOMAIN IN THE NETHERLANDS" THIS IS A FAITHFUL REPRODUCTION OF A TWO-DIMENSIONAL PUBLIC DOMAIN WORK OF ART. PUBLIC DOMAIN IN COUNTRY OF ORIGIN WHERE THE COPYRIGHT TERM IS AUTHOR'S LIFE PLUS 100 YEARS OR FEWER. THIS IS ALSO IN THE PUBLIC DOMAIN OF U.S. BECAUSE COPYRIGHT WAS TAKEN OUT BEFORE 1927 AND NOT RENEWED. THIS PHOTOGRAPHIC REPRODUCTION IS THEREFORE ALSO CONSIDERED IN THE PUBLIC DOMAIN OF UNITED STATES LICENSE: CREATIVE COMMONS 2.0 SHARE ALIKE

"NO DURIENS": AUTHOR/PHOTOGRAPHER: PROJECT MANHATTAN (2013) AUTHOR RELEASED IMAGE IN U.S. UNDER LICENSE: CREATIVE COMMONS ATTRIBUTION-SHARE ALIKE 3.0 FREE TO TRANSMIT, COPY AND DISTRIBUTE WITH NO RESTRICTIONS

CHAPTER 55: "MEDEA" PUBLIC DOMAIN, THE AUTHOR DIED IN 1904. THIS IS A FAITHFUL REPRODUCTION OF A TWO-DIMENSIONAL PUBLIC DOMAIN WORK OF ART. PUBLIC DOMAIN IN COUNTRY OF ORIGIN WHERE THE COPYRIGHT TERM IS AUTHOR'S LIFE PLUS 100 YEARS OR FEWER. THIS IS ALSO IN THE PUBLIC DOMAIN OF U.S. BECAUSE COPYRIGHT WAS TAKEN OUT BEFORE 1927 AND NOT RENEWED. THIS PHOTOGRAPHIC REPRODUCTION IS THEREFORE ALSO CONSIDERED IN THE PUBLIC DOMAIN OF UNITED STATES SOURCE: BIRMINGHAM MUSEUM AND ART GALLERY ENGLAND

CHAPTER 56: SISTINE CHAPEL "ADAM AND EVE": THIS IS A FAITHFUL REPRODUCTION OF A TWO-DIMENSIONAL PUBLIC DOMAIN WORK OF ART. PUBLIC DOMAIN IN COUNTRY OF ORIGIN WHERE THE COPYRIGHT TERM IS AUTHOR'S LIFE PLUS 100 YEARS OR FEWER. THIS IS ALSO IN THE PUBLIC DOMAIN OF U.S. BECAUSE COPYRIGHT WAS TAKEN OUT BEFORE 1927 AND NOT RENEWED. THIS PHOTOGRAPHIC REPRODUCTION IS THEREFORE ALSO CONSIDERED IN THE PUBLIC DOMAIN OF UNITED STATES LICENSE: CREATIVE COMMONS ATTRIBUTION-SHARE ALIKE 3.0

INDONESIAN II HEADER: JAKARTA CANALS: CARPENTER COLLECTION: PUBLIC DOMAIN. LIBRARY OF CONGRESS PRINT

CHAPTER 57: DURER PAINTING: THIS IS A FAITHFUL REPRODUCTION OF A TWO-DIMENSIONAL PUBLIC DOMAIN WORK OF ART. PUBLIC DOMAIN IN COUNTRY OF ORIGIN WHERE THE COPYRIGHT TERM IS AUTHOR'S LIFE PLUS 100 YEARS OR FEWER. THIS IS ALSO IN THE PUBLIC DOMAIN OF U.S. BECAUSE COPYRIGHT WAS TAKEN OUT

BEFORE 1927 AND NOT RENEWED. THIS PHOTOGRAPHIC REPRODUCTION IS THEREFORE ALSO CONSIDERED IN THE PUBLIC DOMAIN OF UNITED STATES LICENSE: CREATIVE COMMONS ATTRIBUTION-SHARE ALIKE 3.0

PUPPET SHOW; SOURCE/AUTHOR: AFRILA SAVITRI (4 NOV. 2015) AUTHOR RELEASED PHOTOGRAPH TO CREATIVE COMMONS ATTRIBUTION-SHARE ALIKE 4.0 INTERNATIONAL LICENSE WITH ATTRIBUTION TO AUTHOR: AFRILA SAVITRI AND REFERENCE TO INTERNATIONAL LICENSE.

CHAPTER 58: KRIS: KRIS AND PHOTOGRAPH OWNED BY TROPPENMUSEUM GIVEN TO WIKIMEDIA AS PART OF COOPERATIVE PROJECT/U.S. LICENSE CREATIVE COMMONS ATTRIBUTION-SHARE ALIKE 3.0 WITH THE ATTRIBUTION: TROPPENMUSEUM, PART OF THE NATIONAL MUSEUM OF WORLD CULTURES. CREATIVE COMMONS CC0

KRIS FORGE: PHOTO BY GUNAWANKARTAPRANTA 2010. AUTHOR RELEASED IMAGE TO CREATIVE COMMONS ATTRIBUTION-SHARE ALIKE 3.0 UNPORTED LICENSE , FREE TO USE WITH ATTRIBUTION OF AUTHOR.

PRINT OF KRIS MAKER: PRINT AND PHOTOGRAPH OWNED BY TROPPENMUSEUM GIVEN TO WIKIMEDIA AS PART OF COOPERATIVE PROJECT/U.S. LICENSE CREATIVE COMMONS ATTRIBUTION-SHARE ALIKE 3.0 WITH THE ATTRIBUTION: TROPPENMUSEUM, PART OF THE NATIONAL MUSEUM OF WORLD CULTURES. CREATIVE COMMONS CC0

CHAPTER 59: ENSOR'S PAINTING: THIS IS A FAITHFUL REPRODUCTION OF A TWO-DIMENSIONAL PUBLIC DOMAIN WORK OF ART. PUBLIC DOMAIN IN COUNTRY OF ORIGIN WHERE THE

COPYRIGHT TERM IS AUTHOR'S LIFE PLUS 100 YEARS OR FEWER. THIS IS ALSO IN THE PUBLIC DOMAIN OF U.S. BECAUSE COPYRIGHT WAS TAKEN OUT BEFORE 1927 AND NOT RENEWED. THIS PHOTOGRAPHIC REPRODUCTION IS THEREFORE ALSO CONSIDERED IN THE PUBLIC DOMAIN OF UNITED STATES LICENSE: CREATIVE COMMONS ATTRIBUTION-SHARE ALIKE 3.0

MOTORCYCLIST: YASSAR ABU GHDAIB ON UNSPLASH

SINGAPORE II HEADING: CHINESE WIFE: CARPENTER COLLECTION LOC USZ62-34390

CHAPTER 60: VESSEL IN SINGAPORE DOCK: PUBLIC DOMAIN IN SINGAPORE AND THE UNITED KINGDOMBECAUSE IT WAS PUBLISHED 70 YEARS AGO AND THERE WAS NO COPYRIGHT RENEWAL. PUBLIC DOMAIN IN THE U.S. BECAUSE IT WAS PUBLISHED PRIOR TO 1927 AND THE COPRIGHT WAS NOT RENEWED.LINCE IN U. S.: CREATIVE COMMONS ATTRIBUTION-SHARE ALIKE 3.0 SOURCE BRITISH GOV. PERMISSION TO USE: PUBLIC DOMAIN PHOTOGRAPH: BRITISH GOV.

CHAPTER 62: LADY JANE PORTRAIT 1831 COLLECTION: NYMPHENBURG PALACE GERMANY: THIS IS A FAITHFUL REPRODUCTION OF A TWO-DIMENSIONAL PUBLIC DOMAIN WORK OF ART. PUBLIC DOMAIN IN COUNTRY OF ORIGIN WHERE THE COPYRIGHT TERM IS AUTHOR'S LIFE PLUS 100 YEARS OR FEWER. THIS IS ALSO IN THE PUBLIC DOMAIN OF U.S. BECAUSE COPYRIGHT WAS TAKEN OUT BEFORE 1927 AND NOT RENEWED. THIS PHOTOGRAPHIC REPRODUCTION IS THEREFORE ALSO CONSIDERED IN THE PUBLIC DOMAIN OF UNITED STATES.

CHAPTER 64: "TREASURE SHIP" SOURCE/AUTHOR (PAINTER) KOSOV VLADIMER (1967) RELEASED IMAGE OF HIS WORK TO CREATIVE COMMONS ATTRIBUTION-SHARE ALIKE INTERNATIONAL LICENSE 4.0 WITH THE ATTRIBUTION OF AUTHOR KOSOV VLADIMER AND REFERENCING THE INTERNATIONAL LICENSE

"U.S. NAVAL EXPEDITION VESSEL": THIS IS A FAITHFUL REPRODUCTION OF A TWO-DIMENSIONAL PUBLIC DOMAIN WORK OF ART. PUBLIC DOMAIN IN COUNTRY OF ORIGIN WHERE THE COPYRIGHT TERM IS AUTHOR'S LIFE PLUS 100 YEARS OR FEWER. THIS IS ALSO IN THE PUBLIC DOMAIN OF U.S. BECAUSE COPYRIGHT WAS TAKEN OUT BEFORE 1927 AND NOT RENEWED. THIS PHOTOGRAPHIC REPRODUCTION IS THEREFORE ALSO CONSIDERED IN THE PUBLIC DOMAIN OF UNITED STATES. SOURCE: UNKNOWN ARTIST UNDER COMMAND OF CAPTAIN CHARLES WILKES

CHARLES FREMONT: THIS IS A FAITHFUL REPRODUCTION OF A TWO-DIMENSIONAL PUBLIC DOMAIN WORK OF ART. PUBLIC DOMAIN IN COUNTRY OF ORIGIN WHERE THE COPYRIGHT TERM IS AUTHOR'S LIFE PLUS 100 YEARS OR FEWER. THIS IS ALSO IN THE PUBLIC DOMAIN OF U.S. BECAUSE COPYRIGHT WAS TAKEN OUT BEFORE 1927 AND NOT RENEWED. THIS PHOTOGRAPHIC REPRODUCTION IS THEREFORE ALSO CONSIDERED IN THE PUBLIC DOMAIN OF UNITED STATES.

CHAPTER 65:" THE SEARCHERS" 1956 FILM POSTER. AUTHOR: BILL GOLD (ARTIST) NOW PUBLIC DOMAIN SINCE COPYRIGHT WAS NOT RENEWED AND ENTERED PUBLIC DOMAIN 28 YEARS LATER

CHAPTER 65:"OPIUM DEN": BANCROFT LIBRARY,UNIV. OF CALIFORNIA, BERKELEY PICTURE 19XX.111:05 PIC HTTPS://OAC.CDLIB.ORG/ARK:/13030/HB829005RD LIBRARY OF CONGRESS PERMANENT LINK:

HTTPS://LOC.GOV/RESOURCE/CPH.3C02090 PUBLIC DOMAIN IN U.S. COPYRIGHT EXPIRED BECAUSE IT WAS PUBLISHED BEFORE 1927 AND COPRIGHT WAS NOT RENEWED LICENCE: CREATIVE COMMONS CCO-PD

"WAITING FOR GODOT" AUTHOR FERNAND MICHAUD TOOK PHOTO AT AVIGNON FESTIVAL (FRANCE) 1978 AND RELEASED PHOTO TO PUBLIC DOMAIN WAIVING ALL RIGHTS. U.S. LICENSE: CREATIVE COMMONS CCO 1.0 UNIVERSAL PUBLIC DOMAIN

CHAPTER 65: MALACCA PORT: AUTHOR/SOURCE: FRANK SWETTENHAM

This image was taken from Flickr's The Commons. *The uploading organization may have various reasons for determining that* **no known copyright restrictions** *exist, such as:*

1. The copyright is in the public domain because it has expired;

2. The copyright was injected into the public domain for other reasons, such as failure to adhere to required formalities or conditions;

3. The institution owns the copyright but is not interested in exercising control; or

4. The institution has legal rights sufficient to authorize others to use the work without restrictions.

U.S. LICENSE: CREATIVE COMMONS ATTRIBUTION-SHARE ALIKE 3.0

CHAPTER 66: "MANILLA OPIUM DEN" LIBRARY OF CONGRESS B&W FILM NEGATIVE/ THE CARPENTER COLLECTION LOC: USZ62-103376 U.S. LICENSE: CREATIVE COMMONS CCO

CHAPTER 68: POSTER OF SWORD FILM: *There are no **known copyright restrictions** exist, such as:*

> 5. The copyright is in the public domain because it has expired;
>
> 6. The copyright was injected into the public domain for other reasons, such as failure to adhere to required formalities or conditions;
>
> 7. The institution owns the copyright but is not interested in exercising control; or
>
> 8. The institution has legal rights sufficient to authorize others to use the work without restrictions.

U.S. LICENSE: CREATIVE COMMONS ATTRIBUTION-SHARE ALIKE 3.0

CHAPTER 69: WANG YU: PUBLIC DOMAIN IN THE REPULIC OF CHINA. ALTHOUGH IMAGE IS BELIEVED TO BE COPYWRITE IN U.S., IT QUALIFYS UNDER U. S. FAIR USAGE FOR THE FOLLOWING REASONS: To illustrate the **subject in question**

- Where no free equivalent is available or could be created that would adequately give the same information

- On the English-language Wikipedia, hosted on servers in the United States by the non-profit Wikimedia Foundation, qualifies as **fair use** under United States copyright law. SOURCE: ttp://archives.thestar.com.my/archives/2012/3/26/lifeliving/f_4jim.jpg

THAILAND III: RECLINING BUDDHA –BANGKOK: CARPENTER COLLECTION LOC USZ62-5320

CHAPTER 70: "TAXI DANCER": PUBLIC DOMAIN THERE WAS NO COPYWRIGHT ON THE LOBBY CARD AND THEREFORE IS IN THE PUBLIC DOMAIN/SOURCE METRO-GOLDWYN-MAYER (MGM) U.S. LICENSE: CREATIVE COMMONS CCO

TAXI DANCERS IN NEW YORK CITY: 1938 PUBLIC DOMAIN: LIBRARY OF CONGRESS. PHOTOGRAPHER NEW YORK WORLD TELEGRAPH PHOTOGRAPHER ALAN FISHER/ SOURCE LOCATION: HTTP//HDL.LOC.GOVLOC.PNP/CPH.3c34893

CHAPTER 73: "MING THE MERCILESS:" PUBLIC DOMAIN FILM CLIP IS COPYRIGHT FREE SINCE IT HAS NOT BEEN RENEWED SINCE PUBLICATION (1938) AND 70 YEARS HAVE PASSED. NOW IT IS THE PUBLIC DOMAIN. LICENSE: CREATIVE COMMONS ATTRIBUTION-SHARE ALIKE 2.0

BIBLIOGRAPHY

"PAUL HARVEY" PUBLIC DOMAIN FILE IS A PRESIDENTIAL MEDAL OF FREEDOM AWARDEE TAKEN BY A FEDERAL EMPLOYEE AS PART OF HIS OFFICIAL DUTIES. AS A WORK OF THE U. S. FEDERAL GOVERNMENT, IT IS IN THE PUBLIC DOMAIN. CREATIVE COMMONS ATTRIBUTION SHARE-ALIKE 3.0 UNPORTED

About The Author

I am a first generation American, born of immigrant Norwegian and Swiss parents. I was the first in my family to attend college (Lafayette College) on a Reserve Officer Training Corps scholarship and a second-generation soldier (my father served in the U.S. Army during World War II). I served three years in the Army and close to two years travelling in Asia. I grew up in the 1960s, the High Noon of the American Empire and see myself as a child of both Woodstock and Vietnam.

The patriotic idealism of the Peace Corps in the Kennedy years dissipated in the societal division and carnage of a senseless war. Yet my generation believed that everything was possible, we could remake America to be that visionary "Shining City on the Hill "our forefathers had envisioned. The Peace, Love and Music of Woodstock seemed to be a harbinger of a new age, of swords into ploughshares.

It is this optimism that inspired my book. It is also my "Bildungsroman", a young man trying to understand the world and himself. I have an insatiable sense of curiosity and wonder about the world, and I have tried to convey this with a sense of humor. This is the Zeitgeist that I want to share with YOU the reader, in the hope that this book will inspire you to get off your rump and discover your own unique Asia. Happy Trails!

About The Book

"Sojourner to Stoner: The Journal" is my record of Southeast Asia in the 1970s. I spent over a year as an officer in the U.S. Army in South Korea and close to two years travelling throughout Asia, first as a backpacker and later as a Hippie (yippee-ki-yay or more appropriately, hippie-ki-yay).

This Journal (YING) is a companion piece to my photography book, surprisingly also called "Sojourner to Stoner: The Photographs" (YANG) (You must buy the two books together; otherwise, the Universe will be out of balance and there will be chaos everywhere).

I have documented a time, the 1970s, before the all-pervading Western culture (sex, drugs, and rock and roll in Levi's) and The Economic Miracle changed Asia irrevocably.

The book is written from a traveller (Sojourner for Stupids) and a stoner (Don't Bogart that Bong) perspective.

Communism, Western culture and the traditional way of life are all fighting for the Soul of Asia. This is my vision of Asia, a bright (albeit smokey) beam of light from a star that has already vanished.

www.ingramcontent.com/pod-product-compliance
Lightning Source LLC
Chambersburg PA
CBHW051309110526
44590CB00031B/4350